THE
ROMAN FORUM SITE
IN LONDON

DISCOVERIES BEFORE 1985

MUSEUM OF LONDON

Peter Marsden

THE
ROMAN FORUM SITE
IN LONDON

DISCOVERIES BEFORE 1985

LONDON

HER MAJESTY'S STATIONERY OFFICE

First published 1987

ISBN 0 11 290442 4

Printed in the United Kingdom for Her Majesty's Stationery Office
Dd. 238636 C25 7/87 48739

FRONT COVER
The second basilica and forum
of Roman London, based upon
archaeological discoveries.

Artist's impression by Ronald Embleton

Symbols used in the drawings illustrating the Roman forum site.

▬	wall or foundation	⬜	wall/foundation retained from earlier phase
▬	foundation only	▨	position of wall/foundation uncertain
▨	wall/foundation conjectured	──	sleeper wall
▨	secondary phase of wall/foundation	- - - -	sleeper wall conjectured
▨	secondary phase of wall/foundation conjectured	⬛	robbed wall
▰	stream: found & conjectured	▱	cut: type (pit, ditch, etc) defined individually
▨	road: found & conjectured	▦	tile/brick
▨	gravel	▨	floor
⬜	gravel conjectured	▨	mortar
‒·‒	limit of excavation		

Contents

1

Introduction

ALTHOUGH THE Roman forum site has had more concentrated archaeological attention than any other comparable area of Roman London, it was not clear until the present study was underway just how outstanding was the dedicated work of many investigators over the last one hundred years. The site work has always been carried out in the difficult conditions of building sites, and usually with no financial support. But the archaeological rewards have been enormous in limiting an archaeological disaster of vast proportions. Office developments have so extensively destroyed the Roman civic centre that without these records it would not now be possible to understand the story of the area even if all that remained was carefully excavated. In particular, the first forum itself would now be unrecognisable. Whilst Gerald Dunning, Frank Cottrill, Adrian Oswald, Brian Philp and others undertook the site investigations, others, particularly Sir Mortimer Wheeler and Ralph Merrifield, tried to understand the significance of the discoveries on a wider basis, and so gave research a sense of direction.

It is curious that most of the investigations have never been properly published, but the decision to write up and publish my own investigations offered an excellent opportunity to examine the whole archaeological evidence. Although the conclusions given in this report are my responsibility, as are most of the site descriptions, any credit must belong to all who have worked in the area. I am particularly glad to have included previously unpublished site reports by Adrian Oswald and the late Gerald Dunning.

When this research report was started there was a large miscellaneous body of archival and published information about many of the sites, most of the information being preserved in the Museum of London. If it was to become meaningful and manageable it was crucial to establish three objectives for each site. Firstly, to reconstruct the sequence of buildings and other features; secondly, to date them as far as possible; and thirdly, to plot out the structures on an accurate master plan of the entire area. Having established the chronology of each site the next stage was to relate all the site chronologies to each other and so obtain a common regional chronology. The result was most encouraging for, bearing in mind that the sites were examined by different people, at different times and under a variety of conditions they were surprisingly consistent with each other in the story that they told.

That story is of 'epic' proportions, for within one lifetime the site was transformed through stages from scrub land to become one of the biggest civic centres in the Roman world. There is no contemporary written record of those events in Roman London, but as the transformation of the civic centre was a mirror of grand ideas on an imperial scale, one cannot help but be aware of the former presence of remarkable, but sadly nameless, men whose ideas took such concrete form. Our archaeological efforts are feeble by comparison yet, but for the dedication of those who examined the sites, all knowledge of these great events would be lost. As this study goes forward for publication I am glad to report that the first major archaeological excavation of part of the second basilica has been started. It covers the north-east part and is already adding new information. Since it covers only a part of the forum site, and will add little to the first forum and the earlier gravelled courtyard, and because its publication will not be possible for another five years, it was decided to go ahead with the publication of this present report. At the time of writing nothing has been found on the new site that conflicts with the conclusions reached.

This report has not been created alone, and there have been important contributions by A. Boddington, P. James, A. Oswald, B. Pye, A. Upson and the late G. Dunning. Very special thanks are due to Sara Parfett (née Paton) and Tracy Wellman. The former accurately plotted the sites on the master plan and copied many of the original drawings, particularly those by Henry Hodge and William Miller, and these are reproduced here. The latter prepared all of the site drawings used in the report. Tony Dyson, Professor S.S. Frere and Ralph Merrifield read the draft and made most useful comments; and Tony Dyson, of the Department of Urban Archaeology of the Museum of London, exercised his usual thorough editorial skills. To all of these I owe a great debt.

Special thanks are due to the late Frank Cottrill and Gerald Dunning, both of whom gave permission to work through and publish their researches, as did the Society of Antiquaries who originally paid these two archaeologists and who strictly speaking own the site records which are now deposited in the Museum of London. The Department of the Environment, and now the Historic Buildings and Monuments Commission, have made generous grants to enable this study to be made, and finally HMSO so kindly agreed to publish the report.

PETER MARSDEN
Museum of London
July, 1986

2

Summary of the Forum site

THE FORUM of Roman London was constructed on the undulating plateau of a former river terrace, overlooking London Bridge (Fig. 1). The site seems to have been located at the north end of the initial settlement area of *Londinium*, and the earliest occupation probably occurred during the early 50s AD. This initial occupation took the form of planned streets, at least at the south end of the forum site, with traces of timber buildings between. There was also an extensive gravelled area which was later to be occupied by the small first forum. The nature of this initial occupation is not clear, but it does bear some resemblance to the early Roman military supplies bases at Richborough and Fishbourne. However, no military objects have been found in pre-Boudican deposits on the forum site.

The initial occupation phase was of short duration, and, at least at the south-east part of the forum site, the area was replanned with timber-framed shops and dwellings later in the 50s AD. These must indicate a definitely civilian phase. One range of shops 56.5m long lay behind a portico fronting the main east-west street beneath Fenchurch Street. In one shop was found a store of grain that had been

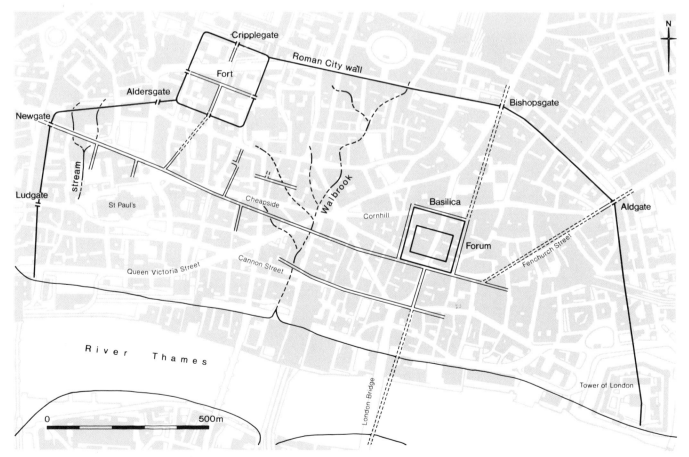

Fig. 1 Outline plan of modern and Roman London, with the main Roman streets, to show the location of the basilica and forum site (only the second basilica and forum is shown).

3

imported from the eastern Mediterranean. The gravelled area continued to be used during this period, and was presumably a market place.

These buildings were destroyed in the Boudican fire of AD 60, but the fact that the burning was limited to the south end of the forum area indicates that much of the site still lay beyond the built-up area of *Londinium* at that stage.

There is inconclusive evidence of activity during the decade or so following the Boudican destruction, though possible traces of a building with stone foundations have been found at the south end of the forum site.

The first basilica and forum complex was built after AD 71, probably about AD 80, and presumably reflects the granting of self-government to the city. The complex measured 104.5m by 52.7m, and was quite small. The basilica, the floor of which was artificially raised about a metre above the forum, measured 44m by 22.7m, and was of simple internal layout comprising a nave between side aisles, and a tribunal at the east end. There may also have been a tribunal at the west end.

The first forum apparently comprised three ranges of chambers around a courtyard, with an external portico in the south wing fronting the main east-west street of the city. Just outside the west side of the forum there was also a small temple, probably of classical type, that was evidently part of the civic centre complex. Each wing of the forum comprised a range of rooms, most of them presumably used as shops, which opened straight onto the courtyard. During its short life the forum, but not the basilica, was probably modified by the addition of an inner portico, and subsequently was extensively rebuilt within the outer shell of the building so that the walls were mostly replaced by brick piers. This may have given the forum a more flexible plan. The first basilica and forum continued to be used while the second basilica and forum was built around it.

The second basilica and forum was probably constructed about AD 100, and it occupied an area measuring 166m by 167m. This is an area five times larger than that occupied by its predecessor, and although of vast extent, being by far the largest civic centre in Roman Britain, it had a fairly simple layout. The huge leap in size perhaps reflects a change in the status of *Londinium*, possibly from *municipium* to *colonia*.

The second basilica measured 52.5m by 167m, and comprised a nave between two side aisles, with a tribunal at the east end at least. Ranges of rooms on the north side of the building presumably contained the administrative offices of the city council.

The second forum lay on the same level as the basilica, and included three wings each 25m wide, each containing a central range of chambers between inner and outer porticos. The inner portico of the south wing was particularly interesting for it was made wider than the other porticos in order to accommodate a row of brick piers which presumably supported statues or monuments of particular significance to *Londinium*. The courtyard had a varied surface of gravel and mortar layers, and in the centre there was a small pool.

The forum had been built on thick dumps of clay and gravel which buried the first forum, and from which have been recovered pottery sherds dating no later than the end of the first century AD. Also, from the All Hallows church site there is evidence of a probable modification to the south wing of the forum during the 2nd century.

Although minor modifications to the basilica and forum have been found, the complex as a whole seems to have retained essentially the same basic plan. Nothing has been found to indicate when it ceased to be occupied. After the Roman period the basilica and forum complex apparently had little effect on later settlement, though the churches of St. Peter, St. Michael, St. Dionis and All Hallows presumably made use of the building materials at hand, and Gracechurch Street was built across its site. Indeed, Lime Street probably owes its name to the lime burning of ragstone quarried from the forum during the early Middle Ages. Although some of the churches may have made use of the ruins by incorporating standing walls into their structure, it is clear that this did not apply to All Hallows church, the nave of which overlay the outer wall of the inner portico of the south wing of the forum.

3

History of discovery

ALTHOUGH THE discovery of Roman structures in the basilica and forum region of London was recorded as long ago as 1785, it was not until 1880–2 that sufficient of the plan was found to indicate the significance of the site. Surprisingly, the records of this Victorian discovery remained unpublished and forgotten until 1915, and it was as recently as 1923 that the building was positively identified as a basilica. Since then much archaeological attention has been given to this area with the aim of elucidating its history. The complexity of this became apparent during the 1930s when parts of a Roman building were found in the courtyard area of the forum adjacent to the basilica. During the 1960s further investigation suggested that this was an earlier 'proto-Forum', whose purpose was obscured by difficulties in accurately plotting the plan of its structure. These difficulties were resolved by a complete replotting of all recorded Roman structures in the forum on an accurate modern map, and the nature of the earlier forum can now be established. Meanwhile, excavations during the 1960s and 1970s also began to define the location and purpose of earlier features, some of which relate to the origin of Roman London.

The Leadenhall Market discoveries, 1880–2

Excavations for the construction of the new Leadenhall Market in 1880–2 revealed the existence of a major Roman building on the site. Little survives in writing of these discoveries, and our knowledge of them derives almost totally from two remarkable sets of drawings; one, unknown until discovered recently, by William Miller (1880–1), and the other, well known for many years, by Henry Hodge (1881–2).

The discovery of Roman walls on the Leadenhall site created a considerable amount of interest as early as 1880, as is shown by the following report, published in *The Builder*.[1]

'Roman London: Treasure Trove
At the last meeting of the British Archaeological Association, Mr. Loftus Brock produced a plan, and described the remains now being excavated on the site

of Old Leadenhall Market. Two long walls of the fifteenth century building are visible, with a series of corbels. A Roman pavement of ordinary brick tesserae has been found over a large part of the surface, and covered with the ashes of some great fire. Above this is the concrete of a second floor, while below, the remains of walls, 5ft thick, have been found, indicating a building of importance. These walls have bands of Roman brick, and one is constructed entirely of that material, pointing to an early period of the Roman occupation.'

It is curious that Miller and Hodge never worked together as far as can be judged, but this may have been a symptom of a rift between archaeologists involved with the site. On the one hand there was Loftus Brock, the British Archaeological Association, and his artist William Miller, and on the other there was John Price, the London and Middlesex Archaeological Society, and his artist Henry Hodge. The rift may simply have been due to a rivalry between Brock and Price, both of whom intended to publish an account of the discoveries. Neither did.

THE WILLIAM MILLER DRAWINGS, 1880–1

The plan exhibited by Brock at the meeting was not published, but clearly it could not have been produced by Hodge whose drawings are dated and show that they were completed later in 1881–2. The recent discovery at Guildhall Library of a series of illustrations of the Roman walls, dated 1880–1 and drawn by William Miller, has almost certainly solved the problem since 'Mr. Miller, Clerk of the Works at Leadenhall', took part in the discussion which followed the exhibition by Loftus Brock at the meeting of the British Archaeological Association on 16 February 1881. Brock 'exhibited a series of plans of excavations' on the Leadenhall Market site, and 'in the discussion which ensued, Mr. Blashill, Mr. Brock, the Chairman (of the meeting), and Mr. Miller, Clerk of the Works at Leadenhall, took part'.[2] These illustrations by the Clerk of Works are of enormous importance since they enable us to check on the accuracy of the drawings by Hodge, and also because they preserve information not otherwise described.

No subsequent reference to the drawings can be found, though it was reported that Brock was preparing a paper on the Leadenhall discoveries[3] and presumably intended to use them. Unfortunately Loftus Brock never did publish his paper, and the fate of the original drawings remains unknown, though photocopies were donated to Guildhall Library by Hugh W. Standen in March 1947.

On 2 March 1881, Loftus Brock described to the Association 'further discoveries at Leadenhall, showing the great extent of Roman building and the thickness of walling. He also exhibited fragments of fresco paintings, with ornamental patterns, of green foliage of a flowing style, on a dull red ground, of the plasterwork of the walls. The building appears to have had the form of a basilica in some respects, with eastern apse, western nave, and two chambers like transepts on the south side'.[4]

THE HENRY HODGE DRAWINGS, 1881–2

Although the drawings made by Henry Hodge of the Roman and medieval structures on the Leadenhall Market site have been well known since their publication in 1915,[5] the circumstances in which he undertook the illustrations have never been clear. Recent research by Mrs J. Alford shows that Henry Hodge was born in 1824, the son of John Hodge a prosperous stationer of the firm of Spalding and Hodge at 145 Drury Lane. Henry became an architect and was an Associate Member of the Royal Institute of British Architects until 1874. In 1849 he married Elvina Garlett, and by 1881, when he recorded the Roman walls at Leadenhall Market, he was living at 4 Suffolk Road, Croydon, and had eleven living children. It is not known why he ceased to be a member of the RIBA in 1874, for until his death in 1898 he apparently considered himself an architect. It seems that in 1876 his career began to change, for not long afterwards he began to produce his numerous illustrations of London buildings and sites. At that time he was working for another architect, W.C. Banks, who was erecting a building in Camomile Street. A Roman bastion containing re-used sculptured stones had been found on the site, and at the instigation of John Price, who was Honorary Secretary of the London and Middlesex Archaeological Society, the complete dismantling of the bastion took place and 'upwards of fifty massive fragments of sculptured stone had to be extracted before the maiden soil was reached'. This work was supervised by Henry Hodge, Bank's assistant, and his efforts were acknowledged in Price's report published in 1880.[6]

As an architect Henry Hodge was well qualified to record the significant features of buried ruins though his artistic style is considered to be rather stiff and lifeless (Plate 9). Perhaps the lack of 'artistic

licence' enhanced the archaeological value of his work. The detail of his records is remarkable, even by modern standards, for he carefully drew to scale plans, sections and elevations of ancient walls. Even more extraordinary are his watercoloured sections of strata, also drawn to scale, for these pre-date Pitt Rivers' strata sections of Cranborne Chase published between 1887 and 1898.[7] Although a recorder, Hodge did not offer any interpretation of what he had drawn.

The earliest known reference to Hodge's Leadenhall drawings occurs in the Minutes of the meeting of the Council of the London and Middlesex Archaeological Society on Monday, 13 February, 1882:

'Mr. John E. Price having kindly offered to the Society on condition of publication a very valuable series of original drawings made on the spot during the demolitions of a portion of the site of Leadenhall Market. It was resolved that the offer be accepted and that the matter should be referred to the publication committee and that Mr. Alfred White be asked to join them.'

On 27 March the publication committee reported to the Council as follows:

'Mr. J.E. Price FSA exhibited the drawings of the Roman remains discovered in Leadenhall Street & on the report of the sub committee appointed to confer with him on the subject it was resolved that a grant of thirty guineas be made out of the Society's funds towards the expense of these illustrations. It was further resolved that the publishing committee take steps to obtain further subscriptions from the City Companies & the public generally & that a form of letter be drawn up for approval to send to each Company.
    It was resolved that the price of the proposed book quarto size, be one guinea to non members.'

A month later, the Council Minutes of 17 April, 1882, include the following statement:

'The Hon. Sec. read the form of proposed letter to the City Companies drawn up by Mr. Wadmore asking for their support made especially towards illustrating the antiquities discovered on the Leadenhall site. Resolved that the same be adopted & sent to the various Companies with such modifications by the Hon. Secretaries to suit the several cases.'

Although Hodge's name is not mentioned the proposed fee of 30 guineas coincides with the thirty illustrations which he completed for that site, while the Minutes suggest that John Price, who already knew Hodge from Camomile Street, had asked Hodge to undertake the illustrations, believing that as the site was so important the London and

Middlesex Archaeological Society would pay the fee. But no further mention of the drawings appears in the Council Minutes; no payment of 30 guineas was ever made, and none of the illustrations was published. Clearly, the whole arrangement described in the Minutes was suddenly abandoned – why?

The likely answer is that it was Hodge himself who refused to sell the drawings to the Society for he did not consider that the fee offered was sufficient. Although interested in ancient architecture, it seems that as he was not a member of any archaeological society he was not especially interested in archaeology. His involvement in archaeological recording, arising from his architectural work and expertise, was evidently on a purely professional basis. Three months later he was to be paid £25 10s 0d by the Corporation of London for four 'plans and drawings of such portions of the buildings of Guildhall' as was considered necessary, 'to retain for preservation amongst the archives of the Corporation.';[8] and in 1888 he was also paid £95 by the Corporation for a set of illustrations of parts of old Guildhall and £15 15s 20d for some rough sketches.[9] On this basis he might have expected a fee in excess of £150 from the London and Middlesex Archaeological Society for the Leadenhall drawings. In this way archaeology lost an opportunity of acquiring this exceptional record of the Roman basilica. The sobering result is that when the account of 'Roman London' was published in the *Victoria County History of London* in 1909, all memory of the drawings of the Roman building found at Leadenhall had gone.

Fortunately the Leadenhall drawings by Hodge were acquired by John Edmund Gardner, a wealthy gas engineer, who was extremely interested in cultural affairs. He was a friend of Dickens and Cruickshank, and commissioned artists to record old London buildings which were to be destroyed by redevelopment. His collection of thousands of illustrations comprised a unique record of disappearing London,[10] and although no record of what he paid Henry Hodge has been found, it is likely that as Gardner employed many such established artists as T.H. Shepherd, J. Carter, R.B. Schnebbelie, H. Lawer, J. Emslie and others, he probably paid Hodge considerably more than the London and Middlesex Archaeological Society could afford. In fact, even before Hodge undertook the Leadenhall drawings he had already been commissioned by Gardner, as a picture by Hodge in the Museum of London shows.[11] The picture has the following pencil inscription in Hodge's hand: 'Bricklayers Arms, Old Kent Road. Sketchd. May 1880 for Gardner Collection'.

When Gardner died about 1899 there may have been a second opportunity of acquiring the Hodge drawings for publication, but this did not happen. Hodge himself was no longer involved for he had died in June 1898, aged 73, in his home at 142 Holmesdale Road, South Norwood, Croydon. Instead, the 'Gardner Collection' was purchased by Major Sir Edward Coates MP. The Guildhall Library may have unsuccessfully tried to purchase the Leadenhall drawings at this time, for some time before 1915 copies of most of the original Leadenhall drawings were made in pencil on tracing paper, and were preserved in the Library. The tracings were discovered about 1914 by Philip Norman, Francis Reader and Frank Lambert, and it was Lambert who in 1915 published some ink drawn copies of the tracings.[12]

Following Sir Edward Coates' death, the entire 'Gardner Collection' as it was still called, was sold, mostly in a huge auction at Sotheby's in 1923. Lot 1902 comprised:

'Leadenhall Market, drawings and plans, by H. Hodge, of the Roman, Saxon and Medieval remains discovered during the preparation of the site for the present Market, 1880–82, mostly in colours (30).' The number in brackets at the end shows that there were still thirty illustrations. A copy of the auction catalogue in Guildhall Library is annotated, and states that the drawings were purchased by 'Nield' – for just £1.[13] 'Nield' was not simply another private purchaser, however, but was apparently bidding on behalf of Guildhall Library, where after forty years the drawings found a safe repository.

Subsequently, the 1928 Royal Commission report on *Roman London* re-published the 1915 illustrations, together with a new copy of the original Hodge plan with all of its detailed annotations. In spite of all of this interest some information about the Roman discoveries remained unpublished until now, particularly some of the cross-sections of walls and all of the strata sections. But even now the full extent of the information contained in the Hodge records has not yet been published, for he also drew and measured in great detail the extensive medieval structures of Leadenhall itself. Without the Hodge drawings the identification of the basilica and forum would have been very much more difficult, and it is a tribute to the architect and artist that as our knowledge of the basilica and forum increases so does our appreciation of the quality of the work which he undertook a century ago.

Subsequent research.

Although Loftus Brock considered that the Roman building recorded by Miller and Hodge 'had the form of a Basilica in some respects', its purpose remained uncertain until 1923 when W.R. Lethaby identified it as 'the civil Basilica of Londinium'.[14] This statement was subsequently supported by R.E.M. Wheeler[15] who, having closely studied the recorded remains, concluded that the basilica may have had two phases of development, and that the forum probably overlay

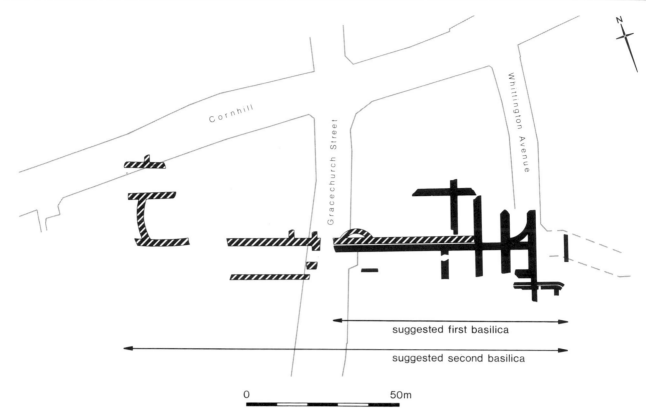

Fig. 2 The two phases of the large basilica as suggested in
1928. Subsequent discoveries do not support this theory.

the remains of an earlier Roman building.

These two phases were indicated by the south sleeper wall of the nave which comprised two walls lying side by side. It was suggested that when first constructed the basilica may have been a modest sized building lying to the east of Gracechurch street, and that the southern of the two walls was part of the original construction. Subsequently, the building may have been extended to the west, with the construction of the northern part of the double wall (Fig. 2). The purpose of the double wall is still in doubt, though for various reasons that will be described later it is unlikely that the great basilica had a 'short' and a 'long' phase. Indeed, there is good reason to believe that the northern of the two walls is the earlier, and that the southern wall was a strengthening foundation.

Wheeler considered that the forum probably lay to the south of the basilica. During the early 20th century a number of new discoveries showed that he was correct, and that the south wing of the forum probably lay just north of Lombard Street. Various other Roman walls were also found, but as they lay within the area of the suggested forum courtyard their relationship to the forum was uncertain (Fig. 3). Wheeler concluded that 'these remains, however, are on a different alignment from the basilica and may

thus belong to a previous layout'.[16] Fifty years later they were identified as parts of a first forum underlying its much larger successor.

Following the publication of the Royal Commission report on Roman London in 1928, R.E.M. Wheeler approached the Council of the Society of Antiquaries, which agreed to sponsor a part-time archaeological investigator to visit building sites in the City. Gerald Dunning took up this post from 1929 to 1934, and by recording Roman walls at 52 Cornhill immediately added a significant new element to the known plan of the second basilica. From this he was not only able to suggest a reconstruction plan of the entire building (Fig. 4), but also he managed to recover for the first time some vital dating evidence, which indicated that the second basilica had been built during the Flavian period.[17] An edited version of his unpublished report, written fifty years ago, is included in this publication (see pp. 82–85), together with a copy of his original drawings. The pottery dating evidence was passed to the Guildhall Museum, but was lost probably when the museum closed during the last war. Fortunately Dunning had drawn and described the significant sherds.

Frank Cottrill succeeded Dunning as the investigator from 1934 to 1937 and recorded Roman features on five sites in the forum area. On two of these, in

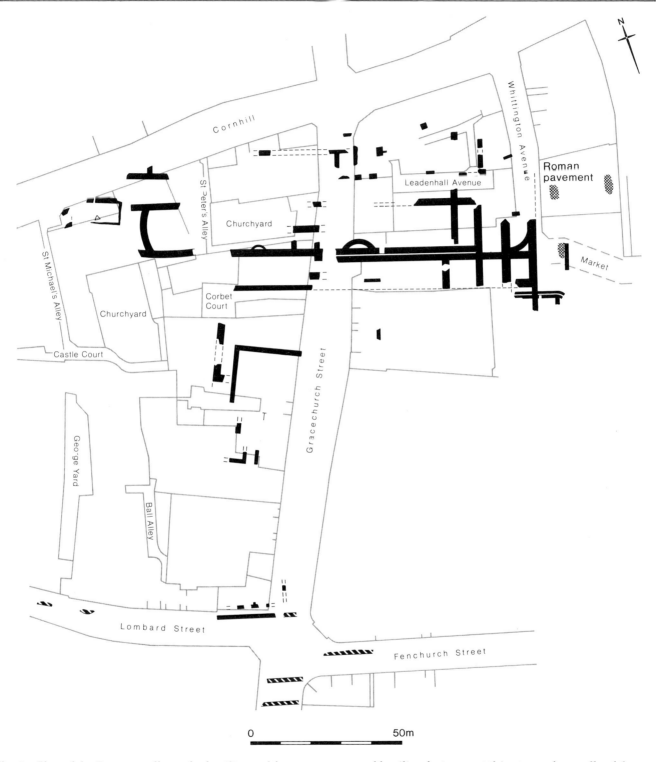

Fig. 3 Plan of the Roman walls on the basilica and forum site as published in the Royal Commission Report on *Roman London*, 1928. Most of the walls belonged to the second basilica, but even at this stage a few walls of the then unidentified first basilica and forum had been found in Gracechurch Street on a different alignment.

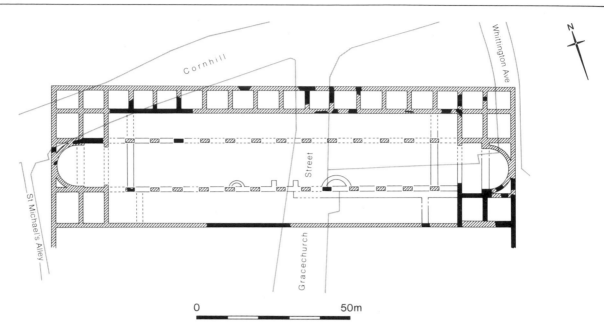

Fig. 4   Reconstructed plan of the basilica proposed by Gerald
Dunning in 1931. Subsequent discoveries support most of Dunnings
views, as is shown by the 1985 reconstruction (Fig. 28).

Gracechurch Street, he recorded substantial Roman structures now identified as parts of the first basilica and forum, and an adjacent small classical temple. Two of the remaining sites, in Birchin Lane and Lime Street, disclosed the main north-south streets which flanked the east and west sides of the second forum, under which he recorded pottery which assisted in dating the construction of the second forum. The fifth site, a small hole in Lombard Street, revealed a Roman wall which is now identified as part of the outer portico of the second forum. Frank Cottrill was himself unable to write up the many sites which he investigated in London, but his records are so clear and well ordered that this has proved to be straight forward, and, indeed, has been completed with his collaboration for publication here.

In 1939 Adrian Oswald of the Guildhall Museum investigated the crucial forum site at All Hallows church in Lombard Street, where he found several superimposed phases of Roman stone buildings. Their significance was unclear, though it can now be shown that they were in essence phases of the first and second forum buildings. Once again, some dating evidence was recovered but lost, probably when Guildhall Museum was closed during the Second World War. Oswald's report could not be published in the circumstances, and it is here reproduced together with copies of his original drawings.

The bombing of London hardly affected the basilica and forum area, and so it was not until 1959 that further rebuilding and archaeological study was undertaken in the area. This was mainly carried out by the writer, who up to 1978 investigated ten sites in the area. These helped to resolve the complex sequence of building phases, and established the early Roman date of the main east-west street beneath modern Fenchurch Street, upon which the frontage of the second forum was aligned.[18] The building, later identified as the first forum, also began to reveal a clearer plan, which suggested that it was a single large structure (Fig. 5).[19] In addition, new discoveries at 69–73 Cornhill and at 3–6 Gracechurch Street enabled the exact position and alignment of the second basilica to be established on modern maps for the first time.[20]

During the 1960s sufficient additional portions of Roman structure had been discovered to enable the layout of the various ancient buildings to be conjectured. In particular, although the purpose of the first basilica and forum had not yet been established, the location of its south-east corner was conjectured by Ralph Merrifield as lying beneath the site of 168–170 Fenchurch Street. When that site was redeveloped in 1968–9 extensive archaeological excavations, undertaken by Brian Philp for Guildhall Museum, revealed the corner as predicted. Philp attempted to correlate his discoveries with other sites in the area on the large scale map published by Charles Goad. This map, however, proved to be inaccurate, and the difficulties of accurately plotting the Roman features unfortunately led to errors of as much as 6m, with the

Fig. 5 Plan of the Roman basilica and forum site published by Ralph Merrifield in 1965. At this stage there was still some doubt about the exact location of the second forum. The existence of the still unidentified first forum was becoming clear as a single building complex between Corbet Court and Lombard Street.

result that his plan of the building underlying the great basilica and forum was inaccurate (Fig. 6); similar problems had also been encountered by Ralph Merrifield.[21] These inaccuracies partly masked the function of the earlier building, though Philp nevertheless suggested that it was a 'proto-forum' which perhaps served some of the functions of the later forum[22]

Although subsequent discoveries occurred on sites in Fenchurch Street, Castle Court and Gracechurch Street, it was clear by 1977 that the best solution to the problems of the various phases was to find a reliable modern large scale map on which to re-plot all the Roman features. Careful checking showed that an enlargement of the Ordnance Survey map was both accurate and sufficiently detailed to

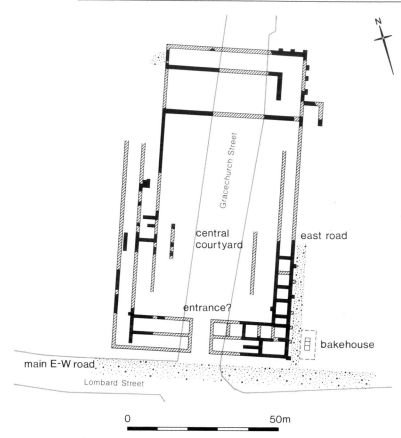

Fig. 6   Plan by Brian Philp of the so-called 'proto-forum', published in 1977. The identification of the first forum and basilica was obscured by the difficulty of accurately plotting the Roman walls. This resulted in the north end being out of position eastwards by more than six metres relative to the south end.

form the basis of a new survey. In addition an electronic calculator proved to be an essential tool in obtaining conversions in scale from the individual site plans to the new general survey. I am particularly grateful to Mrs. Sarah Parfett who so meticulously undertook this new plot (Fig. 7). Although each individual site was plotted independently, it was re-assuring to find that the major discrepancies no longer existed. The resulting plan of the so-called 'proto-forum' was now clearly that of a typical basilica and forum.

    This identification of the first basilica and forum left many problems unresolved, but in 1977 there occurred a remarkable opportunity to link the whole basilica and forum complex together. In that year a telephone cable was laid along the whole length of Gracechurch Street, and the small tunnel through which it was to run lay about 3m below the modern street level, which by coincidence is at the level of the floor of the second basilica and forum (Plates 8, 10, 11, 19. Fig. 8). For the first time these floors were

recorded, together with their relationship to the walls of the basilica and forum. In addition, further parts of the first basilica and forum were revealed, and also earlier Roman features, including the early Roman gravelled area below the forum. It was now possible to see, in the space of a few days, portions of many of the Roman walls that had been recorded by various individuals, including William Miller and Henry Hodge, since the first major discoveries of the great basilica and forum occurred a century ago.

FOOTNOTES AND REFERENCES

1   *The Builder*, 22 January, 1881, p. 110.

2   *Journal of the British Archaeological Association*, 37, 1881, p. 90.

3   Ibid. in Note 2, p. 84.

4   Ibid. in Note 2, pp. 90–91.

5   F. Lambert, 'Recent Roman discoveries in London', *Archaeologia* 66, 1914–15, pp. 227–235.

6   J.E. Price, *On a Bastion of London Wall, or Excavations in Camomile Street, Bishopsgate*, London, 1880, p. 4.

7   G. Daniel, *The Origins and growth of Archaeology*, Pelican ed., 1967, p. 236.

8   *Guildhall Library Committee Minutes*, Vol. 25, 20 June, 1882, under the heading of 'drawings'.

9   *Donations Book of Guildhall Library*, 3 December, 1888.

10 I am grateful to John Phillips, of the Greater London Record Office for this information.

11 Museum of London Accession Number 58.69/10.

12 Ibid. in Note 5.

13 Sotheby's auction catalogue, 1923, of the 'Gardner Collection' of Sir Edward Coates. Guildhall Library.

14 W. Lethaby, *Londinium architecture and the crafts*, London, 1923, pp. 33–42.

15 Royal Commission on Historical Monuments, *Roman London*, 1928, pp. 35–42.

16 Ibid. in Note 15, p. 42.

17 Report by G. Dunning in *Journal of Roman Studies*, 21, 1931, pp. 236–8.

18 P. Marsden, 'Archaeological Finds in the City of London, 1962', *Transactions of the London and Middlesex Archaeological Society*, 21, part 2, 1965, pp. 138–9.

19 P. Marsden, 'Archaeological finds in the City of London, 1963–4', *Transactions of the London and Middlesex Archaeological Society*, 21, part 3, 1967, pp. 209–213; P. Marsden, 'Archaeological Finds in the City of London 1966–8', *Transactions of the London and Middlesex Archaeological Society*, 22, part 2, 1969, pp. 18–20; R. Merrifield, *The Roman City of London*, London, 1965, pp. 136–140.

20 P. Marsden, 'Archaeological Finds in the City of London, 1966–8', *Transactions of the London and Middlesex Archaeological Society*, 22, part 2, 1969, pp. 16–18.

21 R. Merrifield, *The Roman City of London*, London, 1965, p. 135.

22 B. Philp, 'The Forum of Roman London: Excavations of 1968–9', *Britannia* VIII, 1977, pp. 19–21, 35–37.

Fig. 7 Plan of discovered structures of the first forum (hatched) and the second forum (solid).

Fig. 8 The location of sites described in this report. Most of these are now banks with very deep basements leaving only limited archaeological deposits still intact. The limits of the Leadenhall Market excavations in 1880 are not known precisely and therefore are not shown.

Synthesis

4

THE PURPOSE of this synthesis is to draw together the information from each of the forum sites described in detail later in this report, and, together with information from previously published reports, to attempt to trace the overall history of the Roman structures. This is a task with many uncertainties which will never be resolved, for the Roman redevelopment of the site took place at a speed that is remarkable by any standards, while the pace of modern redevelopment has unfortunately destroyed unrecorded most of the archaeological evidence.

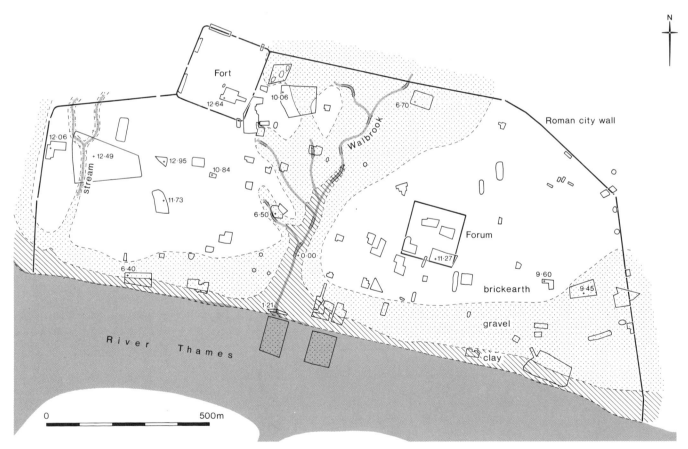

Fig. 9   Map to show the basic geology of Roman London. A bed of brickearth (not shaded) covers the plateau or raised river terrace on which the Roman city was built. This overlies the thick deposits of river gravels (stippled) of an elevated terrace, which in turn overlies London Clay (hatched). Further river gravels (stippled) of the flood-plain river terrace underlie the present River Thames. Individual sites on which the geology has been recorded are shown in outline, and spot levels, in metres above Ordnance Datum, indicate the land forms on the site of the Roman city.

The Roman development took place between the beginning of the Roman occupation of *Londinium* in about AD 50, and the construction of the enormous second basilica and forum by the early 2nd century. This was the span of but a single lifetime, and into this had been compressed an extraordinary amount of labour, resources and money. With such a large body of information to distill it has been essential first to establish the sequence of structural events on each site, and then to integrate these as much as is possible. Fortunately, the Boudican destruction and the first and second forum buildings provide conve-

Fig. 10 A reconstruction of the natural brickearth contours at half metre intervals on the forum site, based upon the spot levels (eg. +12.6) taken on the top of the natural brickearth. These show that the terrain sloped gently down to the east.

nient datum points common to many sites in the forum area, and these have greatly assisted the reconstruction of the overall sequence of development.

There nevertheless remains a small number of poorly described and dated walls which, though suggested to be Roman, do not obviously fit into the reconstruction proposed here. In particular there are the ancient foundations containing Roman brick found beneath the Norman undercroft in Corbet Court in 1871–2,[1] and a massive foundation 2.4m thick, within the nave area of the second basilica, which was found beside Gracechurch Street just south of St. Peter's church.[2] The available records are insufficient to enable their date and significance to be assessed, and consequently they have been omitted from this report.

Geology of the Forum site

The forum was constructed on an elevated river terrace on the north bank of the Thames, about 300m north of London Bridge. The natural surface of the terrace is brickearth, here overlying a thick bed of brown-yellow river gravel which in turn rests upon the London clay (Fig. 9).

Spot levels on the natural subsoil of the forum site show a slightly undulating surface, with a prevailing rise from 11.27m OD in the south to 12.38m in the north. There is also a general slight incline from 10.92–11.33m OD in the east, to perhaps as much as 12.91m in the west (Fig. 10).

These levels were recorded by a variety of people at different times, and it is quite possible that there are some minor errors. Nevertheless, the general pattern is consistent, and indicates a height variation of little more than 1.5m overall. These variations are important in understanding the dumping of materials necessary to level the site for the construction of the second basilica and forum.

Traces of a stream bed have been noted at 50 Cornhill,[3] at 9–12 George Yard and at 34–37 Nicholas Lane.[4] These three sightings present a problem, however, for they appear to represent the course of a single stream. Unfortunately no description is given of the stream, or of its relationship either to the natural subsoil or to the Roman and medieval deposits. Indeed it is difficult to substantiate the existence of the stream, for the published archaeological investigations at 50 Cornhill in 1891 made no mention of it.[5] In addition, the conjectured line of the stream between 50 Cornhill and 9–12 George Yard[6] passes through 1–2 St. Michael's Alley,[7] but Gerald Dunning, who carefully examined this latter site and recorded the natural subsoil and Roman and medieval features, found no trace of the stream. Similarly, the conjectured course of the stream north of 50

Cornhill passes across 68–73 Cornhill, a site carefully investigated by Peter James in 1982, where again no trace of a stream was found. These more recent and much better documented investigations plainly contradict the evidence of the earlier reported sightings of the stream, and no satisfactory explanation for this discrepancy can be offered at present.

The earliest occupation

The earliest Roman settlement on the forum site comprised a major east-west street, now mostly beneath Fenchurch Street and the east end of Lombard Street, together with a zone of occupation along its north side. This zone included a large gravelled area, presumably a courtyard (Fig. 11).

As no trace of prehistoric occupation has been found in the forum area it is clear that it was the Romans who created the first settlement there.[8] Although little detail has been discovered of the earliest structural features, enough has been noted to give a rough indication of the character of the occupation, and to show that it was a carefully planned settlement from the beginning. Unfortunately there is little evidence of the nature of that settlement, whether military or civil.

Prior to the construction of the main features there were, however, slight traces of preliminary Roman disturbance over the natural brickearth. At 168–170 Fenchurch Street these took the form of very thin bands of grey-black loam and carbon,[9] while at 30–32 Lombard Street there was a pit beneath the main east-west street which had been filled with grey clay before the street had been constructed (p. 135). No related structures have been found on either site, though the deposits at 168–170 Fenchurch Street did contain a coin, an *as* of Claudius; probably an imitation that may date from about AD 50 (see p. 71). The apparent absence of structures suggests that these deposits were associated with the clearance of the site as a preliminary to the construction of streets and buildings.

The east-west street was the main feature, its lowest layer of gravel metalling having been laid on the trampled surface of the natural brickearth. It was found at 168–170 Fenchurch Street[10] and at 30–32 Lombard Street (see p. 135), and was about 9m wide. A small roadside ditch with vertical sides, about 0.76m wide and 0.46m deep, was found on the former site.[11]

The large gravelled area was constructed on clean natural brickearth without a trampled surface, indicating that it had been de-turfed before the gravel was laid. The evidence of de-turfing was noted in the Gracechurch Street shaft (Fig. 12). The gravelled area was found in the Gracechurch Street tunnel (p. 100), and its approximate eastern limit was recorded at

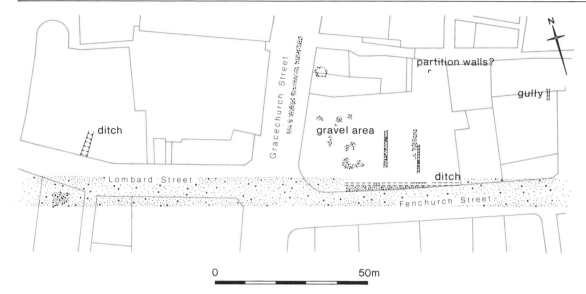

Fig. 11   The earliest phase of occupation on the forum site dates from about AD 50. It comprised a main east-west street, and on its north side a large gravelled 'area' of unknown extent to the north and west. Timber framed buildings apparently lay on the north side of the street, and were themselves probably separated by a narrow north-south street. The heavy stippling of the main street shows where gravel metalling was discovered, and the light stippling indicates the conjectured areas of metalling.

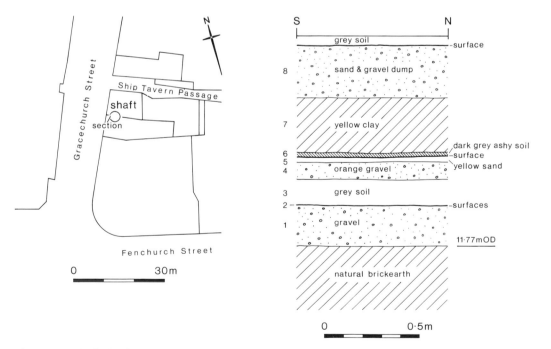

Fig. 12   A shaft dug beside Gracechurch Street disclosed two layers of gravel metalling (layers 1 and 4) of the large gravelled 'area'. The dark grey ashy soil, layer 6, may represent the destruction by Boudica, and the subsequent dumps, layers 7 and 8, are most likely associated with the second forum.

168–170 Fenchurch Street.[12] In general the gravel was 0.075–0.125m thick, and covered an area of more than 37m (north-south) by 25m (east-west).

The occupation zone east of the gravelled area was carefully studied by Philp at 168–170 Fenchurch Street.[13] It had been laid out with timber buildings and streets (Fig. 11). Traces were found of two gravelled north-south streets leading north from the main east-west street, and between them evidence of a timber building. The positions of the west and south walls of this building were marked by six circular post-holes 0.1–0.125m in diameter. The building was at least 6.4m long and probably not more than 7.6m wide. The widths of the north-south streets were not determined, but just beyond the eastern street were found three more post-holes of similar size which perhaps represent the frontage wall of another building. Further north were two clay walls, each 0.1m thick, of a further building, and associated with them was a small circular pit containing the contracted skeleton of a sheep or goat.[14]

This occupation at 168–170 Fenchurch Street was also represented by dumped deposits of clay and gravel; and, as similar deposits were also found at 160–162 Fenchurch Street, together with occupation debris and a gulley, it seems likely that the streets and buildings continued across that site too (p. 94).

The site at 54–58 Lombard Street lies west of the gravelled area, and there appeared to be less evidence of structural occupation here than was found to the east of the gravelled area. However, a major north-south drainage ditch was found, about 1.5m wide and 1.8m deep and with a flattish bottom, which originally drained northwards from the main east-west street (see p. 142). It probably drained water from the roadside ditch during the initial occupation of the site.

The pre-Boudican phase

A major re-planning of the area east of the gravelled courtyard was carried out during the 50s AD, and it was because these new buildings were burnt down during the Boudican revolt of 60 AD that so much of their plan is known. The main area investigated was at 168–170 Fenchurch Street,[15] but a substantial continuation was found to the east at 160–162 Fenchurch Street (see Fig. 13). The re-planning seems to have included three large parallel buildings, two apparently lying back to back between parallel east-west gravelled streets, and the third lying north of the northernmost street. Philp drew attention to one internal north-south wall line that was followed through the three buildings for a distance of over

Fig. 13 Features in the forum area in AD 60, and the known extent of Boudican burning (toned). Heavy stippling indicates discovered gravel metalling, and light stippling shows the conjectured course of the Roman street.

31m, suggesting that the buildings had been planned together as part of a single development.

THE SOUTHERN BUILDING

Of the three buildings, the southernmost was the most extensively recorded. It lay beside the main east-west street under Fenchurch Street, and was about 56.5m long and 14m wide. It seems that a range or ranges of rooms, about 10m wide north-south, extended alongside a verandah or portico beside the main street. Philp has suggested that there might have been a central east-west division in the range of rooms, but this is not necessarily borne out by the excavation of the large room at the east end of the building at 160–162 Fenchurch Street (p. 94). Nevertheless, Philp has pointed out the similar size and form of this building to another building also destroyed in the Boudican revolt at *Verulamium*.[16] This, however, had both large single and smaller double rooms behind the portico. At 160–2 Fenchurch Street only the east end of the Roman building revealed evidence of room size: here two rooms, respectively 7m and 3.3m wide and the former 9.5m deep from north to south, both fronted onto the portico.

The verandah or portico was about 3.2m wide, and extended along the southern frontage of the building beside the main street. Although there was no evidence of the form of its superstructure, it is presumed to have comprised an exterior row of timber pillars which supported a lean-to roof against the main building.

The walls were evidently timber-framed, with an in-filling of wattle and daub or brick at 168–170 Fenchurch Street,[17] and with unfired clay or mud-brick at 160–162 Fenchurch Street (p. 94). It is unlikely, however, that wattle and daub was actually used, rather than mud-brick, since when the excavation of 168–170 Fenchurch Street took place, very little evidence of mud-brick had been recognised in London and burnt clay was frequently assumed to be daub. The walls rested on wooden sleeper beams set in shallow trenches, some of the beams being supported on short timber piles. At the east end of the building load bearing walls lay on the wooden sleeper beams which in turn rested upon foundations of flint and brown mortar. Close to the west end of the building was found a large rectangular block of ragstone seated on a foundation of ragstone and yellow-white mortar. This suggests that a more substantial structure, perhaps a monument of some kind, lay at a corner of the building overlooking the large gravelled area.

Walls were roughly 0.5m thick, and, where seen, were rendered with clay. No painted plaster was found in the burnt debris of the Roman building at 160–162 Fenchurch Street, but instead a rendering of clay onto which a herringbone design had been impressed (Plate 1). Although Philp, generalising about the three Roman buildings at 168–170 Fenchurch Street, said that 'many of the walls had clearly been rendered with thin coats of plaster of which small traces were found in the fire debris',[18] painted plaster is only specified as having been found in the central and northern buildings. It seems unlikely, therefore, that any of the walls of this southern building had a painted plaster rendering. Similarly, there was no trace of window glass associated with any of the buildings burnt in AD 60, even though such should have been found either on the clay floors of the rooms, or in the burnt building debris, had it been in use.

Evidence of the form of the roofing was also forthcoming from this building. It was only at the south end of the easternmost north-south wall at 168–170 Fenchurch Street that an area of broken imbrex and tegula roof tiles were found, indicating that at this point at least the roof was tiled. There was otherwise no trace of roofing material in the fire debris either on that site or at 160–162 Fenchurch Street, suggesting that most of the roof may have been thatched. It would seem that this building comprised a row of shops opening into the street side portico beside modern Fenchurch Street. No evidence of domestic life was found in the building, though this may have been removed in AD 60. However, the general absence of decorated plaster and domestic occupation debris does suggest that the southern building was simply used as a row of shops. This view is supported by the large quantity of grain, imported from the eastern Mediterranean, which was found in the easternmost room of the building at 160–162 Fenchurch Street (p. 151). The proximity of the shops to the gravelled area, presumably a market place, was probably no coincidence; and the water pipe found at 168–170 Fenchurch Street reflects the quality of this early phase of planning.

THE CENTRAL BUILDING

The central building, immediately north of the double wall recorded at 168–170 Fenchurch Street,[19] may have been about 13.4m wide (N-S), and apparently fronted a narrow gravelled street to the north. Little is known about this building except for a north-south wall between two rooms. One room, with a slightly sunken floor, included a south wall which had been resurfaced four times with layers of painted plaster, indicating a span of several years before the burning of AD 60. Although Philp reconstructed the plan of the building as including two rooms, each about 13m long, north-south, it is more likely that there was a corridor or portico fronting the narrow northern street. The plaster perhaps suggests that this building was more domestic in character than that to the south, and that it contained the living quarters of the shopkeepers occupying the latter.

THE NORTHERN BUILDING

Even less is known about the northern building at 168–170 Fenchurch Street, which was probably more than 7.8m wide (N-S).[20] Part of a room with a sunken clay floor was found, together with a clay wall with a painted plaster rendering. In addition, because the burnt building debris of AD 60 filled a circular pit with vertical sides and a flat bottom, 1.22m deep and about 1.63m wide, it is possible that the pit, perhaps used for storage, lay within the northern building.

THE GRAVELLED AREA

The extent of the gravelled area, interpreted as a market place, is not known for certain. Since, however, burnt debris, probably from the Boudican fire, was found at the south and east sides of the All Hallows church site, in Lombard Street (p. 138), it would seem that buildings lay in that area in AD 60, and therefore that the gravelled area did not extend that far west. If so, the gravelled area was about 33m wide east-west and at least 40m long north-south; an area of over 1,320 sq metres. However, on this uncertain evidence, the gravelled area would not have been centrally placed at the north end of the north-south street beneath Gracechurch Street, leading up from the Roman bridge across the Thames. Instead it occupied perhaps one quarter of a cross roads, perhaps skirted on its west side by the street from London bridge which may then have continued northwards towards Bishopsgate. Unfortunately there is now no means of checking this except by excavating beneath Gracechurch Street itself, for the Roman features on neighbouring sites have elsewhere been completely destroyed.

WEST OF THE GRAVELLED AREA

At 54–58 Lombard Street were found traces of burnt debris probably also from the fire of AD 60 (see p. 143), but this was patchy and seemed to be dumped, indicating that the south end of the site had not actually been occupied by any substantial buildings even though it lay beside the main east-west street. A pit was found partly filled with rubbish and sealed by fire debris. The pit was therefore probably partly open in AD 60, and the rubbish, which included pottery and a considerable quantity of fine imported glass, dates from about that time, suggesting the partial use of the site.

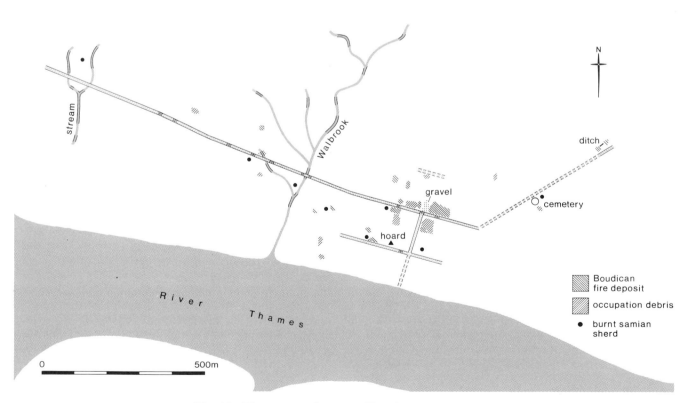

Fig. 14 The supposed extent of Londinium *c.* AD 60. A gravelled 'area' occupies the later forum site, and may at this stage have represented a public market place.

THE URBAN SETTLEMENT AREA C. AD 60

Because the burning by Boudica was confined to a zone roughly 50m wide, north of the main east-west street, on the forum site, it is likely that the northern edge of this zone marks the limit of the main built-up area of *Londonium* in AD 60. The distribution of Boudican fire debris east of the Walbrook suggests that the primary zone of occupation lay south of the forum site between the two parallel east-west Roman streets beneath Fenchurch Street and Cannon Street (Fig. 14).

Although it has long been recognized that the extent of the burnt debris of AD 60 is an extremely valuable indicator of the size of *Londinium* at the time of the Boudican rebellion, until recently maps showing the distribution of the debris have merely been restricted to recording those sites on which evidence of burning, presumed to be Boudican, has been found.[21] Fortunately, sufficient information has been recovered from many other sites to show where burning apparently did not occur,[22] and as a result it is now possible to map this phase of the Roman city in greater detail. Although the dating of fire deposits is often very difficult to determine, and proximity to the natural subsoil and to pre-Flavian occupation deposits is usually the only indication of their probable Boudican origins, the limits of the main settlement area can nevertheless be more precisely defined, at least on the assumption that most buildings in the embryonic city were burnt. Nowhere is this better illustrated than on the forum site.

In spite of the uncertainties and assumptions, the distribution of the fire debris of presumed Boudican origin on the forum site is consistent with the view that the main area of settlement was confined to a fairly narrow zone immediately north of the east-west street beneath Lombard Street. Since no burnt debris has been found in the region further north, it is presumed that the area was not generally occupied by buildings until after AD 60.

The Boudican fire

Sites in the forum area on which burnt debris is indicative of the former presence of buildings in AD 60, are: 30–32 Lombard Street (p. 135); 160–162 Fenchurch Street (p. 96); and 168–170 Fenchurch Street.[23]

Some patchy burnt debris suggesting a scatter or dumping of comparable material soon after the fire and close to the remains of as yet undiscovered buildings, has been found at: 19–21 Birchin Lane (p. 79); 54–58 Lombard Street (p. 143); and 1–2 St. Michael's Alley (p. 148).

In spite of careful examination for possible traces of Boudican destruction, none was found in significant quantity on the following sites, which were presumably not built upon by AD 60: 3–6, 15–16, 17–19 and 83–87 Gracechurch Street; the shaft in Gracechurch Street; the GPO tunnel dug in 1977 beneath Gracechurch Street; and 15–18 Lime Street.

Post-Boudican occupation

There is some rather inconclusive evidence of a phase of building intervening between the Boudican revolt in AD 60 and the construction of the first forum perhaps twenty years later (Fig. 15). The plan of the Roman structures found on the site of All Hallows church, Lombard Street, in 1939 (p. 138) shows that an east-west Roman wall was cut by a north-south wall of the first forum. Unfortunately the east-west wall, which on this evidence is presumed to be earlier, is not further described in the All Hallows site report, and there is no suggestion of how much earlier it was than the forum.

It is possible, however, that it was the western continuation of the north wall of a building found at 54–58 Lombard Street (p. 145), with which it was closely aligned. The foundations of this building were of ragstone and flint with brown mortar overlaid by courses of tiles, and it evidently comprised a range of rooms beside the main east-west street. It was apparently post-Boudican and was probably in existence during the Flavian period (p. 145), and it certainly pre-dates the second forum whose thick clay build-up dumps covered its walls. There was no ragstone demolition debris, and it is possible that a dismantled timber and mud-brick or daub superstructure itself formed part of the clay dump.

If these foundations and the wall on the All Hallows site were parts of the same building, the whole structure could be seen as predating the first forum. However, since demolition at 54–58 Lombard Street seems to have been intended to make way for the second forum, and the wall at All Hallows was cut by the structure of the first forum, it may be that the eastern end of the conjectured single building was demolished before the western so as to accommodate the first, smaller, forum.

It has been suggested that the building may have served an administrative purpose,[24] and, although this may be true, it would be unwise now that the extent of the uncertainties is clear, to draw even tentative conclusions without firmer evidence. Fortunately, more conclusive evidence may yet be found beneath the northern edge of Lombard Street adjacent to the main Roman east-west thoroughfare.

The first Basilica and Forum

An extensive Flavian building complex of four wings surrounding a central courtyard and occupying more than 5500 square m (about 1.5 acres), replaced the earlier gravelled area, and, as recently as 1977, was

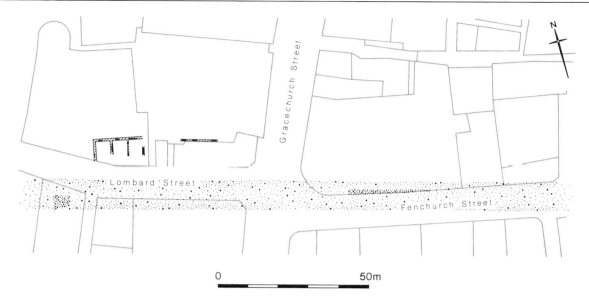

Fig. 15   Traces of a building believed to pre-date the first forum, but to post-date the Boudican destruction.

identified as the first basilica and forum of Londinium.[25] Measuring overall 104.5m long (north-south) and 52.7m wide, the length evidently intended to be exactly twice the width, the complex comprised a basilica in the north wing, and the remaining three wings which opened onto a rec-

tangular forum courtyard (Figs. 16, 17, 18). Two distinctive features of the complex were its flint foundations, and a series of external buttresses, the latter presumably originally supporting decorative architectural elements such as engaged columns. The buttresses were part of the original structure which

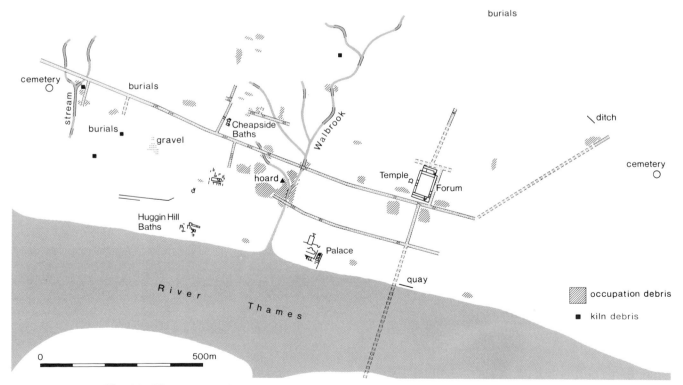

Fig. 16   The supposed extent of Londinium *c*. AD 80–90, with the first basilica and forum occupying a central position within a ring of cemeteries, as if it was then intended that the city should develop equally to the east and west of the forum.

Gracechurch Street

Lombard Street

Fenchurch Street

0   25m

Fig. 17 (*left*) Plan of the first basilica, forum and temple as recorded on individual sites. No adjustments have been made here to co-ordinate these findings. Black represents walls of the primary building phase; light hatching represents conjectured walls of that phase; heavy cross hatching represents recorded walls of a secondary phase; and dense stippling represents street metalling.

Fig. 18 Reconstructed plan of the first basilica, forum and temple, the symbols used being as in Fig. 17. It seems that initially the forum comprised a range of rooms opening out onto a courtyard, but that subsequently an inner portico was added.

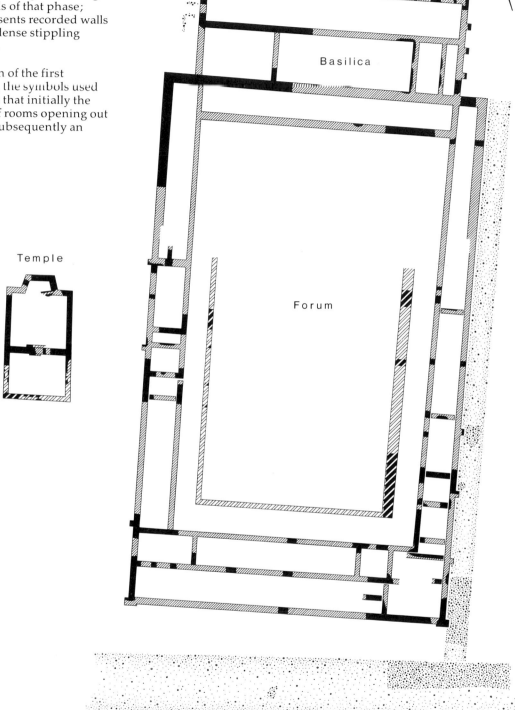

Temple

Basilica

Forum

0   25m

had been built into the outer walls of the basilica, and into the exterior walls of the east and west wings of the forum.

The main access to the forum courtyard and to the basilica was no doubt through the south wing, where there seems to have been a portico (Fig. 18) fronting onto the main east-west street of Roman London, now lying beneath parts of Lombard Street and Fenchurch Street. Indications of a possible entrance in the middle of the west wing (Fig. 18) have also been found, perhaps for access to the small classical temple which lay just outside the forum. This temple had the same unusual flint foundation construction as the basilica and forum, and as it was probably part of the civic centre complex, it will also be included in this report.

THE FIRST BASILICA

The first basilica seems to have comprised a nave and side aisles separated by rows of columns or piers, and at the east end of the nave there was a raised tribunal (Fig. 19).

Construction. From the start of its construction it was evidently intended that the basilica should dominate Londinium, for its floor was built on an artificial platform of dumped debris raised to about a metre above the surrounding area. With the floor lying at 13.61–13.77m OD, irregularities in the underlying natural surface, which varied from 11.33m OD

at 83–87 Gracechurch Street (at the west end of the basilica) to 12.1m OD at 3–6 Gracechurch Street (at the east end), could be removed, though about 0.6m of made-ground had already accumulated over the natural brickearth at 79 and 83–87 Gracechurch Street.

A construction programme was evidently devised to integrate the dumping and building activities in several clearly defined stages. Firstly, the positions of the foundations were presumably marked out, mostly about 0.9m wide, for trenches of that width were dug down through the earlier man-made deposits and the natural brickearth into the underlying natural gravel. The basilica foundations were dug down to two different levels: those of the nave and the 'shoulders' of the forum were dug to between 8.8m and 9.2m OD; and the shallower foundations of the aisles and of the presumed tribunal to between 9.65m and 9.8m OD. The greater depth of the nave foundations evidently reflects a greater weight of superstructure than was intended for the side aisles.

The foundations were constructed of alternating layers of flints, freshly quarried from the chalk and set in brown mortar. Courses of tiles were usually laid at about the level of the natural brickearth, between 11.15m and 12m OD, above which were built several roughly faced courses of ragstone. A triple course of bonding tiles lay above this, followed by further courses of ragstone and of bonding tiles, all set in brown mortar. The effect of this was to construct low walls of ragstone with courses of bonding tiles up to about 13.77m OD. The facings

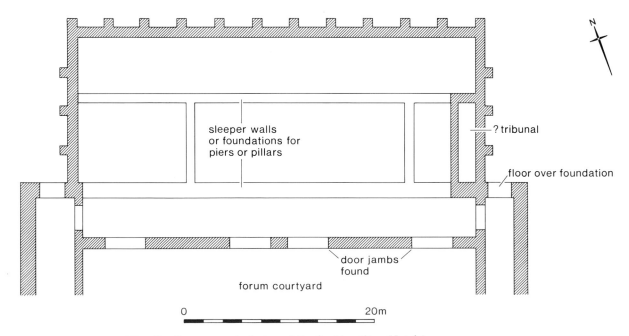

Fig. 19 Reconstructed plan of the first basilica. Hatching represents wall superstructure; no hatching indicates foundations with no superstructure.

were deliberately rough, presumably because, although the walls were constructed above the contemporary ground level, it was intended to bury them with dumps of clay etc. upon which the basilica floor would be laid.

Pressure from the dumped debris within the basilica may explain why the outer walls were buttressed on the outside, at intervals of about 3m. Each buttress was 0.9m square, and shared the same foundation construction of flints and brown mortar as the wall foundations into which they were bonded. Their upper part, above the flint foundation, was entirely of layers of red tiles.

The enormous quantities of brickearth, rubbish, rubble and gravel that were dumped inside the building to raise the floor level to about 13.77m OD were found at 83–87 Gracechurch Street. Construction of the walls seems to have continued as the dumping progressed, for at 83–87 Gracechurch Street layers of mortar were found interleaved between the dumped deposits. Indeed, one layer of mortar was described ·by Frank Cottrill as 'a mass of white material, lime? – with some stones – a place for making cement?' (see p. 120).

The construction and dumping process appears to have been complicated at 3–6 Gracechurch Street by the presence of an extensive pit-like excavation beneath the north aisle. The west side of the pit coincided with the west wall of the aisle, and it is not certain if the pit was earlier than or contemporary with the basilica. Part of it seems to have been contemporary with the basilica because the fill layers were piled against the basilica foundation (p. 121), suggesting that an underground room may have existed below this part of the north aisle. Alternatively, this may have been an earlier pit across which the walls were built, and which was filled in with the dumping intended to raise the floor level generally in the basilica. It is likely that some further and clearer evidence has survived below Gracechurch Street.

Description of the first basilica. The basilica measured externally 44m long and 22.7m wide, and overlooked the north side of the forum courtyard. With the exception of its south wall, only the foundations had survived. Nevertheless, although it is difficult to reconstruct the form of the superstructure on this evidence, the foundation plan indicates that it was a fairly conventional building with a nave and side aisles, probably separated by parallel rows of columns or piers erected on deep foundations. It is this plan (Fig. 19) which enables its purpose to be identified.

Exterior. A series of projecting brick buttresses, constructed on foundations of flint and mortar bonded into the wall foundations, had been constructed against the outer faces of the north, east and,

presumably, west walls of the basilica. Although only three have been recorded projecting from the north wall, their spacing at approximately 3m intervals shows that there were originally twelve along this wall. Three more, also spaced at intervals of about 3m, were found against the east wall, and were presumably mirrored by a further three against the west wall (Fig. 19). It is likely that their main purpose was to help retain the raised floor level inside the building.

As the upper part of the foundations was built of ragstone and courses of tiles, and the buttresses were built entirely of tiles, it is likely that this form of construction continued above the final floor level of the basilica.

The Nave. The width of the nave between its two foundations was 8.38m and it is likely that these foundations, which separated the nave from the side aisles, carried pillars or brick piers supporting the roof (Plate 3). The nave foundations, which were about one metre wide, were 0.5m deeper than the exterior foundations of the aisles. This strongly suggests that the roof of the nave was appreciably higher than the roofs of the aisles, and that there was a clerestory to admit daylight into the nave. No trace of the pillars or piers was found to suggest their construction and spacing, but presumably they were no wider than the foundations.

Three foundations have been located crossing the nave, the easternmost lying only 2m from the east wall of the basilica. The base of this foundation was at 9.8m OD, showing that it was 0.6m shallower than the nave foundations. This presumably indicates that it carried less weight, and is probably best interpreted as the front wall of a tribunal or raised dais from which meetings were supervised. If this was the case then the wall probably stood no more than about 2m high.

Another foundation crossed the nave 5.18m west of the conjectured tribunal, its base lying at 9.19m OD, at the same great depth as the nave foundations. Thus this may have supported columns in front of the tribunal, but as there was only a very limited space across the narrow nave it is perhaps more likely that its purpose was merely to help stabilise the north and south foundations of the nave.

The purpose of a third foundation found crossing the nave further to the west is unknown, and there is no description of its construction.[26]

The floor of the nave was found only at 83–87 Gracechurch Street, where its surface lay at 13.77m OD. This comprised a layer of cream coloured cement about 0.2m thick, containing occasional brick fragments, above a mixed rubbish deposit.

The North Aisle. Measuring 42.18m long and 5.64m wide internally, the north aisle appears to have been a completely open chamber. No transverse partitions have been found suggesting sub-division into offices or other apartments. Its floor was of exactly the same cream coloured concrete as in the nave, and at the same level (85–87 Gracechurch Street). The foot of its north, east and west foundations lay at about 9.7m OD, about 0.5m above the base of the south wall which separated the aisle from the nave. This presumably means that the nave foundations supported a greater weight than did those of the north aisle.

The South Aisle. This was narrower than the north aisle, being 4.42m wide, and, as the foot of its foundations lay at 9.72m OD, about 0.5m above those of the nave foundations, it would seem that, like the north aisle, this carried less weight than did the nave.

Because the south aisle fronted the forum courtyard, it is to be expected that it contained the entrances into the basilica. Two entrances have been recorded, in both of which traces of flooring were found. One lay at the east end of the south wall of the basilica, adjacent to the east wing of the forum. Its western door jamb was found, and the sill of the opening was traced for a distance which suggests that the doorway was about 4.88m wide, though the eastern jamb was not found. The western door jamb was constructed of red tiles for some depth below the door sill, and may indicate that the jamb above the door sill was also constructed of tiles. Above the door sill itself, constructed of a layer of tiles above courses of ragstone, was a floor surface of white cement about 0.013m thick, overlying a layer of mortar and ragstone chips. As this lay at 13.61m OD, only 0.16m lower than the flooring of the nave and north aisle, it is presumed that this was also the approximate level and construction of the flooring of the south aisle.

A second doorway was found under Gracechurch Street close to the centre of the south wall of the basilica (see p. 101). In this case it was an eastern door jamb, much of which had been robbed away, the lowest 0.33m of the jamb being constructed of a corner of ragstone overlaid by three courses of tiles set in pink mortar. The door sill itself, like the other doorway, also had a single course of tiles which was overlaid by a white mortar floor at about 13.2m above OD.

Apart from two further doorways which probably existed in the south wall (see below, 'Superstructure of the basilica'), it seems likely that doorways may also have existed at the east and west ends of the south aisle, to give access to the east and west wings of the forum. Unfortunately, the site of the suggested doorway at the west end of the aisle had been destroyed at 7–9 Gracechurch Street, while at the east end, on the site of 83–87 Gracechurch Street, the wall remains to be excavated.

Superstructure of the Basilica. The care with which the basilica was planned is shown by the fact that the width of the building was exactly half its length. Such regard for proportions is an important clue to the degree of care that was exercised in constructing the superstructure.

Although it is not possible to judge the form of the roof with certainty, the significantly greater depth of the nave foundations implies that the roof of the nave was appreciably higher than the roofs of the aisles. A clerestory, supported on pillars or piers supported on the foundations which separated the nave from the sides aisles, would have admitted daylight into the nave (Fig. 19).

More certain, however, are the entrances from the forum courtyard to the building. Since a doorway into the forum courtyard existed at the east end of the south aisle, symmetry would demand a matching doorway at the west end. A more imposing central double entrance is suggested by the doorway that was discovered just off centre. The combined entrance was probably about 10m wide, each opening perhaps being about 4m wide.

The absence of administrative offices is important, for this shows that the *curia* and other municipal offices were located elsewhere. The suggested doorways in the east and west wings of the forum imply that at least some of those offices may have been located in the forum. If the overlapping of the east and west wings of the forum with the ends of the south aisle of the basilica was not to facilitate access between the two buildings, it would be difficult to account for their arrangement.

Later Phases of the Basilica. No evidence of any modification to the plan of the basilica has been found, for whenever its foundations have been examined they invariably exhibited a uniform construction. Sufficient of this building has been examined to conclude that had any major modifications occurred, traces of them would have been detected. This contrasts with the forum where clear evidence of major modifications has been recorded.

One minor alteration to the basilica, however, was recorded at 83–87 Gracechurch Street in the eastern doorway of the south wall of the south aisle, where a deposit of sand and gravel was found overlying the original concrete floor; above this was a new white mortar floor 0.038m thick.

THE FIRST FORUM

From its varying methods of construction and from the straight joints between some of its walls and foundations, the first forum appears to have been constructed in three main phases. It is not certain to what extent these 'phases' were merely stages in one planned phase of construction, or different schemes of reconstruction. However, the criteria by which they are judged include the architectural integrity of the whole complex.

Phase 1 The primary phase of the forum has been divided into phases 1A and 1B. In phase 1A the forum apparently comprised two side wings (east and west) without cross-walls (with one exception in the west wing), and a south wing with a range of rooms behind a presumed portico fronting the main east-west street of *Londinium*. In phase 1B, a number of cross-walls were added to the east and west wings, and at least two north-south cross walls were constructed within what is believed to have been the portico of the south wing. Because of the similarity of foundation construction it seems most likely that phases 1A and 1B are different stages in a single building phase, though in the former the foundations are bonded together, while in the latter they are separated by straight joints.

Construction. The foundations of phases 1A and 1B were constructed of flints freshly quarried from the chalk, and set in yellowish-brown mortar. The base of the foundations lay roughly at 10.5m or 10.6m OD, though Philp recorded the south end of the extreme east wall of the forum as lying at about 11.31m OD. However, the drawn section from which this level is obtained[27] is incomplete, and it is quite possible that the foundation may have been deeper than supposed, so as to accord with the level of the other forum foundations.

Courses of tiles lay at about the apparent contemporary ground surface, and the base of these varied in level from 12.06m to 12.76m OD in the east, west and south wings. The differences may be accounted for by the uneven natural surface, which in general dropped in level by about 0.46m from beneath the west wing, where the natural surface lay at about 12.16m OD, to 11.70m OD under the east wing. In addition, an uneven accumulation of 'made ground' above the natural surface probably contributed to the differences in tile levels.

The East Wing. In phase 1A, the east wing measured internally 74.5m long and 4.27m wide, and comprised an elongated rectangular compartment with walls 0.91m thick. The construction of the walls included a triple course of bonding tiles which was overlaid by at least two courses of ragstone; and the foundations below, of mortared flints, were 1.52m deep and 0.93m wide in the southern half of the wing.

In phase 1B, a series of cross-walls was added to the wing, and as these had a construction of mortared flints identical to the pre-existing north-south walls against which they abutted, it is very likely that they were part of the original scheme for the east wing. Indeed, the addition of internal walls in this way, as part of a single construction scheme, is exactly paralleled in the east wing of the Flavian palace in Cannon Street.[28] The cross foundations in the forum were all about 0.76m wide, and they divided the east wing into a series of chambers of unequal size. Five cross-walls were found at 168–170 Fenchurch Street (Fig. 20), and one more was found in 1982 at 79 Gracechurch Street (see p. 117).

Three buttresses were found projecting from the external face of the east wall of the wing at 168–170 Fenchurch Street. These measured 0.91m long and 0.76m wide, and their foundations were of flint and mortar with an upper construction of bricks. They probably belonged to phase 1A, as did the south-east corner buttress and also the buttresses of the basilica. The three buttresses were 9.70 and 19.70m apart, and Philp suggests that the probable existence of three further buttresses of the same dimensions would give an original spacing of about 4.27m.[29]

The north end of the east wall at 83–87 Gracechurch Street had been robbed, and the robber trench was 1.8m wide, indicating that the wall was substantially thicker here than was the case in the southern part of the wing. Its true thickness was probably about 1.37m thick, like the north wall of the same wing and the northern wall of the west wing. One possible reason for this thickening is that the north end of the forum, like the basilica, apparently lay on a terrace (see below p. 31) about a metre above the southern part of the forum, and this required additional support.

No certain trace of any internal flooring has been found in the east wing, and at 79 Gracechurch Street, excavated by A. Upson in 1983, any original flooring appears to have been removed before the gravel make-up was dumped for the second forum (see p. 117). A mortar surface at about 12.2m OD was found immediately west of the east wing at 79 Gracechurch Street, and was overlaid by the second forum dump (Plates 4, 5). This surface suggested that the floor within the east wing in the southern part of the forum was also at about this level.

Possible traces of a cement floor were found by Cottrill over the north wall of the east wing, just east of the basilica, at 83–87 Gracechurch Street, suggesting the former existence of a doorway at that point. The pink mortar surface lay at about 13.64m OD, which was about the level of the terrace or platform upon which the basilica floor was constructed.

There is little indication of decorative embellishment, such as statues and monuments, in the forum. The only element so far found is a shallow masonry foundation 1.83m × 0.38m that was built against the west wall of the east wing. This is believed to be the base of a decorative feature facing into the forum courtyard.[30]

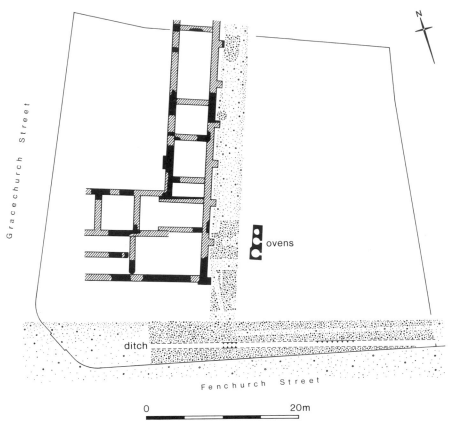

Fig. 20   168–170 Fenchurch, showing features of *c.* AD 80. Solid shading represents recorded walls, and hatching represents conjectured walls.

The West Wing. The west wing was also probably 74.5m long, and 4.43m wide internally, and, although not so carefully recorded as was the east wing, its main external walls are presumed to date from period 1A. The outer wall, forming a 'shoulder' at the north end of the west wing, was found in 1912 on the site of 7–9 Gracechurch Street, and was 1.37m thick.[31] The base of the foundation descended to a depth of 8.2m below the present street level (*ie* to about 9.44m OD), while its thickness, greater than that of its continuation to the south, suggests that it too was supporting a greater weight, as was its counterpart which formed a 'shoulder' to the east wing. This great L-shaped wall in the west wing extended eastwards as the foundation separating the nave of the basilica from its south aisle. It appears to have rested upon a foundation whose base lay at about 9.44m OD, and above that was 0.76m of flints lightly set in occasional splashes of mortar; 1.52m of rough ragstone, which was overlaid by a double course of bonding tiles; ragstone 0.9m thick; and a further double course of tiles, the base of which lay at about 12.72m OD. This massive wall may reflect the extent of the raised terrace that lay beneath and apparently in front of the basilica.

The remainder of the west wing, further south, was found at 15–16 Gracechurch Street in 1912, and at 17–19 Gracechurch Street in 1934–5. Little information was recovered from the former, but on the latter

Frank Cottrill recorded much detail (see p. 114). The main north-south walls, presumably belonging to phase 1A, were based on flint foundations 0.86m wide (west wall) and 0.76m wide (east wall). The base of the foundations lay at 10.4m–10.6m OD, about a metre above the level of the base of the main L-shaped wall at the north end of the wing.

In only one case were the foundations of a cross-wall found to be bonded into the north-south walls. This was located at 17–19 Gracechurch Street (p. 115), and although it is clear that it too must be of phase 1A, insufficient of the superstructure of any of the walls remained for this to be reconstructed with certainty. Nevertheless, it seems possible that it was intended as part of a side entrance leading through the wing. It is perhaps significant that its position lay opposite a small classical temple, found at 17–19 Gracechurch Street, which stood just west of the forum.

Although a further cross-foundation abutted a north-south wall at 17–19 Gracechurch Street, showing that it was of phase 1B, most of the cross-walls were not sufficiently well recorded for their phase to be established. Such descriptions as exist seem to indicate that they all had flint foundations, showing that they could belong to either phase 1A or 1B.

Traces of buttresses on the west wall of the west wing were found at 17–19 Gracechurch Street and at All Hallows church, Lombard Street (p. 139). On the former site traces of two external projections, presumed to be buttresses, were found 13.3m apart. Assuming that the buttresses were of the standard 0.76m width, as occurred along the east wing, and that there was an intermediate buttress, then the spacing would have been 6.27m. At All Hallows church, however, the interval between two buttresses was about 10.6m; and, allowing for an intermediate buttress, would indicate a spacing of 4.92m compared with an interval of 4.27m suggested by the east wing. It is not certain which was the 'correct' spacing, though it should be pointed out that the 4.92m dimension suggested at All Hallows would require a buttress both where the southern buttress was actually found at 17–19 Gracechurch Street, and also at the extreme north end of the west wall. Although no buttresses were noted at the north end of this wall at 17–19 Gracechurch Street, the circumstances of the building site observations may have made this difficult. However, an interval of 4.92m would be compatible with a buttress at the southwest corner of the forum, matching that which occurred at the south-east corner. As a buttress existed just short of the conjectured corner position on the All Hallows site, it must be assumed that for some reason the arrangement was slightly modified at this point.

On present evidence it would seem that the spacing of 4.92m is the more correct measurement along the west wing, though, if so, it is difficult to account for the west wing possessing sixteen buttresses, and the east wing eighteen. Perhaps there was rather more variation in the spacing of the buttresses than the few known measurements allow, but as very little, if any, of the west wing survives in the ground, it is unlikely that these conclusions can be checked.

The South Wing.   The south wing measured approximately 52.4m long and about 12m wide, and fronted the main east-west street of *Londinium* from which it was set back about 8m. Although remains of the wing have been found at 168–170 Gracechurch Street, in the GPO tunnel dug under Gracechurch Street in 1977, and at All Hallows church in Lombard Street, little more than the foundations have been observed.

The wing comprised two east-west ranges of chambers set within three parallel east-west walls. The northern range was about 4.65m wide internally, and at the east end had two cross foundations forming a room 4.57m × 4.35m. The foundations, of flint and mortar, were bonded into the main east-west foundations, showing that they were of phase 1A. Comparisons with other fora suggest that this was one of a series of rooms in the wing, but there is no definite evidence at present. Although the south range was about 5m wide internally, the absence so far of any recorded cross-walls in phase 1A suggests that it was planned as a portico perhaps with a row of

pillars supported on the southernmost foundation beside the main street. Two flint and mortar foundations discovered in the south range at 168–170 Fenchurch Street, however, were evidently of phase 1B because they abutted both each other and the main east-west walls with straight joints. Such structures would seem to have broken the integrity of the range as a portico, but the information at present is too limited for a satisfactory reconstruction. In general the lower parts of the tile and ragstone walls were 0.76m wide, and set on flint foundation 0.81m thick. No definite evidence of flooring has been found. Deposits beneath the presumed floor level have been recorded up to 11.83m OD,[32] and as they were overlaid by dumped debris for the second forum it is likely that the flooring of the south wing lay at about 12m OD.

Courtyard.   Although the surface of the forum courtyard has not been recorded, its levels are probably reflected by adjacent internal floors and other surfaces within the basilica-forum complex. It would seem that the courtyard lay at two levels, the upper suggested by floors in the doorways of the basilica, which lay at 13.2m OD and 13.6m OD. These gave access to the north end of the courtyard, and it was clear at 83–87 Gracechurch Street that the 1m thick dumping of debris, which artificially raised the ground level under the basilica, extended at least a little further into the area immediately to the south, under the north end of the courtyard.

Sites further south in the forum, at 17–19 Gracechurch Street and at 168–170 Fenchurch Street, showed no evidence of dumping; and at 79 Gracechurch Street a careful archaeological excavation demonstrated not only that there was no dumping, but also that here the ground surface of the first forum lay at about 12.3m OD (p. 117). Most of the courtyard, therefore, seems to have stood on the lower level.

The only possible clue to the form of the courtyard surface in the lower area is derived from a shaft dug during 1978 in the Gracechurch Street frontage of 168–170 Fenchurch Street, just south of Ship Tavern Passage (p. 101). The two pre-forum gravelled surfaces were disclosed above the natural brickearth, the upper at 12.46m OD. Deposits, apparently dumped, overlay this, and the next definite trampled surface lay at 13.27m OD. On the basis of these levels alone it would seem most likely that the upper pre-forum gravelled surface may have been re-used to create part of the forum courtyard.

It is uncertain where the 1m change in level occurred, but it was evidently between nos. 79 and 87 Gracechurch Street. The thickening of the external east and west walls of the forum may be a clue, for on the lower level at 168–170 Fenchurch Street and at 17–19 Gracechurch Street the walls were only 0.86–

0.91m thick. But on the upper level, at Nos. 83–87 and 17–19 Gracechurch Street, continuations of the same walls were 1.37m thick. The extent of the thick walls may therefore reflect the extent of the upper terrace. At 17–19 Gracechurch Street the thick wall was traced as far south as Bell Inn Yard, and on present evidence it would seem most likely that the change in terrace level occurred roughly there. Flights of steps may be presumed to have led from the lower to the upper terrace, as occurred in the forum at Caistor by Norwich[33], and perhaps they were originally situated opposite the entrances into the basilica.

THE STREETS

Although the forum entrance probably lay in the south wing, beside the main east-west street of *Londinium* and opposite the north end of the north-south street leading to the Roman London bridge, it is to be expected that streets also bounded the other three sides of the basilica-forum complex. Possible traces of east, north and west streets have been found, though their stratigraphic relationships to the basilica and forum remains to be demonstrated. As the east-west streets to the north of the basilica (at 3–6 Gracechurch Street) and south of the forum (at 168–170 Fenchurch Street) overlay the natural sub-soil, and clearly pre-dated the first basilica and forum, it would seem that they determined the length of the complex. However, the streets to the east (at 168–170 Fenchurch Street) and west (at 3–6 Gracechurch Street) overlay the remains of earlier Roman building and rubbish deposits, and it may be assumed that they were built at the same time as the forum.

It was usual for a basilica and forum to be constructed at the junction of two arterial streets leading to gates, as occurred at Verulamium, Cirencester and Caistor by Norwich. However, as for example at Silchester, this was not always the case. Although it is clear that the first London forum lay beside the arterial east-west street, the *decumanus*, below Lombard Street and Fenchurch Street, it is far from certain that it lay next to a north-south arterial street, the *cardo*. Such a street, had it existed, would have presumably led through the Bishopsgate area to become the start of Ermine Street.

The north-south street on the east side of the forum was examined in 1968 at 168–170 Fenchurch Street (Fig. 20), and found to be 3.66m wide with just one layer of gravel metalling not more than 0.3m thick.[34] This could only have been a minor street for it was clearly not designed to carry heavy traffic, and an absence of remetalling evidently reflects very limited use. Some use, though, is suggested by the existence of buildings nearby. Immediately east of this street, and just north of the main east-west Roman road beneath Fenchurch Street, Philp found six brick ovens at 168–170 Fenchurch Street, which he

suggested were part of a bakery.[35] Traces of a more substantial building with a ragstone wall and herringbone tiled pavements were found at the east end of Leadenhall Market (see Fig. 30, no. 7).[36] This should be contemporary with the first basilica and forum, for it lay on the line of and below the level of a later north-south Roman street which fronted the east side of the second forum. As it lay a little to the north-east of the first basilica it need not necessarily have used the eastern street beside the first forum as a regular means of access.

The presumed street on the west side of the forum is perhaps a more likely candidate for the main north-south street, for at the only site on which it appears to have been found, just west of the first basilica at 3–6 Gracechurch Street, there were six layers of gravel metalling indicating a much heavier use (p. 104). Indeed, the fact that this western street was flanked on its far side by a temple is also indicative of its importance.

THE TEMPLE

A building believed to have been a temple of classical type was found on the site of 17–19 Gracechurch Street, lying 11.88m to the west of the forum (Fig. 81). Unfortunately it was not possible to establish with certainty what lay between the temple and the forum, though had there been any substantial masonry walls it is likely that they would have been noted. The temple itself was 20.7m long, 10.66m wide, and was orientated approximately north-south. Its foundations were constructed of quarried flints, exactly as were used in the first forum and basilica; and because this is an unusual construction in Roman London it is reasonable to assume that it was built as part of the forum-basilica complex, and was for municipal use.

The temple comprised a *cella*, with an angular apse in the north wall, and in the south wall there was a doorway, one jamb of which had survived, suggesting that the opening was originally 4.1m wide. Two southward projecting *antae* of unequal length enclosed a portico, in which was found a ragstone and mortar foundation only 0.5m deep. Although rather shallow, this may have been sufficient to support a pillar on either side of the doorway, thus affecting the architectural style *distyle in antis*.

In spite of the excellent archaeological record of the temple made by Frank Cottrill, it was not possible for him to record enough, during the building operations in 1934–5, to establish the original height of the temple. The absence of any plaster wall rendering of floor within the *cella* might suggest that the interior of the building had been filled with dumped materials to raise its floor level. However, the door sill in the south wall lay at 12.92 OD, suggesting that in its first phase the temple floor was not raised in this way. Although the ground level around the temple exterior was not recorded, the base of the tile superstructure which overlay the flint foundation is presumed to reflect the ground level. This lay between 12.6m and 12.8m OD, and the temple walls were standing about 0.6–0.8m high (ie, to about 13.4m OD).

In a subsequent phase, not necessarily connected with any rebuilding of the forum, the portico of the temple was enclosed by brick walls with shallow foundations only 0.5m deep. The purpose of this enclosure is not certain, but it seems most likely to have retained the dumped debris which supported a staircase leading up to a now raised temple floor.

There is no pottery or coin evidence to date the construction of the temple and its modifications; but as part of the civic centre pre-dating the second forum it may be presumed to date from the building of the first forum and basilica.

LATER PHASES OF THE FIRST FORUM

Although definite evidence of alterations to the first forum has been found, there remains considerable difficulty in establishing the structural sequence because many of the later features were not physically related to each other. These subsequent phases are mainly identified by their relationship to the primary phase of the forum, and by their construction which is significantly different from that of the original forum.

In particular there are groups of brick piers which occur mostly in rows following the wall lines of the first forum (Figs. 21, 22). Brian Philp suggested that they formed part of a monumental entrance to the second forum, but he did not discuss his reasons for that attribution, or indicate how they related to that forum, or indeed describe what his 'tentative reconstruction' plan might have looked like.[37] On his own admission, this reconstruction was made by 'ignoring those piers which seem random',[38] and it is clear that the information available in 1969, when Philp excavated the south-east corner of the first forum, was insufficient for satisfactory interpretation.

It is now certain that most of the piers pre-date the second forum, for they were constructed before the dumping of clay, gravel and building materials which raised the ground level by about a metre to accommodate the second forum. This was recently demonstrated at 79 Gracechurch Street where a thick dump of gravel overlay the first forum. On that site was also found a robbed pier (pier 11) which had been constructed upon a wall of the first forum before the dumping for the second forum had occurred (p. 117. Plates 4, 5). In fact Philp's own record of his site at 168–170 Fenchurch Street confirms that the piers were earlier than the second forum, for the base of their brick facing lay between

12.36m–12.8m OD,[39] while the truncated top of the dumped deposits underlying the floor of the second forum lay about a meter higher, at 13.4m OD.[40]

Not only is it clear that most of the piers pre-dated the second forum, but it is also certain that almost all of them respect the wall positions of the first forum, and therefore follow its basic plan. In fact some piers even used the walls of the first forum as their foundations, showing that their builders knew the layout of that forum, which would not have been possible once the dumping associated with the second forum had occurred. The piers must therefore belong to an intermediate stage or stages between the primary construction of the first forum, and the building of the second forum.

The intermediate structures appear to comprise four distinct groups:

(1) An inner portico. A foundation of flint and ragstone which was constructed close to the east, west, and perhaps the south, wings of the forum, suggests that an inner portico had been added to the forum. It is because its construction included ragstone that it is assumed to be of a secondary phase.[41]

Several piers of brick set in yellow mortar have been found on this flint and ragstone foundation beside the east wing (Figs. 21, 22, piers 7 and 9 at 168–170 Fenchurch Street), and others (piers 6, 7, 12, 13, and 14) have been found following the conjectured line of the foundation beside the south wing (at 168–170 Fenchurch Street and at All Hallows, Lombard Street, see Figs. 21, 22). On the latter site the alignment of the piers was incorrectly recorded, as was an adjacent wall of the second forum. By correcting the position of this forum wall, the first forum piers also fall into line with those found at 168–170 Fenchurch Street.

Unfortunately there is very little information about this inner portico foundation, and nowhere is its full width recorded. At 17–19 Gracechurch Street its outer (i.e. eastern) edge lay 5.33m east of the phase 1 west wing (p. 115), and at 15–16 Gracechurch Street the inner edge lay roughly 3.7m east of the wing. This suggests that the foundation was about 1.63m wide. Two observations on the foundation beside the east wing (at 168–170 Fenchurch Street and at 77–79 Gracechurch Street) place its inner edge about 4m west of the wing. On the latter site the foundation, carefully investigated during archaeological excavations, was found to be of ragstone and yellow mortar, and was nearly 2m wide. Its surviving top surface lay at about 12.3m OD, and along its eastern side was the impression of a course of tiles 1m wide, as if a tile wall had been built along the top of the foundation. The impression of the tiles in the mortar was traced throughout the length of the foundation exposed, and was therefore too extensive to represent the remains of a pier.

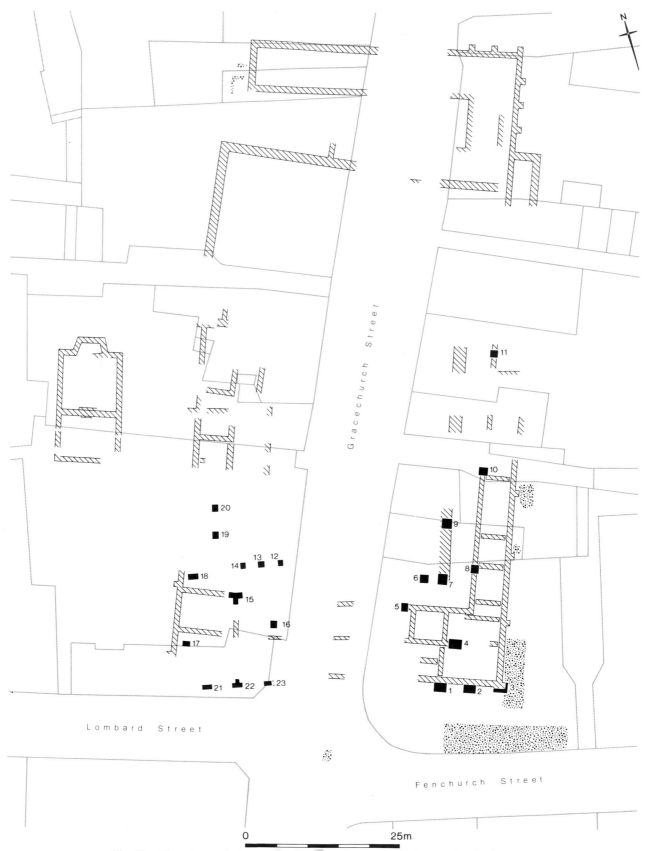

Fig. 21   The phase of piers of the first forum as recorded on individual sites.

Fig. 22 The piers shown on a reconstructed plan of the first forum. Their location generally upon the walls of the primary phase of the forum (not hatched) seems to indicate that most of the walls had been demolished before the piers were constructed. The absence of piers on the exterior buttressed walls of the forum (hatched) suggests that these walls were not demolished.

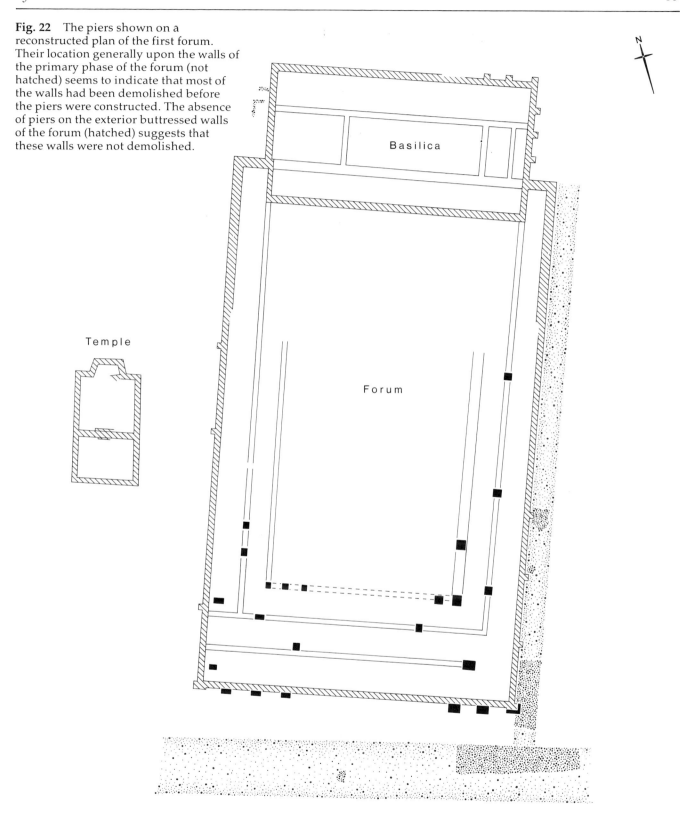

Basilica

Temple

Forum

0   25m

No evidence of the inner portico foundation has been found to the north of the south wing. However, a line of brick piers (piers 6, 7, 12, 13 and possibly 14) recorded 4m to the north of the wing, suggests that the foundation did exist and that it supported these piers.

The general relationship of the piers to the inner portico foundation is not clear, but the report on 168–170 Fenchurch Street[42] suggests that each of the piers, particularly pier 9, had an individual foundation of stone which overlay the continuous foundation. If so the piers may represent a separate rebuilding of the inner portico.

(2) Piers on the inner forum wall of phase 1A. A series of brick piers has also been found constructed on top of the phase 1A inner or western wall of the east wing at 79 Gracechurch Street and at 168–170 Fenchurch Street (piers 8, 10 and 11) (Fig. 23). Other piers have been found on the northernmost wall of phase 1A in the south wing at 168–170 Fenchurch Street (pier 5), and on a continuation of this wall line at All Hallows, Lombard Street (pier 15); and also close to the eastern wall of phase 1A in the west wing at All Hallows, Lombard Street (piers 19 and 20). These last piers, when adjusted for planning error, would coincide very closely with the assumed position of the inner wall of the west wing.

The piers are generally a little wider than the phase 1A wall upon which they are built, indicating that they were not part of the original construction. This, together with their apparent lack of relationship to the phase 1 cross-walls in the east and south wings, suggests that the piers were constructed after the demolition of the phase 1 forum wall and the cross walls.

(3) Piers beside the south wall of the south wing. Six brick piers (piers 1, 2, 3, 21, 22 and 23) have been found close to the south wall of the south wing, suggesting that they formed part of a rebuilt portico fronting onto the main east-west street of Roman London. Three piers were found at 168–170 Fenchurch Street,[43] and three more (piers 21–23) on the Barclays Bank site at the corner of Lombard Street and Gracechurch Street. [44] On the former site they were lying against and partly over the south wall of the forum, as if to give a portico frontage, and on the latter they seem to have been built about 2.5m south of the forum wall line (Fig. 24). They seem to represent a line of piers or pillars, spaced at centres of about 4.72m, which diverged from the original frontage line of the forum in phase 1A. This divergence is clear in the row of three piers (piers 21–23) found on the Barclays Bank site.

Fig. 23 Walls and piers of the first forum at 168–170 Fenchurch Street. Piers not hatched occurred only as foundations; recorded pier superstructure is represented in black, and where conjectured is shown hatched. The rebuilding of piers 6 and 7 is not represented since this is believed to belong to the second forum (see Figs. 25, 26 and 53).

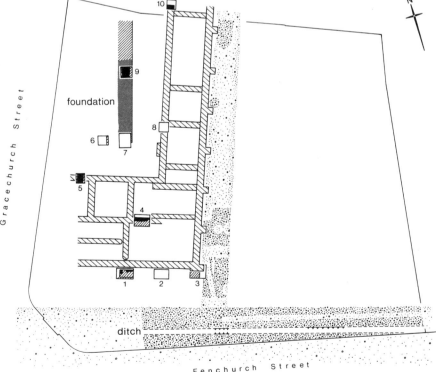

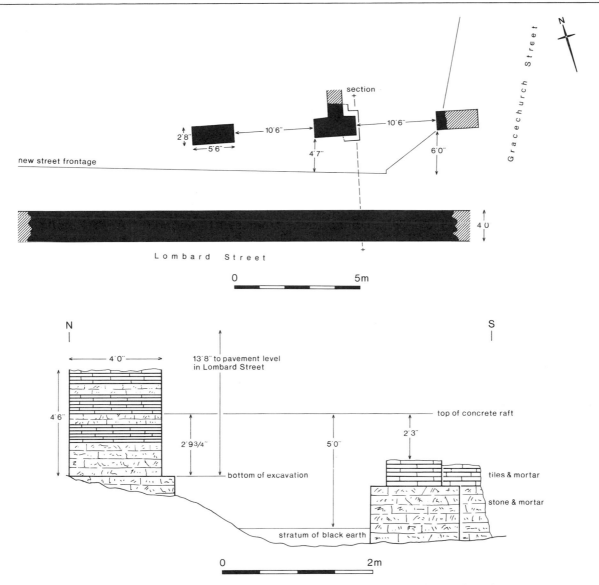

Fig. 24 Three piers (piers 21–23, Fig. 21), believed to be of the first forum, found in Lombard Street in 1925. They are on a different alignment from the south wall of the second forum, also shown on this plan, indicating that the piers and the wall belonged to separate building phases.

The westward divergence of the piers from the south wall of the forum may be explained by a small change in the alignment of the main east-west street beneath modern Lombard Street.[45] Before the first forum was built, and during the period of the second forum, buildings were aligned on the main street as described in this report (Fig. 21). The first forum, however, was at variance from this alignment by about 3°. It is difficult to understand how such a change could have occurred, unless the street line itself was temporarily changed when the first forum was constructed. The diverging line of piers, however, seems to indicate a change back to the orginal street line during a rebuilding of the first forum.

(4) Piers within the south and west wings. Four piers have been found within the south and west wings of the first forum, at 168–170 Fenchurch Street (pier 4), and at All Hallows, Lombard Street (piers 16–18). On present evidence they seem to have been placed randomly, and their significance is not clear. Pier 4 used a phase 1 foundation as its foundation, indicating that some demolition had occurred in the wing before the construction of the pier.

CONCLUSION

The piers overlying the phase 1 forum foundations show that at least one major phase of rebuilding had occurred. Although the final form of this rebuilding is unclear, there seems to be a pattern in the positions of the piers that makes it possible to suggest the form of the reconstructed forum.

The external east and west buttressed walls of the forum seem to have remained standing during the rebuilding, for no piers have been found constructed upon either wall. The ranges of rooms within the east and west wings appear to have been abandoned with the demolition of the cross walls, and a row of piers was built on the inner foundations of each wing (piers 8, 10, 11, 19 and 20). Each of these wings had probably resembled a covered ambulatory with openings in the side facing the forum courtyard, as existed in the Forum II phase at Caistor by Norwich.[46] It is possible that temporary stalls were erected in this wing, for these would explain the presence of a further row of piers, built on a continuous ragstone and flint foundation, as if a portico lay between each wing and the courtyard (piers 7 and 9).

The relationship of the piers to the ragstone and flint foundation of the portico is uncertain, but Philp's account suggests that the piers had their own ragstone foundations which were built on top of the continuous foundation.[47] The implication is clearly that the continuous foundation and the piers each belong to two separate phases. If so, then there was an intermediate phase between the phase 1 forum and the reconstruction which introduced the piers.

The south wing is a little more difficult to understand, but it too seems to fit into the pattern outlined above. Many of its cross-walls were demolished, and in the rebuilding piers were constructed on the foundations of its inner wall (piers 5 and 15), an an inner portico was added (piers 6, 7, 12 and 13). The extent of the internal demolition is not clear, but the rebuilding is represented by piers 4, 16, 17 and 18. It is certain that a new portico was constructed fronting the main east-west street of Roman London (piers 1, 2, 3, 21, 22 and 23).

It is assumed that the piers all represent a single phase of rebuilding of the forum, primarily because the life-span of the first forum was limited to approximately twenty years, and additional phases of redevelopment would be difficult to accommodate. The possible construction sequence may be summarised as follows:

(1) The east, west and south wings were built in period 1.

(2) An inner portico was perhaps added, built on a continuous foundation of flint and ragstone.

(3) The internal walls of the three wings of the forum were demolished and replaced by a more 'open-plan' layout with roofs supported on piers.

At some stage, not necessarily as part of a reconstruction of the forum, the small external temple was modified by the addition of various walls with ragstone foundations. In its initial phase 1 construction it seems that the temple may not have had a raised podium floor, because the door sill remained at ground level. However, enclosing walls with shallow ragstone foundations and a tile superstructure were built on the south side of the temple, suggesting that the floor of the *cella* was raised by in-filling the chamber, and that the new walls supported a flight of steps to the new floor level. To the north and west of the temple were traces of walls with ragstone foundations suggesting that a walled enclosure may have been built around the temple. Immediately to the south of the temple was an area of hard gravelled metalling of unknown extent which at some stage was re-resurfaced (p. 113). Presumably this was the forecourt of the temple upon which the altar was situated.

The Second Basilica and Forum

At the end of the first or early in the second century a new basilica and forum complex was built, five times larger in extent than its predecessor. Measuring 166m × 167m it was by far the largest building of its type in Britain, and was one of the largest in the Roman world (Figs. 25, 26). It undoubtedly took some years to build, and to ensure the continuing facilities of a civic centre, the first basilica and forum seems to have remained in use until the second basilica and much of its forum had been completed around it (Fig. 27).

The second basilica was 52.5m wide and 167m long externally, and internally included a great hall 32.75m wide which comprised a nave 13m wide between two side aisles. Two ranges of rooms have been identified along the north side of the hall in the central and western parts of the basilica, but the portions of walls found at the north-east end are at present too fragmentary for satisfactory interpretation.

The forum comprised three wings surrounding a large courtyard measuring 84.8m (N-S) wide and 116m (E-W) long. In the centre was apparently a shallow pool about 7m wide (N-S), and probably more than 14m long. The east and west wings were each about 25m wide, and comprised a central range 8.5m wide which presumably originally contained shops and perhaps offices. Each of these central ranges was flanked by an inner portico about 5.6m wide and an outer portico about 6m wide. The south wing, which fronted the main east-west street of Londinium, was also about 25m wide, but had somewhat different internal dimensions. Although its outer portico was 5.5m wide, the central range was only 7m broad, and its inner portico was 8.84m.

This was about 3m wider than the inner portico of the other wings, and it seems to have been designed to accommodate a row of monuments erected on piers constructed alongside the north wall of the portico. The width of the portico between these piers and the central range was about 6m, which is in accord with the width of the inner portico of both the east and west wings.

The floor level of the forum courtyard lay about 3.3m below the level of the present Gracechurch Street (*ie* at about 14.30m OD), and although there was some variation in the primary floor level of the courtyard and the basilica due to unequal settlement of the ground, it is clear that they were both intended to lie at the same level.

The construction of the second basilica and forum involved the dumping of an enormous quantity of brickearth, gravel and building materials, so as to raise the land surface by about a metre overall. Allowing for the already elevated parts of the first forum and basilica and also for the natural land contours it seems that about 20,000 cubic metres of materials were dumped over the remains of earlier buildings. This is equal to the loads of more than 2800 standard 7cu.m tipper lorries today, and does not take into account the gravels that were transported to construct new streets to the east, west and north of the new basilica and forum. These streets would have needed some further 3000cu.m of gravel. The mass clearance of earlier buildings around the first basilica and forum is suggested by the structures that have been found below the dumped deposits. The demolition certainly included a small classical temple (see p. 113), a baker's shop[48] and a building with a herringbone-tiled floor (see Fig. 30, no. 7).

The magnitude of this building project is staggering, and in such contrast with the very modest first basilica and forum that political considerations must surely be taken into account (see p. 76).

CONSTRUCTION OF THE SECOND BASILICA AND FORUM

The construction of the second basilica and forum complex, which occupied an area five times larger than the first complex, must have taken several years. It would seem from the archaeological evidence that the redevelopment of the site was carefully planned in six distinct stages (Fig. 27). The intention was evidently to retain the facilities of the first basilica and forum until sufficient of the second building had been completed for it to replace its predecessor. The first basilica and forum was then demolished, and the south wing of the second forum was completed.

The first stage must have involved the demolition of all the buildings on the site of the new basilica and forum, excluding the first forum and basilica complex. Although this meant the demolition of roughly four acres of the city centre surrounding the first basilica and forum, few traces of the demolished buildings have been found, probably because most private buildings in first century *Londinium* were timber framed with daub and mud-brick wall infillings. These are not easily detected on building sites, but the existence of such occupation is indicated by the many rubbish deposits pre-dating the second basilica and forum. The few traces of these earlier buildings include some ovens, presumably of a baker's shop, found beneath the dumped debris of the second forum at 168–170 Fenchurch Street;[49] a stone wall and herringbone-tiled floor found in 1880–1 just east of the second basilica, under Leadenhall market[50] (see Fig. 30, no. 7); and the remains of a stone building found at 54–58 Lombard Street, also beneath the dumped brickearth of the second forum (see p. 145).

The second stage involved levelling the site to raise it roughly to 14.30m OD, which was to be the floor level of the new basilica and forum. To achieve this it was necessary to dump an enormous quantity of clay, gravel and building debris over much of the site of the complex. This dumped brickearth has been identified at 168–170 Fenchurch Street,[51] at 160–162 Fenchurch Street (see p. 97), at the south end of 54–58 Lombard Street (see p. 146), and at 52 Cornhill (see p. 85). At the north end of 54–58 Lombard Street, the dumped debris consisted of building material (see p. 114) and, at 77–79 Gracechurch Street, of gravel (see p. 117, Plate 5).

However, the preparatory work for the second basilica also involved some levelling, for at 68 Cornhill some of the earlier deposits had been dug away, apparently for the construction of a new street along the north side of the basilica. The street surface lay at 12.8m OD, roughly 1.5m below the floor level of the basilica, and it was presumably this change in ground level which accounted for the series of external buttresses along the north wall of the building (see p. 88).

The third stage was the construction of the second basilica itself, together with the east and west wings of the forum. The foundations comprised ragstone set in extremely hard white or buff concrete. The thickness of the basilica foundations varied, as did their depths which ranged from 2.4m to 4.4m below the floor level of the building. The forum foundation at 54–58 Lombard Street seems to have been constructed before the clay dumping occurred (see p. 146).

The fourth stage seems to have involved the demolition of the first basilica and forum. Philp reported that at 168–170 Fenchurch Street the second forum foundations had in most cases cut through the walls of the earlier first forum, but that in two places they overrode them.[52] Philp also said that the stone walls of the first forum (his 'proto-forum') 'had only

Fig. 25 Plan of the second basilica and forum, the walls having been
separately plotted on each site without any co-ordination. Heavy cross
hatching on walls at the south-east corner of the forum represents
structures recorded by Hodge *c.* 1880 at St. Dionis Backchurch, and the
solid lines on the same site indicates the position of the same walls
when they were recorded in 1976. For the position of Rooms A and B in
the basilica see the caption to Fig. 30.

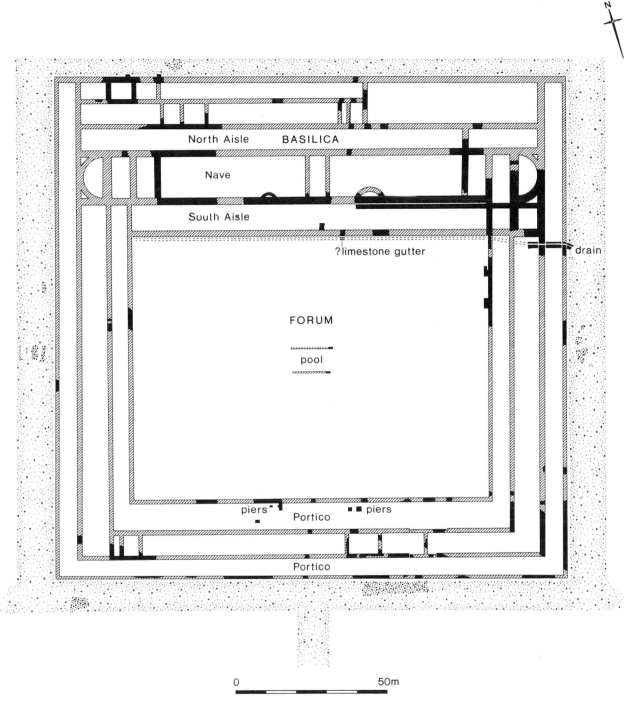

Fig. 26 Reconstructed plan of the second basilica and forum. The great width of the inner or nothern portico of the south wing of the forum is particularly clear, suggesting that there was a continuous row of piers along and within its northern side, of which only four piers have been found.

Fig. 27 Suggested stages in the redevelopment of the basilica and forum site, *c.* AD 100.

1. First Basilica and Forum in use

2. Second Basilica and Forum built around first Forum

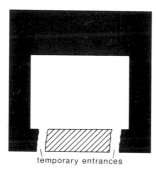

3. First Forum demolished. Second Forum entrance built

temporary entrances

4. Temporary entrances blocked

Basilica

Forum

the counterpart of a second break to the west of the site of the first forum and recorded in Lombard Street by another straight joint or wall termination in the same central range (p. 146). These breaks seem not to have occurred at the same points in the foundations of the accompanying inner and outer porticos of the wing.

The most logical explanation of these gaps is that in the fifth stage they gave access to the central area of the new enlarged forum during the demolition of the first forum, and that after the demolition was completed they enabled traffic to bypass the building of the new forum entrance. Once this was completed the gaps were filled in the sixth stage, and the new inner and outer portico walls of the south wing were built.

DESCRIPTION OF THE SECOND BASILICA

Although the recovery of the plan of the second basilica of London has been the subject of much effort on site for a long time, little attempt has been made to interpret the plan overall. In fact Gerald Dunning stands alone in this matter, even though his brief study was published more than half a century ago, in 1931.[53] Subsequent discoveries have confirmed some of his and others' conclusions, such as the existence of a nave and two side aisles; but other suggestions, such as the construction initially of a shorter basilica, have not been confirmed.[54] In general, however, the more recent discoveries have added considerably to the plan of the northern part of the building.

The basilica was 167m long and 52.5m wide externally, and, despite its huge size, the main part of its layout was comparatively simple. The building comprised two main parts: the great hall, which consisted of a nave, side aisles and tribunals; and the ranges of rooms situated along the north side of the hall (Fig. 28).

The Nave. The nave was about 13.7m wide, and was separated from the side aisles by two parallel rows of brick piers constructed on sleeper walls of ragstone and hard buff mortar. The northern sleeper wall was 2m thick, and was found in 1881–2 on the site of Leadenhall Market (see Fig. 30); in 1891 at 50 Cornhill;[55] in 1929 at 52 Cornhill (see p. 84); and in 1923–4 at 45–47 Cornhill.[56] The southern sleeper wall was 2.1m thick and was found both at Leadenhall Market and at 3–6 Gracechurch Street in 1883–4 (see p. 56) and in 1964 (see p. 106), and at 50 Cornhill in 1891.[57]

been dismantled to just above foundation level and no doubt the materials (were) re-used'. He interpreted this demolition as part of the scheme to build the second forum, prior to the dumping of clays to raise the floor level. It would now seem, however, that the walls of the first forum had been demolished much earlier, when its piers were reconstructed. These piers were found standing above the foundations of the first forum, and were surrounded by dumped debris as if the dumping had occurred inside the first forum while the building was still standing. The dumping was found at 79 Gracechurch Street (p. 117), and at All Hallows, Lombard Street (p. 137). Dumping was not necessary on the site of the first basilica since the floor of that building was already elevated by more than a metre (see p. 39).

The fifth and sixth stages are indicated by straight joints across the course of the south wing foundations, which suggest a carefully phased programme of construction. It is clear from the excavations at 168–170 Fenchurch Street and at 54–58 Lombard Street that the central range of this wing was built in two distinct stages. At the former site a break was found just east of the position of the first forum, and was represented by an infill 9m wide between two transverse straight joints. This seems to have been

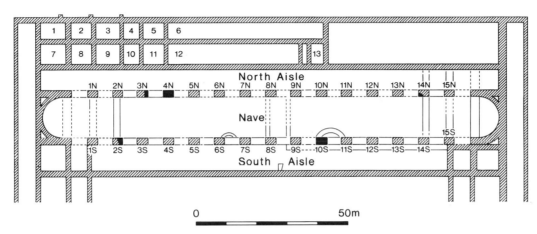

Fig. 28 Reconstructed plan of the second basilica. The hatching represents superstructure, and the four piers (Piers 4N, 14N, 2S and 10S) shown in black are those whose superstructure was actually recorded. The impression of Pier 3N was also found thereby giving the true spacing of the piers.

Three pairs of transverse foundations crossed below the nave, evidently to help stabilise the main sleeper foundations. One pair, each member 1.37m thick, lay almost half way along the length of the nave, at 3–6 Gracechurch St. (see Fig. 46); and the other two pairs, their foundations about 2m thick, were situated at each end of the nave (at the east end at Leadenhall Market, and at the west end at 45–47 and 50 Cornhill). It is unlikely that they supported any superstructure. A further strengthening of the southern sleeper wall was recorded by Hodge in 1881–2, in the form of two projecting apsidal foundations situated in intermediate positions under the nave between the central and the end pairs of cross foundations (see Fig. 41).

The two sleeper walls supported a series of brick piers, each about 3m long and 1.5m wide. Traces of five piers have been found, their positions indicating that there were originally fifteen piers on each sleeper wall, spaced at intervals of 5m.

Pier 10S was the most complete, its brickwork, 1.52m wide and 3.04m long, being laid over a slightly larger stone plinth (Fig. 29). This pier is a Scheduled Ancient Monument, and is preserved in the basement of a shop at the north-west corner of Leadenhall Market. The plinth was incorrectly described by Hodge in 1881–2 as constructed of brick. However, Miller correctly described it as of stone (Fig. 30. Plate 14).

Pier 2S was found at 50 Cornhill, where its brick superstructure was seen to be built on a plinth of sandstone ashlar overlying the ragstone sleeper wall.[58]

Pier 3N was found at 52 Cornhill by Dunning who merely found traces of its ragstone plinth just east of the conjectured position of its brick structure (see p. 84).

Pier 4N was preserved at 52 Cornhill, for much of its ashlar plinth, measuring 3.4m × 1.8m and composed of oolitic limestone and ragstone, bore clear traces of its brick superstructure measuring 3.2m × 1.42m (see p. 84. Plate 13).

Pier 14N was recorded by Hodge at Leadenhall Market, without comment on its function. Near the east end of the north sleeper wall he noted some 'limestone blocks 2'3" (0.68m) wide and 11" (0.3m) thick', which clearly formed part of the plinth of this pier (see Fig. 30).

For many years a puzzling feature of the basilica was the double sleeper wall at the south-east part of the nave. Once interpreted as part of an earlier and shorter basilica which was later enlarged,[59] this is now disproved by the subsequent re-interpretation of the first and second forum buildings. The evidence for the 'double foundation' appears in Hodge's survey of discoveries at Leadenhall Market (Figs. 29, 30) and is now supported by Miller's survey (Figs. 43, 44). The difficulty with these drawings, however, is that none shows any straight joints with adjoining walls at the east end of the double foundation. Further excavation at that point, if the opportunity ever arises, could be carried out with great profit. Nevertheless, it would seem that at some stage after the construction of the basilica, a second foundation was constructed to strengthen the south sleeper wall, as if the foundation supporting the piers was found

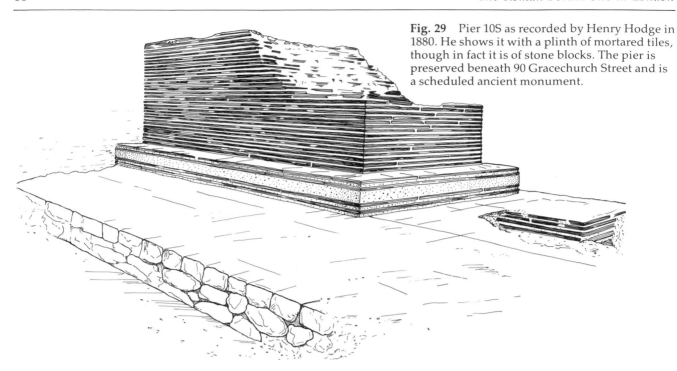

Fig. 29 Pier 10S as recorded by Henry Hodge in 1880. He shows it with a plinth of mortared tiles, though in fact it is of stone blocks. The pier is preserved beneath 90 Gracechurch Street and is a scheduled ancient monument.

to be insufficient. Fortunately, the recently discovered Miller drawings of 1880–81 include an elevation of the north face of the southern of the two sleeper walls on the Leadenhall Market site. This is the face on the opposite side to the additional foundation, and it shows that the wall, although below the floor level of the basilica, had been patched with bricks – apparently evidence of the damage which would explain the position of the additional foundation on the south side for further support. It is particularly interesting to note that the brick patching also coincided with the conjectured positions of some of the brick piers, indicating that they at least may have been rebuilt after the strengthening of the foundation.The rebuilding of some of the piers is also indicated by pier 10S, for this was partly set upon the additional foundation.

According to Hodge, the continuous length of the top of the south sleeper wall west of Gracechurch Street was only 1.4m wide (Figs. 46, 47). This is puzzling, for although it was wide enough to support the brick piers, it was of insufficient width to carry their stone plinths, and is in contrast with the south sleeper wall to the east of Gracechurch Street and with the north sleeper wall at 52 Cornhill (see p. 83), which were of sufficient width to support the stone plinths. Another discrepancy was also noted in the rough ragstone and mortar top of the south sleeper wall found in the GPO tunnel under Gracechurch Street in 1977. Although its north and south faces were not found, its position did not exactly accord with that of the sleeper wall as previously observed to either side of this point, though the north sleeper wall and the north wall of the north aisle were in

their correct positions. Instead, the south sleeper wall which was apparently of one build, lay in line with the centre line of the double foundation further to the east. The significance of these varying constructions is uncertain.

It is difficult to judge the original height of the nave, but as the foundations of the sleeper walls were a little deeper than those of the side aisles, it would seem probable that the piers supported the greater weight of a clerestory above the roof levels of the aisles. The tops of the openings between the piers were evidently arched, as is indicated by a fallen piece of masonry, found at Leadenhall Market, which Hodge described as a 'Block of oversailing bricks like an arch on red loose mortar or concrete'.

The South Aisle. Since 1966 there has been doubt about the existence of a south aisle, particularly as the southernmost Roman wall recorded by Hodge in 1883–4 at 3–6 Gracechurch Street, and long believed to be its south wall, was found to be the north wall of the earlier basilica (see Fig. 77). This interpretation of course explained why this wall was not parallel to the southern sleeper wall of the second basilica. The only other suggested portion of a southern wall of the second basilica was also recorded by Hodge at the south-west end of the Leadenhall Market site. He described it as a 'rag wall' of indeterminate date (*ie* it is not coloured pink as are the certain Roman walls shown on Hodge's original plans): it must be assumed, therefore, that it was dissimilar to the other Roman walls and foundations on the site. Thus it was that when further rebuilding excavations were carried out at 3–6 Gracechurch Street in 1966, and still no

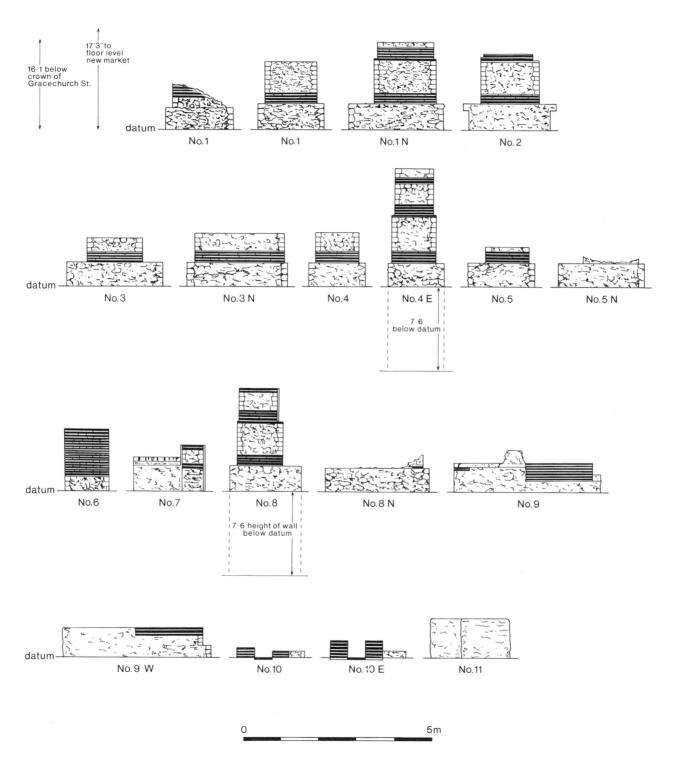

Fig. 31   Copy of Roman wall sections on the Leadenhall Market recorded by Henry Hodge in 1880–81.

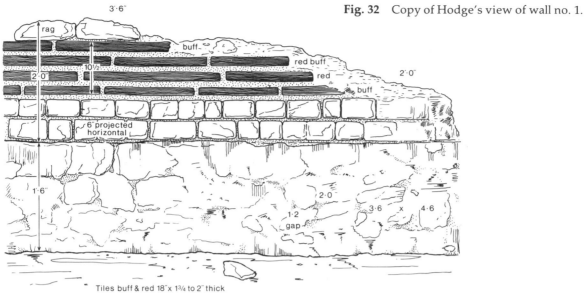

Fig. 32 Copy of Hodge's view of wall no. 1.

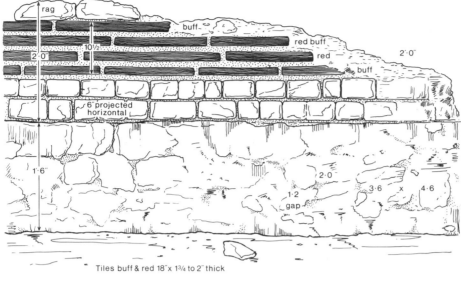

Fig. 33 Copy of Hodge's view of wall no. 6.

Fig. 34 Copy of Hodge's view, facing west, of wall 1N and of upstanding walls 4E and 8.

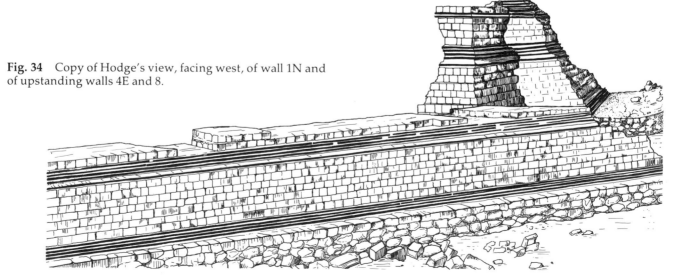

Facing stones 6" 5' 6' 5' wide

2·10

Fig. 35 Copy of Hodge's view, facing west, of wall 1 and the drain 10E. In the background is wall 2.

Fig. 36 Copy of Hodge's view of part of wall 3.

4 courses 10½
1¾ tiles 1·8 x 1·0½

1·9 set off

M.... ground taken out later

Fig. 37 Copy of Hodge's view of walls 3 and 4, with a detail of wall 2. The sketch of walls 3 and 4 shows earth apparently containing blocks of masonry, probably from the demolition of the basilica.

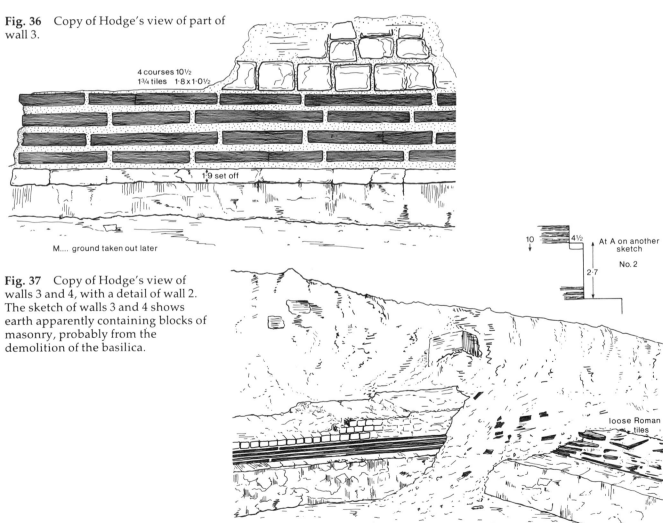

10
4½

At A on another sketch

No. 2

2·7

loose Roman tiles

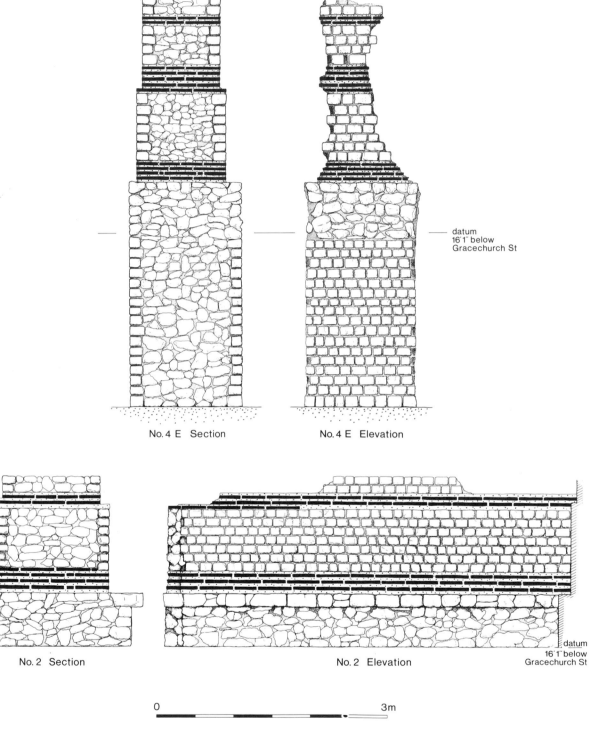

datum
16'1" below
Gracechurch St

No. 4 E   Section   No. 4 E   Elevation

No. 2   Section

No. 2   Elevation

datum
16'1" below
Gracechurch St

0   3m

Fig. 38   Copy of Hodge's views of walls 4E and 2.

trace of a southern wall of the basilica was found (though the area was disturbed by deep modern sub-basements and foundations), it seemed likely that that southern sleeper wall formed the basilica's southern frontage.

The excavation of the GPO tunnel beneath Gracechurch Street in 1977 gave a particularly welcome opportunity for further clarification without the encumbrance of deep modern basements, and, in the event, definite evidence of a south aisle and its outer wall was found. The south aisle was 8.8m wide, but the fact that its southern wall had been partly robbed out, probably in post-Roman times, may explain why the wall had previously proved to be so elusive on neighbouring sites. The robber trench was 1.85m wide, but fortunately the base of the tunnel cut through a deeper, unrobbed part of the foundation constructed of ragstone set in very hard white concrete. There is no doubt about the identity of this as the south wall of the basilica, for the floors of the great hall were located immediately to the north of the robber trench, and an entirely different sequence of forum surfaces lay immediately to the south.

With the discovery of the south wall of the second basilica it is now possible to offer an explanation of an apparently isolated foundation recorded by Hodge under the frontage of 3–6 Gracechurch Street, immediately north of the recently discovered south wall. Of the west face of this structure Hodge comments; 'This was a finished face or end of the wall. No tile courses.' The foundation did not extend as far east as the GPO tunnel only 5m away, and it is therefore likely to have been simply a strengthening of the foundation of the south wall of the basilica.

The North Aisle. The north aisle was about 6.3m wide and appears to have been fairly featureless, though a cross foundation was found north of pier 14N. The north wall of the north aisle was 1.47m thick in the Gracechurch Street tunnel in 1977, (Fig. 48) and, at 52 Cornhill, 1.5m thick (Figs. 63, 64). On both sites it contained several courses of bonding tiles below the basilica floor level, above which were courses of ragstone.

Floors of the Nave and Aisles. Loftus Brock, a nineteenth-century antiquary, described Roman flooring seen on the Leadenhall Market site in 1881–2 as follows: 'A Roman pavement of ordinary brick *tesserae* has been found over a large part of the surface and covered with the ashes of some great fire. Above this is concrete of a second floor, while below the remains of walls 5ft thick have been found'.[60] This may be the pavement or pavements shown by Hodge in his sections 'At Arch B' and 'At M wall' (Figs. 40, 41). It would seem from Brock that the tessellated pavement was the earlier of two floors, and were present throughout a major part of the basilica.[61] This was not borne out by the discoveries either in the Gracechurch Street tunnel in 1977, or at 52 Cornhill, where no tessellated pavement was found in association with the nave or aisles. As the relationship of the mosaic pavement to the basilica generally remains unknown it is not now possible to interpret its significance.

It was very difficult to establish levels relative to Ordnance Datum in the tunnel beneath Gracechurch Street (Fig. 51) but in general it seems that the first basilica floor lay roughly at 14m OD (about 3.60–4m below street level). The tunnel, dug across the south aisle, the nave and the north aisle of the basilica, showed that despite minor variations in the floor sequence, mainly due, it would seem, to localised repairs and variations in the materials used, the nave and aisles had a common floor (Figs. 48–50, sections 1–7).

The earliest floor was of a fairly soft white mortar or concrete, about 0.55m, thick containing fragments of tiles, lumps of ragstone and pebbles (Plates 10, 11). It extended across the south and north aisles fairly

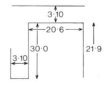

Fig. 39 Copy of Hodge's view, facing north, of walls 4 and 5.

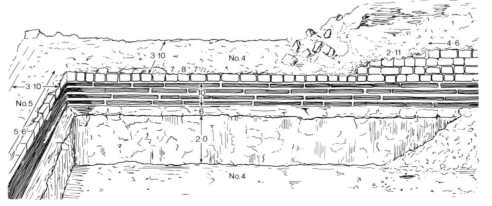

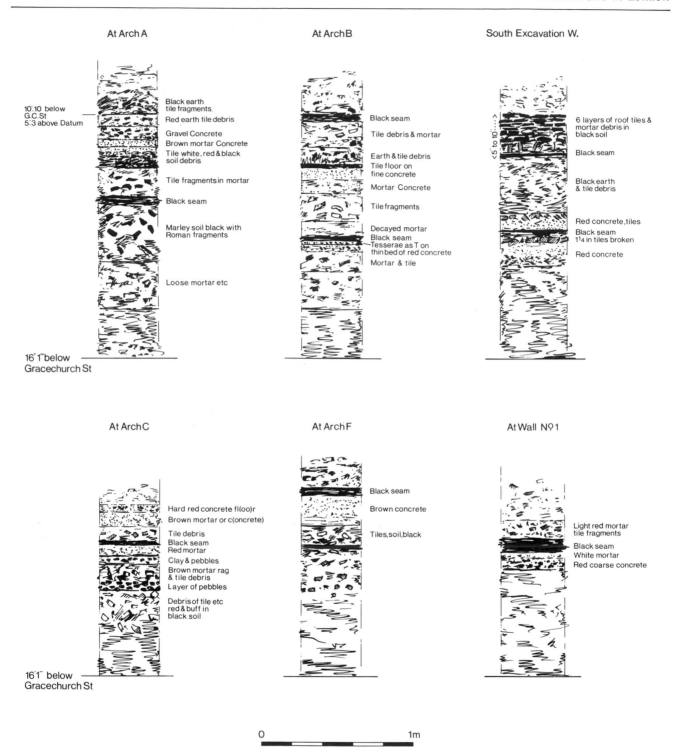

At Arch A

10'.10 below
G.C.St
5'.3 above Datum

Black earth
tile fragments.
Red earth tile debris

Gravel Concrete
Brown mortar Concrete
Tile white, red & black
soil debris

Tile fragments in mortar

Black seam

Marley soil black with
Roman fragments

Loose mortar etc

16' 1" below
Gracechurch St

At Arch B

Black seam

Tile debris & mortar

Earth & tile debris
Tile floor on
fine concrete

Mortar Concrete

Tile fragments

Decayed mortar
Black seam
Tesserae as T on
thin bed of red concrete

Mortar & tile

South Excavation W.

<5' to 10"--->

6 layers of roof tiles &
mortar debris in
black soil

Black seam

Black earth
& tile debris

Red concrete, tiles
Black seam
1¼ in tiles broken

Red concrete

At Arch C

Hard red concrete fl(oo)r
Brown mortar or c(oncrete)

Tile debris
Black seam
Red mortar
Clay & pebbles
Brown mortar rag
& tile debris
Layer of pebbles

Debris of tile etc
red & buff in
black soil

16'1" below
Gracechurch St

At Arch F

Black seam

Brown concrete

Tiles, soil, black

At Wall № 1

Light red mortar
tile fragments

Black seam
White mortar
Red coarse concrete

0   1m

Fig. 40   Copy of Hodge's watercoloured sections of strata, drawn to scale, at
various points shown on Fig. 30.

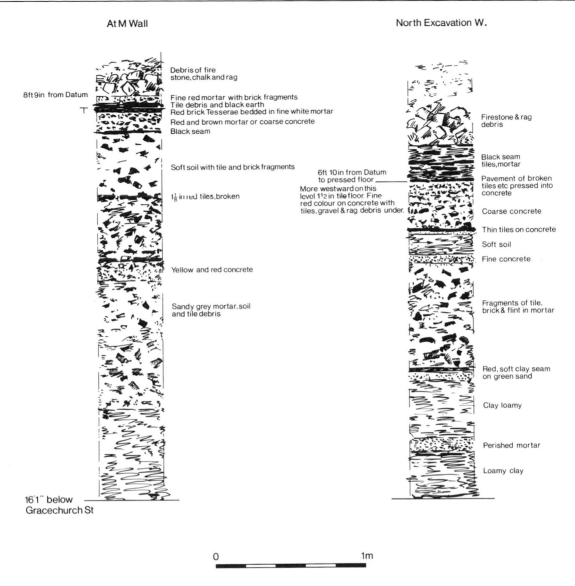

At M Wall

8ft 9in from Datum

Debris of fire
stone, chalk and rag
Fine red mortar with brick fragments
Tile debris and black earth
Red brick Tesserae bedded in fine white mortar
Red and brown mortar or coarse concrete
Black seam

Soft soil with tile and brick fragments

1⅛ in red tiles, broken

Yellow and red concrete

Sandy grey mortar, soil
and tile debris

16′1″ below
Gracechurch St

North Excavation W.

Firestone & rag
debris

Black seam
tiles, mortar

Pavement of broken
tiles etc pressed into
concrete

Coarse concrete

Thin tiles on concrete

Soft soil

Fine concrete

Fragments of tile,
brick & flint in mortar

Red, soft clay seam
on green sand

Clay loamy

Perished mortar

Loamy clay

6ft 10in from Datum
to pressed floor
More westward on this
level 1½in tile floor. Fine
red colour on concrete with
tiles, gravel & rag debris under.

0   1m

Fig. 41   Copy of Hodge's watercoloured sections of strata, drawn to
scale, at various points not shown on his site plan.

horizontally, but sagged down perhaps by as much as 0.80m in the centre of the nave. It passed directly across the top of the south sleeper wall, but close to the north sleeper wall had been partly removed during the Roman period. The shallow excavation to remove the floor was overlaid by a subsequent Roman mortar floor. A thick layer of soft brown mortar mainly underlay the white mortar floor, as if to give it a foundation, and butted up against the sides of the sleeper walls. It is possible that this was an earlier floor, but no really convincing surface was seen, and it would have left the rough top of the sleeper wall exposed. The brown mortar was absent from the centre of the nave, where the thick white mortar floor was found to overlie dumps of clean pebbly brickearth.

About 0.50m above the thick white mortar floor was a floor of pinkish-white mortar 7–10cms thick. It was particularly distinctive because it included many fragments of red brick. This was traced across the south aisle, most of the nave, and also across the north aisle where it was a pale pink colour.

Between the two floors was an ever changing sequence of deposits, including hard trampled surfaces. For example, a section in the south aisle revealed a bed of hard rammed gravel flooring 0.11m thick overlying the thick white mortar floor. This in turn was overlaid by a 0.27m thickness of layers of

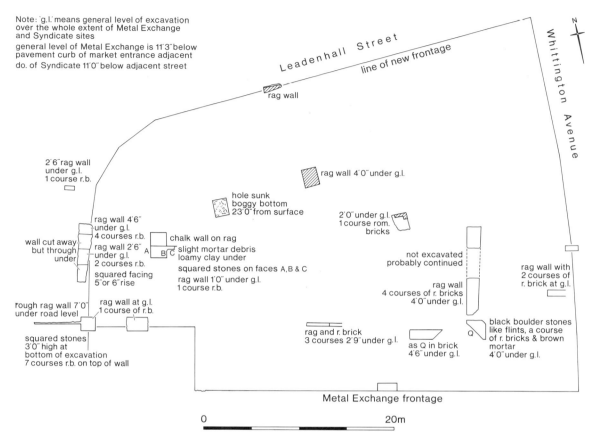

Fig. 42 Copy of Hodge's plan and notes made in 1880–81 on the site immediately north of Leadenhall Market.

mortary soils, none of which resembled floors, except the uppermost which was a layer of hard mortary earth only 0.02m thick. This was overlaid by 0.05m of dark soil, above which was the white mortar floor containing the tile fragments.

The rapid variation in the deposits is illustrated by a section only 2.72m north of the last, still in the south aisle. The thick white mortar floor was here overlaid by a deposit of grey earth only 0.04m thick, containing a few pebbles. Above it was a hard pebbly grey earth 0.13m thick, with some tiles and bones. This seemed to be a trampled floor surface, unlike the overlying three layers of grey earth with pebbles and mortar, none of which were compacted. Last in the sequence was the slightly pink mortar floor 0.10m thick, containing small brick fragments, which overlay the grey earth, its surface 0.40m above the first thick mortar floor. In all of the sections the upper mortar floor appeared to be overlaid by grey soil containing destruction debris of the basilica.

Portions of the mortar floor of the nave and north aisle were recorded by Dunning at 52 Cornhill (see p. 85) as composed of pink concrete mixed with crushed brick and chalk. This floor, only 0.15m thick,

overlay the stone plinth of pier 4N. There was no trace of a white mortar floor over 0.50m thick, and it is possible that the pink concrete was an extension of the second mortar floor exposed in the tunnel.

Wall decoration of the Nave and Aisles. The excavation of the tunnel along Gracechurch Street did not reveal any wall plaster debris in the nave and aisles, even though this was deliberately sought to determine the nature of any wall decoration. Dunning's record of 52 Cornhill makes no reference to wall plaster, and Hodge's and Miller's records of Leadenhall Market similarly say nothing about the basilica wall renderings. On this basis it would seem that in the great hall the brick and stone wall faces may have remained exposed during the use of the building.

The Eastern Tribunal. The southern half of an apsidal chamber at the east end of the nave was recorded by Hodge at Leadenhall Market in 1881–2. It was originally about 8.5m deep and probably 15.2m wide, and was presumably a *tribunal* at the east end of the great hall of the basilica. Most of what survived was only the ragstone foundation, though a little of the superstructure remained with a construction of ragstone and courses of tiles. No evidence of flooring was recorded, though it is likely that any floor was originally raised above the level of the nave, in accordance with normal practice in other basilicas.

The Western Tribunal. Dunning has suggested that another tribunal lay at the west end of the nave[62], as was the normal practice in basilicas. At present this is entirely conjectural as no part of it has been found, its site lying beneath the church of St. Michael Cornhill.

Rooms A and B. At the east end of the south aisle were what seem to have been two square rooms, both of which were recorded by Hodge on the Leadenhall Market site (Fig. 30 caption).

Room A measured 7.5m E-W by 7.8m, and was illustrated by Hodge (Fig. 30). Part of its north wall had survived to a height of more than 2m above its foundation, but no evidence of a floor was recorded.

Room B was 6.8m wide E-W, but no sign of a southern wall was found. Although it may have opened into the inner portico of the east wing of the forum, the stability of the building probably required that the foundation of the south wall of the basilica was carried across, forming the south side of this room. The north-west corner of the room was sketched by Hodge (Fig. 39), and as the walls were faced with ragstone and courses of tiles, and were mostly below the level of the floor in the adjoining south aisle, it is possible that this was a slightly sunken room. However, no evidence of a floor was recorded, and the relationship of the north wall of the room to the double south sleeper wall remains unknown until these walls can be re-excavated.

On the assumption that another tribunal lay at the west end of the basilica, it is to be expected that two rooms similar to A and B lay at the west end of the south aisle. However, this spot lies beneath St. Michael's churchyard and has not been excavated.

Northern part of the Basilica. The reconstruction of the plan of the northern part of the basilica has been helped enormously by establishing the location of both the north side of the north aisle, and the position of the north wall of the building. Definite evidence of the latter was discovered as recently as 1982 in an archaeological excavation by Peter James at 68 Cornhill (see p. 88). Thus the plan of the basilica north of the great hall was seen to have comprised a zone about 17m wide (N-S) which extended along the whole length of the building.

Although portions of walls have been found on a number of sites in this area, it is only from Gracechurch Street westwards that a coherent plan can be considered. An east-west wall evidently passed through the centre of at least the western part of the zone, apparently separating two ranges of roughly square rooms, each measuring approximately 6.25m (N-S) by 6.5m (E-W) internally.

Parts of thirteen rooms have been found from Gracechurch Street westwards (see Fig. 28). The rooms were found at 68–73 Cornhill (see p. 86) and at 50–52 Cornhill (see p. 83).[63] The northernmost row of rooms was bounded by the north wall of the basilica. This was 1.6m thick above the foundation, and was strengthened by external buttresses at intervals of approximately 9m (see p. 86). The north-south walls of all the rooms were constructed of ragstone with courses of bonding tiles, and were generally about 1.5m thick (Plate 12). Unfortunately, no evidence of any floors, wall superstructure or decoration has been found.

The extent of the rooms further east is unknown, but it seems that the central east-west wall continued at least as far as the east side of Gracechurch Street. It was recorded at 69–73 Cornhill in about 1894 as being about 1.8m wide at foundation level, with apparently an offset of 0.3m above the foundation to the wall face on the south side (see Fig. 52). The central wall was also found at 56–7 Cornhill in 1922, where a small piece of red painted wall plaster was found adhering to its north face.[64]

The place of greatest survival is, as might be expected, beneath Gracechurch Street, and it is from there that most is known about the superstructure. The evidence of Room 13 was found just east of St. Peter's church during the construction of a sewer in 1848–9, and while laying telephone cables in 1922 and 1977 (Fig. 28, 52).

Part of the central east-west wall was found, together with a north-south wall on its south side, thus forming a corner of perhaps another square room (Room 13, Figs. 28, 52). These were recorded on the *City Sewer Plan* 210 in 1848–9, together with the note: 'In the inside of these two walls there was an old pavement which extended from wall to wall; it was 1½in (0.038m) thick and it laid on a bed of concrete 6in (0.15m) thick a specimen of which I brought to the office.' The north-south wall was of ragstone and was 1.5m thick, and its top lay at a depth of 3m.

In 1922 the central east-west wall was again found, slightly to the east of the sewer excavation, approximately in the centre of Gracechurch Street. It was about 1.4m thick and about 4m below street level. At a depth of 3–3.5m were five rows of tiles between courses of squared ragstone, and somewhat higher were two further rows. The upper part of the south face was plastered and painted, apparently with square or oblong panels in black outline on a yellow ground with touches of red. A later Roman wall, 0.84m thick and aligned north-south, abutted against the south face of the central wall, and at a

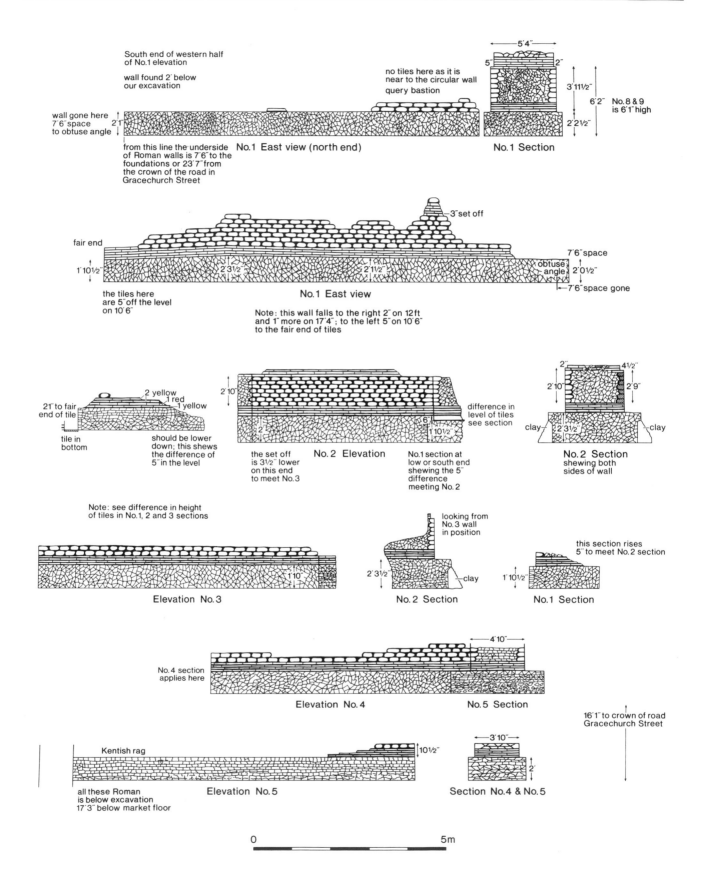

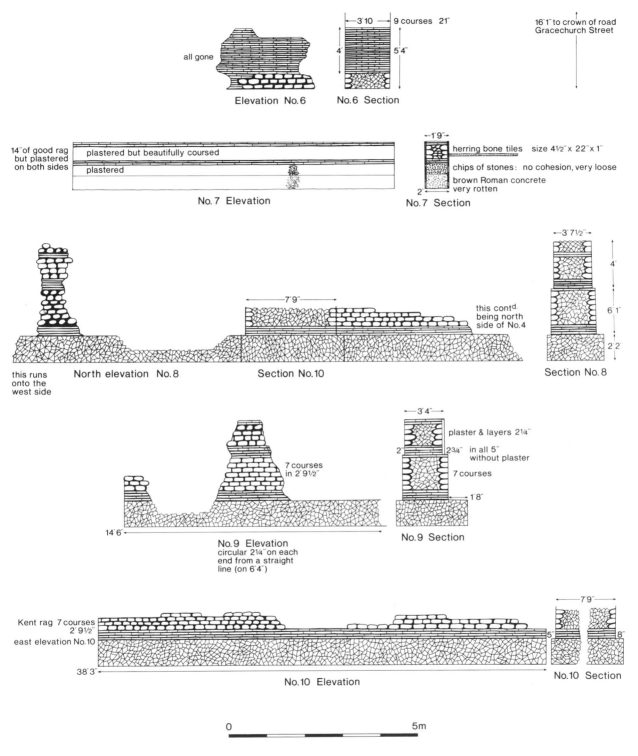

all gone

Elevation No.6

No.6 Section

9 courses 21″
3′10″
4′
5′4″

16′1″ to crown of road Gracechurch Street

14″ of good rag but plastered on both sides

plastered but beautifully coursed

plastered

No.7 Elevation

1′9″

herring bone tiles   size 4½″ x 22″ x 1″

chips of stones: no cohesion, very loose

brown Roman concrete very rotten

2″

No.7 Section

this runs onto the west side

North elevation No.8

Section No.10

7′9″

this contd. being north side of No.4

3′7½″
4′
6′1″
2′2″

Section No.8

7 courses in 2′9½″

No.9 Elevation
circular 2¼″ on each end from a straight line (on 6′4″)

14′6″

3′4″

2″

2¾″

plaster & layers 2¼″
in all 5″ without plaster

7 courses

1′8″

No.9 Section

Kent rag 7 courses 2′9½″

east elevation No.10

No.10 Elevation

38′3″

7′9″

5″

8″

No.10 Section

0   5m

Fig. 45   Copy of Miller's sections and elevations of Roman walls at Leadenhall Market, the positions of which are shown on Fig. 43.

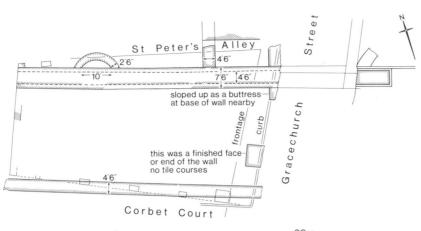

Fig. 46 Copy of Hodge's plan and notes of Roman walls at 3 Gracechurch Street, 1881.

Fig. 47 Copy of section by Hodge of the south sleeper wall of the second basilica at 3 Gracechurch Street, 1881.

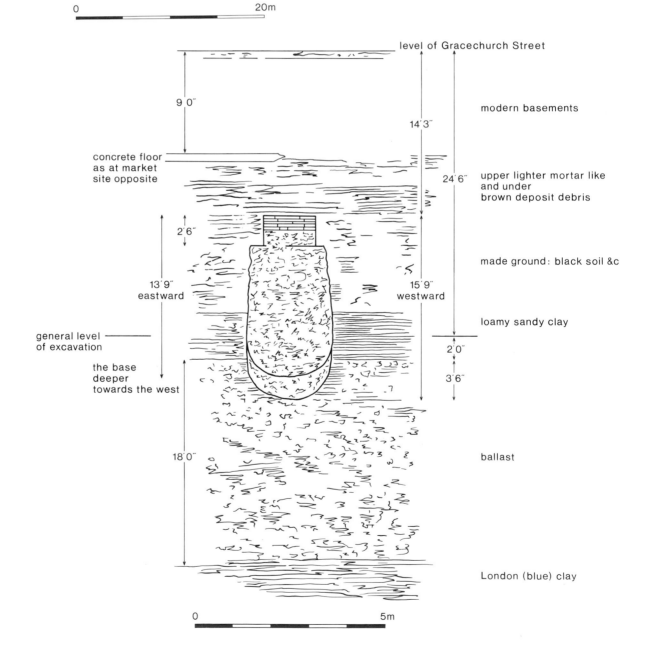

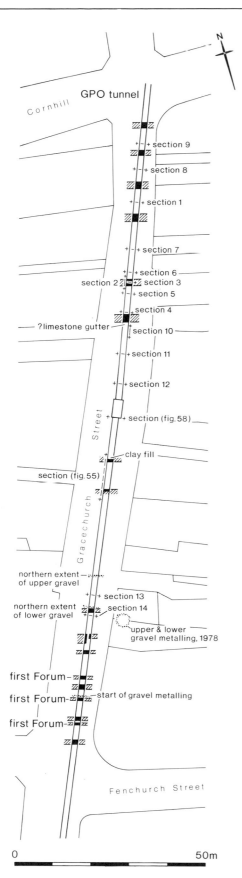

Fig. 48 Plan of the main Roman features recorded in the GPO tunnel dug beneath Gracechurch Street in 1977. The sections are shown on Figs. 49, 50, 51, 54, 55 and 58.

depth of 3.8m contained a double course of tiles. At this level on the west side of the later wall was a white cement floor several inches thick. The footings of the wall here apparently did not exceed 4.4m in depth. Both sides of this north-south wall had been plastered and painted, but only the west face could be examined. This was decorated, like the south side of the east-west wall, but only the lower part of the panels could be seen. The ground level on the west side of the north-south wall had subsequently been raised to a height of 1.2m above the original floor, and a rough brick tessellated pavement laid.[65]

The east-west wall was again found in 1977 when the GPO tunnel cut through it immediately east of the 1922 excavation, and there also revealed the east side of the later north-south wall. Unfortunately the east-west wall was a long way from the tunnel access shaft, and there was no accurate means of estimating its depth below Gracechurch Street. The east-west wall was 1.31m thick above the 1.66m wide foundation of ragstone and buff mortar. At the base of the wall were four courses of tiles set in buff mortar, and above them were courses of ragstone as far as the base of another course of tiles 1.18m above the foundation. An offset of 0.053m was recorded on the south face of the wall about 1.12m above the foundation, and at this level south of the wall were two superimposed mortar floors. The lower floor, of white pebbly mortar, was 0.13m thick and was immediately overlaid by a pink mortar floor 0.03m thick. This floor extended southwards to the north wall of the north aisle, and was presumably part of the 'old pavement' which was found in 1848–9. Although deposits below the floor were obscured by modern timber shuttering immediately south of the E-W wall, a section close by showed that the white mortar floor, 0.18m thick, and the pink mortar floor, 0.025m thick, overlay large dumps of ragstone, mortar and clay, and it would seem that they were the earliest floors in the room.

The east side of the ragstone and buff mortar north-south foundation was evidently a later Roman phase of construction since it was at a higher level. Indeed, only the lowest 0.4m of its foundation had remained at the top of the tunnel, and, judging from the 1922 record, the bottom of the foundation apparently lay 4.4m below the level of Gracechurch Street. This was also at about the level of the mortar floor, which, if the 1922 measurement is correct, lay at approximately 13.50m OD.

In conclusion, these records of discoveries beneath Gracechurch Street between 1848 and 1977 show that a room 10.41m wide (N-S) lay immediately north of the north aisle, and that originally it had a

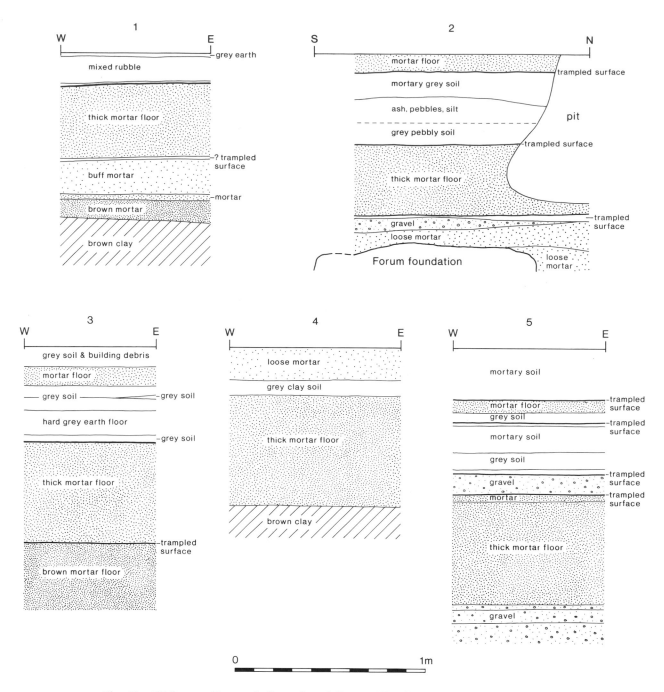

Fig. 49 GPO tunnel beneath Gracechurch Street, 1977. Sections across the aisles of the second basilica, as drawn in the tunnel. The exact depth of the tunnel beneath Gracechurch Street could not be determined, but was at approximately 3 metres. The thick white mortar primary floor of the basilica was clearly visible in all sections, and is also shown in Plates 10 and 11.

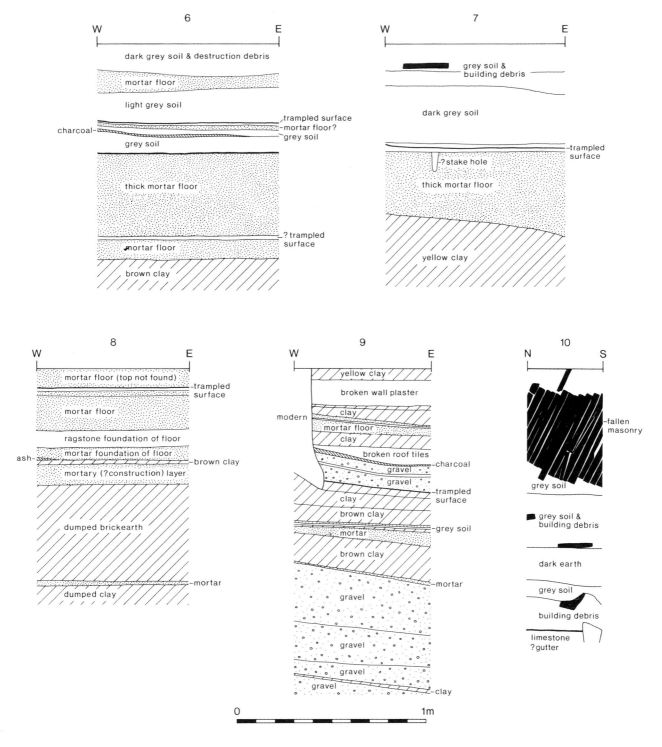

Fig. 50 GPO tunnel beneath Gracechurch Street, 1977. Sections across the nave (6 and 7), the northern range of rooms (8 and 9), and the southern threshold of the basilica (10) with its limestone ?gutter and fallen masonry.

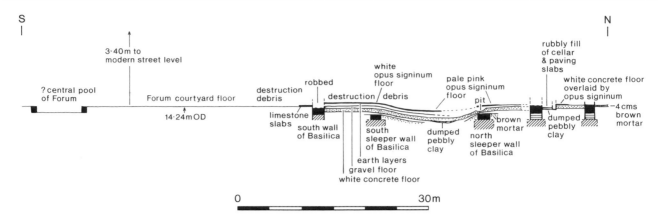

S

N

?central pool
of Forum

3·40m to
modern street level

Forum courtyard floor

14·24m OD

destruction
debris

robbed

limestone
slabs

south wall
of Basilica

destruction / debris

white
opus signinum
floor

south
sleeper wall
of Basilica

earth layers
gravel floor
white concrete floor

dumped
pebbly
clay

pale pink
opus signinum
floor

pit

brown
mortar

north
sleeper wall
of Basilica

rubbly fill
of cellar
& paving
slabs

white concrete floor
overlaid by
opus signinum

dumped
pebbly
clay

~4 cms
brown
mortar

0   30m

Fig. 51 Sketched north-south section across the basilica and the northern part of the forum courtyard compiled from daily observations as the digging of the GPO tunnel proceeded beneath Gracechurch Street. The 'rubbly fill of cellar & paving slabs' are recent features whose presence beneath the street is puzzling. Not to scale.

white mortar floor which was re-surfaced with pink mortar. The north-south wall found in the 1848 excavation was 1.5m thick, and probably formed the west side of the room. Subsequently, the north-south wall, found in 1922, was constructed with a white cement floor on its west side. The painted walls, with black lines on a yellow ground, seem to belong to this phase. As this north-south wall, only 0.84m thick, lay very close to the 1.5m wide north-south wall found in 1848, it must have formed a very small room indeed. The west wall found in 1848 appears to have remained standing as its surviving top, at a depth of 3m, lay above the white cement floor, at a depth of 3.8m. Subsequently, the room on the west side of the north-south wall was re-floored with a plain red mosaic pavement.

The GPO tunnel of 1977 also revealed another room lying on the north side of the central cross wall. It had a floor of brown pebbly mortar 0.04m thick, at about the same level as the earliest mortar floor in the room described above. Above this was a thin layer of brown mortary clay, and then a layer of broken wall plaster one piece of which was painted with a black line on a white ground. Yellow clay lay above this. No further Roman walls were encountered for a distance of 6.45m north of the central east-west wall, at which point there occurred the dark earth filling of what seemed to be a robbed wall trench. This was about 1.67m wide, and lay exactly where the north wall of the basilica is now known to have stood. Modern sewers and other obstructions were found immediately north of that point, and the archaeological deposits had been destroyed.

Traces of walls have been found to the east of Gracechurch Street where they were recorded by Hodge in 1881–2, but in general the archaeological record is too fragmentary to judge their significance. In spite of this it would seem that the north-south wall found under the then frontage of Gracechurch Street formed the east side of the two rooms described above as having been found beneath the modern street. Hodge described it as: 'Rag wall 4ft 6in under G(round) L(evel). 4 courses R(oman) B(rick). Wall cut away but through under . . .' (see Fig. 42).

East and West Porticos. It is likely that a portico lay beyond the east and west ends of the basilica, but no evidence of this has been found. Although the outer porticos of the east and west wings of the forum could have stopped at the south wall of the basilica, no trace of this was found at Leadenhall Market and it is assumed that the eastern portico continued northwards. The outer eastern portico wall was found immediately south of the basilica on that site, and was described by Hodge as being 3ft 10½in (1.18m) thick. It was associated with a brick drain and was sketched by Hodge who shows it with a brick superstructure. The eastern portico was 5.79m wide internally.

THE SECOND FORUM

The East Wing. The east wing of the second forum was about 25m wide overall, and comprised a central range, 8.5m wide, which presumably contained shops, between an inner or western portico, 5.6m wide, overlooking the forum courtyard, and an outer or eastern portico about 5.9m wide. Unfortunately, the plan of the east wing is extremely fragmentary, not merely because the building has been recorded on only a few sites, but also because it was extensively robbed probably during the Middle Ages (Figs. 25, 26).

The foundations of the wing were constructed of ragstone and buff concrete, the base projecting into the gravels which underlie the natural brickearth.

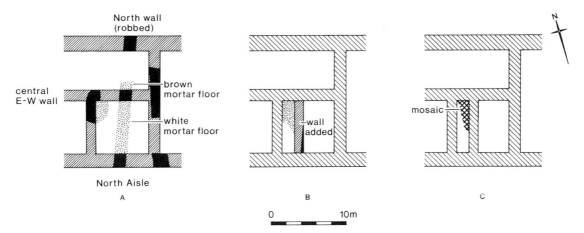

Fig. 52 Room 13 (see Fig. 28), disclosed in 1848–9, 1922 and 1977 beneath Gracechurch Street, preserved clear evidence of rebuilding or refurbishment of part of the basilica during the Roman period. The structural sequence was probably as shown in A, B and C, but no dating evidence was found.

The superstructure seems to have been of squared ragstone with courses of bonding tiles.

The Central Range. The central range of rooms apparently extended southwards from Room A at the east end of the south aisle of the basilica (see Fig. 30). Elsewhere it is recorded only at its south end at 160–162 Fenchurch Street (including 23 Lime Street) and on the neighbouring site of 22 Lime Street. On the former site the foundation of the eastern wall of the central range was only 0.83m wide (see p. 97), and its superstructure, recorded at 22 Lime Street, was 0.74m wide. The west wall of the central range was rather more substantial at 22 Lime Street,[66] for its foundation was 1.47m wide, with a superstructure of four courses of ragstone overlaid by four courses of tiles. No other clue to the form of the superstructure was found, and it is unclear why the thickness of the two walls of the central range was so unequal.

The Eastern Portico. The eastern or outer portico was 5.87m wide at Leadenhall Market (see Fig. 30), and 5.31m wide at 22 Lime Street (see p. 92). At 160–162 Fenchurch Street it was believed to be 7.25m wide (p. 97), but in fact the position of the inner or western wall of the portico was only roughly established on that site, and cannot be regarded as certain.

The external or eastern wall of the outer portico was found on four sites: at Leadenhall Market (Fig. 30), where it was partly built of ragstone but, where it incorporated a brick drain leading under the wing from the forum courtyard, it included many courses of brick (Fig. 35); at 15–18 Lime Street (p. 132); at 22 Lime Street, where it had been robbed (p. 91); and finally at 160–162 Fenchurch Street, immediately north of the south-eastern corner of the forum (p. 97. Plate 18). On each site it was about 1.5m wide, and although primarily built of ragstone, close to the south east corner it was constructed entirely of bricks, the actual corner having been robbed away.

At 22 Lime Street the faced superstructure of the inner or west wall of the portico lay at 13.3m OD, but tile courses and offsets suggests that there may have been floors at higher levels. Nevertheless, within the portico area a series of mortar floors which were unrelated to the walls may have been portico floors rather than those of an earlier building. The lowest, of pink mortar 0.1m thick, lay at 13.18m OD; the next, of buff mortar 0.06m thick, lay at 13.44m OD; and finally there was another pink mortar floor 0.1m thick at 13.74m OD. Further south, at the south-east corner of the forum at 160–162 Fenchurch Street, there were found many floors and trampled surfaces lying between 13.18m and 14.29m OD, though in general the lowest floor lay at 13.41m OD. There was a considerable amount of sand associated with the surfaces, perhaps strewn around from time to time to help keep the portico dry. A hollow in the floor seemed to be a wheel rut, suggesting that there was a vehicle entrance from the main east-west street at the south end of the portico (p. 99). However, any such access may have been impeded by a monument which apparently lay within the outer portico at 22 Lime Street. Philp recorded it as a ragstone foundation of uncertain date within the Roman period about 1.22m wide which was only seen in section.[67] It did not extend either to excavations 4m to the north or about 1m to the south, and is therefore interpreted as an isolated structure.

The Western Portico. The external wall of the inner or western portico, found at 83–87 Gracechurch Street, did not appear as a continuous wall on that site, but as the walls and foundations had been extensively robbed, it was impossible to determine the original form of the structures (p. 129). The external portico wall appeared as a robbed trench 1m wide in the central and southern parts of the site, but surviving traces of the original foundation showed that it was constructed of ragstone and yellow mortar, which rested upon the top of the natural gravel. However, this wall terminated near the north end of the site, and another wall, also robbed, apparently lay immediately on its west side and continued northwards. This was 1.24m wide, but was not as deep as the adjacent wall.

The southern continuation of the external wall was also found at 22 Lime Street where it was 1.1m wide with four courses of tiles above a thicker foundation of ragstone and yellow mortar.[68] Hodge also recorded it just south of this point, on the site of St. Dionis Backchurch, in about 1878, and showed that there were three courses of squared stones above a rough foundation (Plate 2).

At 83–87 Gracechurch Street a foundation was observed in section within the portico. It was of ragstone and yellow mortar and was 1.32m thick. It is possible that it was part of a cross wall within the portico, but this is unlikely since these were not normally placed in this location. Instead, it is rather more likely to have been the foundation of a pier or monument; further excavation should elucidate the matter since the relevant deposits probably survive.

In conclusion it seems likely, on the present very limited evidence, that the central range of the east wing may have stood to a greater height than the porticos, and that the range was illuminated by windows in a clerestory. The porticos were presumably roofed below this, the external walls of the porticos supporting columns or piers to carry the roof. Unfortunately no evidence of columns or piers has yet been found, though it is likely that the external wall of the outer portico which supported some of them stood a metre or so in height above the surrounding ground level.

The West Wing. Very little of the west wing has been found, but the evidence suggests that it was about 25m wide, and similar in plan to the east wing. Traces of the west wing have been found only at 1–2 St. Michael's Alley, and at 19–21 Birchin Lane. An inner or eastern portico, found on the former site, was 5.5m wide (p. 148). It lay between two walls, each 1.5m thick, of which the easternmost was merely a foundation of ragstone and hard yellow mortar. The western wall seems to have formed one side of a central range in this wing, and Gerald Dunning suggested that, although built of ragstone and hard yellow mortar, it was a sleeper wall supporting a pier (p. 149). The outer wall of the western or outer portico was found at 19–21 Birchin Lane, beside the main Roman street which flanked the west side of the forum. The wall had been robbed, the trench being 1.2m wide (p. 82).

The South Wing. The south wing of the forum was also about 25m wide, but its internal arrangement was a little different from that of the east and west wings (Figs. 25, 26). Although, here also, there was a central range of chambers between the porticos, both the central range and the south portico were narrower than their counterparts in the east and west wings. This created a wider inner portico, evidently to accommodate a row of brick piers adjacent to the north or external wall of the portico. It is presumed that these piers supported a row of statues or other monuments (Fig. 53).

In general, only the ragstone and hard buff mortar foundations of the forum walls had survived, though in many cases even these had been robbed. Thus there is almost no trace of wall superstructure, except for the external portico wall found beneath Lombard Street in 1933 (p. 133) and the piers (p. 137).

The Central Range. The central range of chambers measured 6.75m wide internally, and was bounded by two east-west foundations 1.22m thick. At 168–170 Fenchurch Street the base of the southernmost of these lay at 10.97m OD, about 2.5m below the floor of the outer or southern portico. Three north-south transverse foundations, each also 1.22m thick, crossed the central range and created two chambers measuring 10 × 7m and 14 × 7m.[69] It is presumed that these were used as shops, though their large size suggests that they may have been sub-divided. At 54–58 Lombard Street, rather smaller chambers, one 4.8m wide (E-W), were found, but as the foundations had been robbed away during the Middle Ages it was not possible to determine the construction of the cross walls.

The Southern Portico. The outer or southern portico was only 5.5m wide, with an external wall 1.22m thick (Plate 15). The portion recorded in Lombard Street was faced with ragstone and bonding tiles between 13.35 and 14.57m OD (p. 133), suggesting that the portico floor lay within this range of levels. In fact, at 168–170 Fenchurch Street, Philp found an *opus signinum* floor at 13.51m OD,[70] which is likely to have been the portico floor for, on the almost adjacent site of 160–162 Fenchurch Street, the lowest general portico floor lay at 13.41m OD. These floor levels indicate that the external portico wall found in Lombard Street in 1933 was standing above the portico floor level, presumably as a dwarf wall. No indication of its superstructure has been found, though it is likely to have carried brick piers or pillars to support the roof. As this low wall would have restricted access to the portico from the main east-west street, there were presumably entrances from the street at intervals. The main entrance was no doubt in the centre of the south wing, where the main access through the wing to the forum courtyard is believed to have been situated. A second entrance

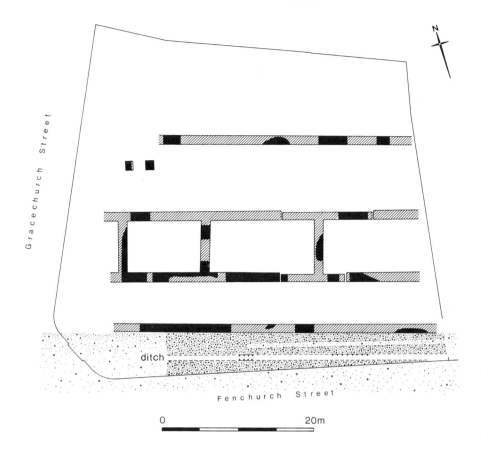

Fig. 53 168–170 Fenchurch Street, showing part of the south wing of the second forum. The straight joints and wall thickness variations indicate that a gap in the central range had been filled-in, presumably at a late stage in the construction of the forum (see Fig. 27).

close to the south-east corner is suggested by a wheel rut in the portico floor at 160-162 Fenchurch Street (p. 99).

The Northern Portico. The north or inner portico was 8.5m wide, and has been found at 168–170 Fenchurch Street and at All Hallows, Lombard Street. On the latter site the northern or external wall of the portico was found to form a corner with a north-south wall (p. 136). As it is exceptional in the forum for the porticos to include cross walls it is likely that this formed the west side of the main entrance into the forum courtyard. Indeed, assuming that this was so, and that the entrance was centrally placed, it would seem that the entrance way through the south wing was about 20m wide. Discoveries in the GPO tunnel beneath Gracechurch Street in 1977 included three of the four main east-west foundations of the south wing of the forum, and showed that they continued under the presumed forum entrance.

To judge from Oswald's plan of the site of the church of All Hallows, Lombard Street, a brick pier stood beside the north-south wall in the inner portico (Fig. 100). This was one of two piers found on that site which seem to have been associated with the second forum, and which were evidently of such

importance that space was made for them by creating a particularly wide northern portico. A continuation of these piers was found by Philp at 168–170 Fenchurch Street (Fig. 53), and it seems that there was originally a row of pillars or monuments perhaps along the entire north side of the portico. It is no doubt significant that the space between the piers and the south side of the portico was about 6m – the same as the widths of the inner porticos of the east and west wings.

The two piers on the All Hallows church site were built upon the stumps of piers of the first forum. A thin white mortar layer, overlying the walls of the first forum, butted up against these two piers at the base of the rebuilding. Below the mortar layer, the brick pier included yellow mortar; above it, pink. These rebuilt piers were placed asymmetrically upon the earlier bases (p. 137).

Two further piers were more exactly recorded at 168–170 Fenchurch Street,[71] and here too the lower parts were constructed of tiles set in yellow mortar; the upper parts in pink mortar.

The rebuilt pier 6 was offset to the east by 0.31m from the original build. On this site also were found thin mortar spreads, probably representing a phase of building rather than a floor, which ran up against the piers close to the base of the pink mortar at about 13m OD, indicating that the portico floor level lay just above this.

It was from beneath the mortar at All Hallows that Oswald recovered some crucial dating evidence of Hadrianic pottery, suggesting that the piers and the portico were constructed not earlier than about AD 120 (p. 136). The dating of the forum as a whole is discussed later (p. 74).

The white mortar layer, found in the northern portico on the All Hallows Church site, also stopped flush against a T-shaped pier situated roughly in the middle of the portico. Although built throughout with yellow mortar, this pier seemed to represent two phases of construction, for one part of it followed the alignment of the first forum, while another part followed the second forum. A coin of Hadrian was found in the mortar, but it is not known in which part of the structure it lay (p. 137). The absence of pink mortar, however, indicates that its rebuilding need not have been contemporary with the construction of the other piers in the portico, and therefore that the coin need not reflect the date of construction of the second forum.

In conclusion, it would seem that the south wing also comprised a central range of shops, perhaps with a clerestory above, and that porticos lay on either side with roofs at lower levels. The greater width of the inner or northern portico strongly suggests that the row of piers or monuments along its north side was an integral part of the wing from the beginning. Unfortunately, no certain indication has been found of what they supported, other than the portions of a stone column, found loose above the mortar floor on the All Hallows church site, which Oswald described as being 'part of one of the pink mortar bases' or piers (p. 138. Plate 17).

The Forum Courtyard. The courtyard of the second forum measured approximately 116m (E-W) by 84.8m, and its surfaces were recorded in some detail in the GPO tunnel excavated beneath Gracechurch Street in 1977. Previously, its mortar floors had been recognised only at 54–58 Lombard Street, approximately at 13.72m and 14.32m OD (pp. 114, 147), but this limited record was an insufficient basis from which to draw any general conclusions about the nature of the courtyard as a whole.

Much of the GPO tunnel was dug at about 3m below Gracechurch Street, enabling the forum courtyard surfaces to be traced for at least 50m south of the basilica frontage. For the first time it was possible to obtain a view of the general character of the central and northern parts of the courtyard, but further south the tunnel was dug at a downward incline below the surfaces, so as to pass beneath the modern sewers at the junction of Gracechurch Street and Lombard Street. Consequently there is no information about the southern part of the courtyard.

An access shaft to the GPO tunnel, opposite the south end of 83–87 Gracechurch Street, revealed the earliest courtyard surface at 14.24m OD, and it is clear that the courtyard remained consistently at about this level northwards to the front of the basilica. Sections showed that there were substantial dumps of gravel and other materials immediately beneath the surfaces, and that in the central area of the courtyard there had been many re-surfacings, which raised the courtyard surface by up to 0.74m. In contrast, the layers were fairly indistinct in the northern part of the courtyard, north of the modern Ship Tavern Passage, as far as the basilica itself (Fig. 54).

The general impression gained was that this part of the courtyard was not so frequently re-surfaced as was the centre, presumably indicating that the area near the basilica was not so heavily used. In the central region the courtyard surfaces were very varied but of limited extent, and it seemed that there was no single sequence of floors. The effect was of patching and re-patching, primarily using mortar, generally buff but sometimes pink, and gravels. The variation in the surfaces is best illustrated by two sections through the courtyard, recorded only a few metres apart (Fig. 54, Sections 13, 14). In general, the surfaces were overlaid by grey soil before being re-surfaced, and it is presumed that the soil was derived from deposits of silt and rubbish from the use of the courtyard.

A flat limestone slab 0.6–0.7m thick and about 2m wide (N-S) was found on the courtyard surface immediately in front of the south wall of the basilica. It was not possible to examine it in sufficient detail to establish its purpose, but it seems likely that it was a rain drip gutter such as existed along the frontage of the basilica at Wroxeter.[72] This would explain the function of the brick drain that was recorded by Hodge under the east wing of the forum (Figs. 30, 35), for this continued the line of the limestone slab, and evidently drained rainwater from the courtyard into the roadside ditch on the east side of the forum.

Near the centre of the courtyard, the GPO tunnel cut across a sunken structure which was lined with ragstone walls backed by stiff impervious clay (Fig. 55). There is little doubt that this was a shallow pool. Only its north and south walls were located, each about 0.5m thick and 7.43m apart. The walls were constructed of ragstone and buff mortar, and were faced towards each other with squared ragstone blocks, while the outer faces were rough and backed by stiff clay below the pink mortar floor of the surrounding courtyard. Traces of two courses of tiles set in pink mortar were found at the top of the walls, roughly level with the pink floor.

Originally the pool was more than 0.7m deep, its inward wall faces being rendered with pink mortar.

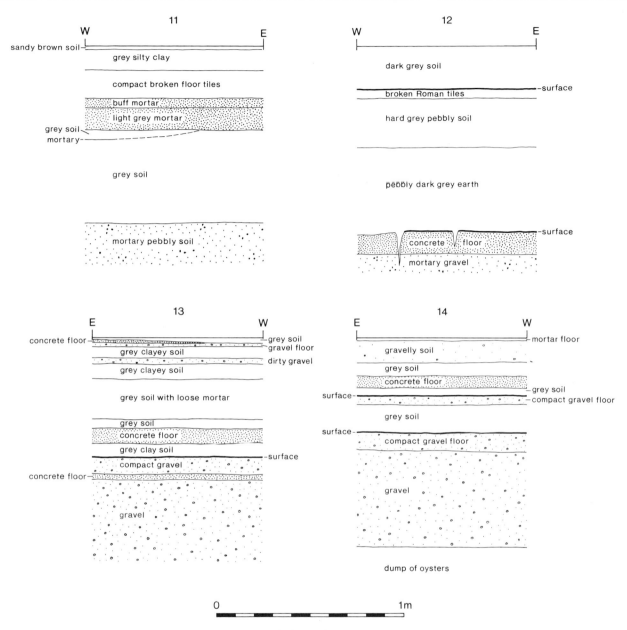

Fig. 54 GPO tunnel beneath Gracechurch Street, 1977. Sections showing the variations in floor surfaces of the forum courtyard (See Fig. 48).

The original floor was not discovered, but subsequently the pool was re-floored with *opus signinum* above a layer of buff mortar. This was repeated in due course, the new *opus signinum* overlying a layer of ragstone set in buff mortar. At this stage, the walls were rendered again with pink mortar onto which tiles were set, and a possible quarter-round moulding of pink mortar was placed at the junction of the walls and the floor. Later the pool was given yet another floor, this time of chalk above a layer of impervious brown clay (Plate 19). Finally, this was superseded by the latest floor, which was of *opus*

signinum, and it was this that was overlaid by dark grey soil of the period after the abandonment of the pool.

The size of the pool is difficult to judge, though it is reasonable to assume that it was centrally placed within the courtyard. The GPO tunnel in which it was found lay 7m to the east of the central north-south axis of the forum, and so it is likely that the pool exceeded 14m long east-west.

Possible indications of monuments within the courtyard have been found at 83–87 Gracechurch Street and at 1–2 St. Michael's Alley. A massive

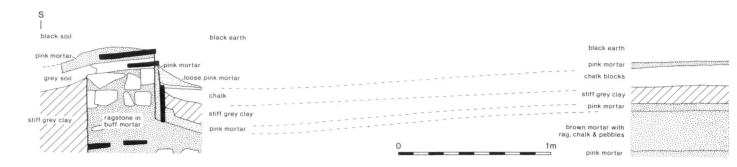

Fig. 55 GPO tunnel beneath Gracechurch Street, 1977. Section across the pool in the forum courtyard. The walls of the pool were lined on the inside with pink mortar, and on the outside was a sticky impervious puddled brown-grey clay (probably London Clay). Inside the pool were several floors (For location see Fig. 48).

foundation of ragstone, yellow mortar and a single course of bonding tiles was found on the former site, close to the west portico of the east wing. Unfortunately, the shape of the foundation was neither clearly defined nor stratigraphically related to the second forum (p. 129). On the latter site was a foundation of ragstone and yellow mortar 0.9m wide. It lay close to the eastern portico of the west wing, but otherwise its relationship to the second forum remains unknown (p. 148).

A particularly important discovery, representing a roughly life-size figure which may have stood in the forum, is a bronze hand which was found in 1867 on the site of 'The Spread Eagle' inn, now part of 83–87 Gracechurch Street (Plate 20). The bronze hand is now in the Museum of London.[73]

STREETS SURROUNDING THE BASILICA AND FORUM

Streets have been found on all four sides of the basilica and forum, thus creating an insula measuring about 170m square (Figs. 25, 26). The north, east and west streets were probably constructed as part of the basilica – forum project, but the southern street was in existence from the beginning of *Londinium* in the mid-first century AD. The central point of the south wing of the second forum was shared by that of the first forum, the focus evidently being determined by the north-south street which led up from the Roman bridge crossing the Thames. All the streets were constructed with cambered surfaces of hard gravel metalling, and it is clear that at least some were associated with side drainage ditches.

The southern street has already been described, for it was found in the GPO tunnel beneath Gracechurch Street in 1977 (p. 100), at 30–32 Lombard Street (p. 135), and at 168–170 Fenchurch Street.[74] This street was a little more than 4.6m wide at 30–32 Lombard Street, though it is not clear how many of

its gravel surfaces were contemporary with the second forum. However, as the many surfaces of gravel metalling survived up to about 2.3m thick at 168–170 Fenchurch Street, they evidently reflected a long life, part of which must have been associated with the second forum. Judging from excavations at 160–162 and 168–170 Fenchurch Street, the edge of the Roman street lay about 3m from the outer forum portico.

The northern street, also about 5m wide, lay between side ditches, and was uncovered in an excavation by Peter James at 68 Cornhill (p. 88). Pottery of the period AD 85–120, found in the lowest road metallings, show that it was constructed at about the time of the second forum. Although only five gravel surfaces had survived, a timber-lined drain on the north side of the street was found to contain pottery of the late 3rd–early 4th century, and indicated that the street had continued in use until at least that period.

The eastern street was probably rather broader, its gravel metalling having been found at 15–18 Lime Street, with a width of over 7m (p. 131). It did not lie directly against the side of the forum for its timber-lined side drain was found 3m beyond the outer portico of the east wing, at 160–162 Fenchurch Street (p. 100). This street probably continued northwards towards Bishopsgate Street, since a thickness of about 0.75m of gravel metalling was found overlying the natural brickearth against the east side of 139–144 Leadenhall Street. It should be mentioned, however, that the low level of this metalling relative to the natural subsoil might place some doubt on the interpretation of this discovery, for at 15–18 Lime Street occupation deposits containing Flavian pottery were found beneath this street (p. 132).

Little is known about the western street, which has been found at 19–21 Birchin Lane and at 4 Castle Court. On the former site the gravel was found with a width of perhaps 10–12m, though it is likely that some of this was not road metalling but was instead gravel dumping intended to level the site before constructing the road (p. 79). On the latter site were found several undoubted surfaces of hard gravel

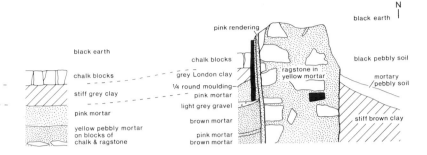

metalling, but these merely show that further excavation is required to elucidate the exact width and limits of the street (p. 82). Pottery found beneath the street in Birchin Lane shows that it was probably a post-Boudican construction (p. 82) and that, like the eastern and northern streets, it was not one of the earliest streets of Roman London.

LATER HISTORY OF THE BASILICA AND FORUM SITE

There is very little information relating to the subsequent history of the basilica and forum site until the late Saxon period, and absolutely no archaeological evidence to date the period when the complex ceased to be used and became a ruin. The latest floors in the basilica and forum are covered by dark earth (eg at 54–58 Lombard Street, Fig. 85; and in the 1977 GPO tunnel beneath Gracechurch Street, Fig. 50, section 10). In the basilica area this included fallen blocks of mortared brickwork from the superstructure of the building. Hodge illustrated similar debris in his sketches of the Leadenhall Market site (Fig. 37), and noted on his plan that one particular block seemed to be part of an arch (Fig. 30). As would be expected, no large portions of building debris were found in the dark earth overlying the forum courtyard, as exposed in the GPO tunnel dug in 1977 beneath Gracechurch Street. However, as the tunnel approached within about 10m of the south frontage of the basilica, substantial portions of building debris began to be encountered. These were in the form of bricks with mortar adhering to them, and, at one point close to the south wall of the basilica, was found part of a very large piece of fallen mortared brickwork.

It is the streets, both Roman and medieval, that provide an important clue to the later history of the site. Only the Roman street on the south side of the forum continued in use into medieval and later times as parts of Lombard Street and Fenchurch Street. In contrast, the Roman streets on the east, west and north sides of the basilica and forum faded from existence, presumably during the Saxon period, and

new streets, Cornhill and Gracechurch Street, came into existence crossing the basilica as if the ruins of that building no longer presented an obstacle (Fig. 56).

Cornhill (Fig. 57), which cuts across the north-western part of the basilica, first appears as the name of a district by the early 12th century, and as a street name in 1193–1211.[75] Gracechurch Street, which crosses the basilica-forum complex from north to south is recorded by the early 13th century. Thus by this period, at the very latest, the Roman buildings were no longer an obstacle to the main routes from Cheapside to Aldgate, or from London Bridge to Bishopsgate. This may have been the case by the mid-11th century, since the church of St. Peter 'within London', which stands almost at the intersection of both streets, was in existence by 1040, and St. Michael's church, adjacent to Cornhill, is recorded probably by the later 11th century.

The excavation of a shaft giving access to the GPO tunnel beneath the centre of Gracechurch Street in 1977 was of great interest in this connection, since it made it possible to seek early street surfaces opposite No. 83 (Fig. 58). The result was surprising for no street surfaces were found lower than modern disturbances, caused by the laying of service pipes and cables, at a depth of 0.68m below the present street (which lies at 17.64m OD). Instead, a dark grey organic deposit 2.68m thick was found, which included bone and leather fragments and, towards the bottom, some tile and ragstone. The lowest part of the deposit lay upon the surface of the forum courtyard at 14.28m OD. The deposit was not obviously stratified, but seemed to have been formed partly in water within the courtyard area over a long period of time.

The absence of any medieval street surfaces would indicate that there had been little change in level over a period of at least nine centuries. The alternative possibility is that the shaft had been dug through the centre of a large pit which had destroyed the earlier stratigraphy. On balance this seemed an unlikely explanation for there were no obvious tip lines, and the silts and soil were so compact that a

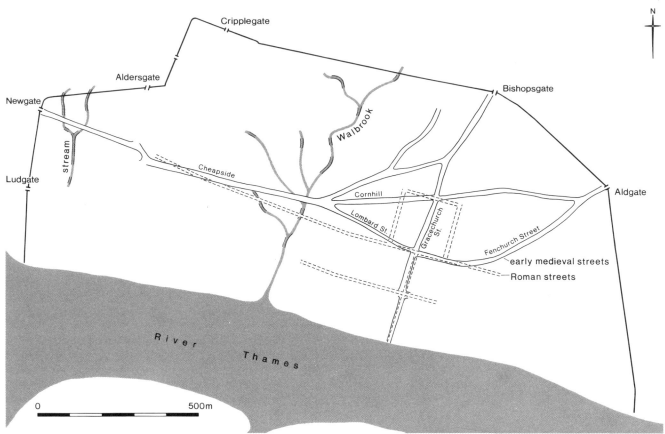

Fig. 56 Plan of London showing the layout of Roman streets around the forum, and the late Saxon – early medieval streets which appear to disregard the forum, suggesting that by the 11th century its ruins no longer impeded communications.

Saxon or medieval date seemed most likely.

The indicated level of the earliest street, not lower than about 17m OD, should also be considered with the evidence of a Norman house found at the south side of Corbet Court in 1872 in the courtyard area of the former forum (Fig. 57).[76] Although the sills of the windows in the undercroft lay at about 3.35m below Corbet Court, at *c.* 14.3m OD, it is possible that the contemporary ground level was higher and that, as with the windows of the west crypt of Guildhall, light wells were originally provided.[77] The fact that the floor of the room above the undercroft lay at about 17m OD, comparable with the suggested early street level, perhaps gives a closer indication of the early medieval ground surface.

It may be significant that St. Michael's church, Cornhill, lies on the presumed site of the western *tribunal* of the basilica, and that St. Peter's church lies in the centre of the northern part of the basilica, a place sometimes reserved in other basilicas for a municipal shrine.[78] Merrifield has suggested that a Christian chapel could have been established in the basilica at this point,[79] and was later adapted as the church of St. Peter. This might account for the later medieval tradition that the church of St. Peter had been founded by a King Lucius in AD 179.[80]

Whatever is made of the tradition itself, the church was evidently considered to be of great and special antiquity, while of the four churches in the immediate area of the forum three are certainly of Saxon origin and all were built upon the ruins of the basilica and forum buildings, rather than within the courtyard. At the very least, it is likely that their location was determined partly by the availability of building materials, and perhaps also by existing standing structures. Without excavation it is impossible to determine whether the earliest churches of St. Peter and St. Michael made use of the basilica structure. St. Dionis Backchurch (recorded *c.* 1100) and All Hallows, Lombard Street (recorded 1035) both overlie the forum, and All Hallows was excavated and recorded by Adrian Oswald in 1939 during the demolition of the church. He established that the Saxon church straddled the exerior wall of the north portico of the south wing of the forum, showing that it did not make use of any surviving walls,[81] though the Roman ruins may have offered more solid and drier ground on which to build than sites within the courtyard.

Another important feature of the site is the

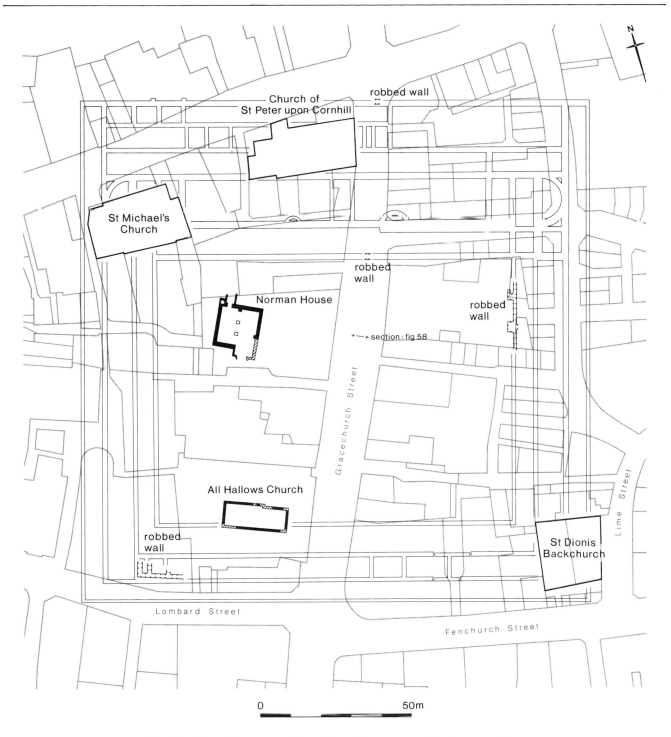

Fig. 57 Plan of known early medieval structures on the forum and
basilica site. The late Saxon church of All Hallows, although built with
Roman building materials presumably robbed from the forum, clearly
did not use any standing walls of the forum. The three other churches
were constructed on the ruins of the basilica and forum, though
whether or not they reused standing Roman walls is not known.
However, it is interesting that St. Peter upon Cornhill church was
allegedly founded in AD 179.

extensive robbing of the forum walls, and of the north and south walls of the basilica, for building materials. To judge from the pottery recovered from the robbed foundation at 54–58 Lombard Street this occurred probably during the 12th century (see p. 146). The extent of the robbing perhaps implies that many Roman walls were still visible as late as the 13th century, and that the area had not yet been intensively built upon, allowing easy access to the old walls. Dr. Marc Fitch recently pointed out that the name of Lime Street, just east of the forum, was

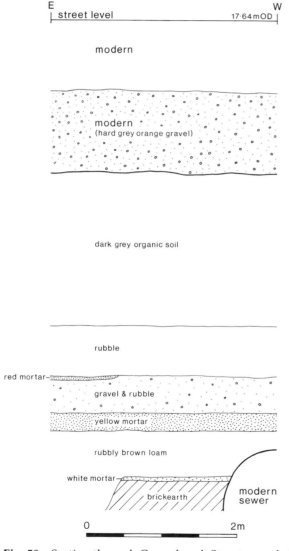

Fig. 58 Section through Gracechurch Street recorded in an access shaft dug in 1977 for the GPO tunnel (for its position see Fig. 57). The mortar layers represent the floors of the courtyard of the second forum, and the rubble above perhaps represents the destruction of the forum. The 'dark grey organic soil' presumably pre-dates Gracechurch Street, which was in existence early in the Middle Ages, and perhaps was formed during the Saxon period in a marshy pond surrounded by the ruins of the basilica and forum.

evidently derived from lime being burnt and sold in the area, where the only substantial local source of limestone was the forum.[82] Lime Street was in existence by 1170–87, and there is a documentary record of a person named Ailnoth, who was a *calcerius* or 'lime-burner' and a 12th century tenant in the ward.[83]

In conclusion, it is suggested that at the end of the Roman period the basilica and forum fell into ruins, and that the former courtyard became a marshy hollow until drained and filled with dumping in late Saxon and Norman times. The Roman streets around the north, east and west sides of the basilica and forum were forgotten, and by the 11th century Gracechurch Street and Cornhill had been constructed over the Roman ruins. The ruins probably provided a convenient location for building the four churches, if not for the use of still standing Roman walls, then for the proximity of stone and brick rubble to be used as building materials. By the 12th century the former courtyard was sufficiently dry for an impressive stone house to be built there with an undercroft, but the main development of intensive settlement took place a little later, as is indicated by the preponderance of 13th century rubbish pits at 160–162 Fenchurch Street.[84]

Discussion and dating evidence

The interpretation of the history of the forum site depends in some measure upon the ability to date accurately the phases of its development. But as those phases occurred mainly within the first 50–80 years of the Roman period in Britain, it is difficult to establish reasonably precise dating on artifactual evidence alone. Indeed, for some phases dates are still unavailable from this source, and are indicated only in relation to other, approximately dated, phases. Thus, as the dating evidence for the sequence of building phases is of primary importance from the sites as a whole, only key dating groups of objects are relevant to this report. Since those objects are few and mostly published, it is not necessary to republish them other than in a summary form. Some of the groups of objects are available for consultation in the Museum of London, Department of Urban Archaeology.

THE EARLIEST PHASE

The first phase of occupation on the forum site has provided some of the earliest stratified Roman pottery found in the City,[85] and seems to relate to the origin of London itself. Only at 168–170 Fenchurch Street, in the Gracechurch Street shaft (p. 101) and in the GPO tunnel beneath Gracechurch Street (p. 100) have the earliest deposits been examined in any detail. They suggest that the initial settlement was carefully planned with streets and buildings laid out on a rectangular plan, with metalled areas alternating with timber structures along the north side of the main east-west street. The large gravelled area of this phase, also beside the main street, is interpreted as a courtyard.

The precise date of these earliest structures is not known, but associated with them are samian sherds of the period Claudius – Nero. Perhaps more important is a coin, an *as* of Claudius, which is tentatively identified as a barbarous copy,[86] perhaps dating from the latter part of the reign of Claudius, *c* AD 50.[86] This was found in a deposit underlying the earliest streets and buildings, and could date the structures to the AD 50s rather than to the 40s. This also accords with other evidence from London, both pottery and coins, which suggests that *Londinium* was founded *c* AD 50–55.[88]

The nature of that earliest occupation on the forum site is far from clear because the plan of the buildings and streets is so incomplete (Fig. 11). Nevertheless, the planning of the settlement is suggestive of Roman military authority, but insufficient is known to show whether it was a military fort, a supplies base, or the military planning of a civilian town. Philp has suggested that it was a military camp,[89] but Merrifield is less certain, suggesting that the military-style planning of streets and buildings was not necessarily for a camp or even for a supplies base.[90] Because there was a military supplies base at Richborough at the same time, Wacher has doubted the need for a further base in London, and wrote that 'it is reasonable to suppose that a supplies base in London was at best short-lived'.[91]

On the assumption that *Londinium* was founded *c* AD 50, there are two main possible interpretations of the earliest phase of occupation. The first is that it was a short-lived military base, situated closer to the frontier than Richborough, and intended to supply the military advance under the governor, Publius Ostorius Scapula, beyond the Foss Way in the early 50s. On this basis the timber structures found at 168–170 Fenchurch Street could have been storage buildings, an interpretation supported by the basic plan of streets and buildings which somewhat resembles the early military supplies base at Fishbourne.[92] The second is that it was part of a new civilian city-port planned by the military authorities, and which, following the advance beyond the Foss Way, was intended to help replace the military presence in south-east Britain with a Roman urban population. However, unlike the other new cities *Camulodunum* and *Verulamium*, *Londinium* probably had no large native settlement from which to draw its population, though a concentration of Iron Age coins west of London suggests that a native British settlement of some kind perhaps lay in that region some time before the Roman invasion, though it may

have ceased to exist by the time the Claudian invasion occurred.[93] A civilian origin of London might account for the complete absence of Roman military objects associated with pre-Boudican deposits in the forum area, though the discovery of military objects elsewhere, particularly in Southwark, shows that the civilian or military nature of that earliest phase of settlement remains unresolved, and only further excavation on the few remaining sites in the area might clarify how *Londonium* originated.

PRE-BOUDICAN

The construction of extensive new Roman buildings and streets immediately east of the gravelled courtyard, at a stage prior to the Boudican revolt of AD 60, shows that major replanning had already occurred in at least this part of *Londinium*. The changes have only been studied at 168–170 Fenchurch Street, and there is no means of knowing if they reflect a change of status, as perhaps from a military to a civil administration. Three parallel buildings were partly recorded at 168–170 Fenchurch Street, and in each was found an internal wall on a common north-south line suggesting that all were planned as a unit.[94] This in turn implies the existence of a planning authority which, at this stage, probably before London had a fully self-governing local authority, was likely to have been under military control. The much discussed comment by Tacitus[95] on the status of *Londinium* about AD 60 does not help for it merely states that the embryonic city was not then a *colonia*.[96]

Only the southernmost building at 168–170 Fenchurch Street has been recorded in sufficient detail for its purpose to be identified (Fig. 13). It was apparently a range of shops that opened onto a narrow portico beside the main east-west street of *Londinium*. The evidence that these were shops is twofold: firstly, its layout was very similar to a range of shops found at *Verulamium* which were also built before the Boudican fire of AD 60;[97] and secondly, the room at the extreme east end contained a considerable quantity of grain that had been imported from the eastern Mediterranean and was presumably being stored for sale (see p. 97 and Appendix, p. 151).

Interpreting the significance of the grain is difficult, for on the one hand it is unlikely that it had been imported from such a distance simply to make bread, but on the other hand it was not so significantly superior in quality to British grain as to justify, under normal circumstances, the trouble and expense of shipping it from the eastern Mediterranean to seed new crops. It is most likely, therefore, to have been a special importation to meet a specific need.

Whatever the difficulties in interpreting the grain, however, it would seem that the block of shops may represent a single or a corporate developer, though differences in the method of construction (*eg* stone foundations at the east end, timber foundations at the west end, and a portion of tiled roof in the western half of the building) presumably indicate the individual needs and tastes of the occupant. The building of similar size at *Verulamium* had a somewhat varied construction too, also suggesting a similar ownership pattern, and the discovery of such buildings in these two cities indicates that property developers were perhaps as important an element in the creation of new Roman towns in Britain as they are in modern towns.

The settlement of *Londinium* on the eve of the Boudican rebellion appears to have comprised a cosmopolitan trading population, with imported goods flooding into the city from many parts of the Empire.[98] The pit group at 54–58 Lombard Street, containing a considerable amount of fine table glass, both coloured and painted, is indicative of this trade (p. 142). The main settlement area, however, to judge from the extent of the fire debris, apparently lay primarily between the two east-west streets beneath Fenchurch Street and Cannon Street, and was therefore closer to the waterfront where port facilities were also being developed.[99] By AD 60 the site which was to accommodate the forum apparently overlay the northern edge of the main settlement area, for Boudican fire debris is only encountered at the south end of the site.

A market place was an essential element in any trading settlement, and presumably existed in *Londinium* from an early stage. The large area of gravel metalling overlying the natural subsoil on the forum site continued in use until the Boudican fire, and is likely to have served this purpose. This interpretation is particularly favoured by the continued use of the gravelled area during the undoubtedly civilian pre-Boudican phase, and by the subsequent use of the site for the forum. From the beginning of *Londinium*, therefore, part of the forum site had been set apart for public use. It is also of interest to note that since the gravelled area lay at the northern edge of the embryonic city of the 50s AD, it was possibly intended as part of a long-term development plan for the city, which was to include the construction of buildings to the north of the market place where no Boudican burning was found.

The dating evidence of the buildings burnt in the fire of AD 60, and of the neighbouring gravelled area at 168–170 Fenchurch Street, comprised pottery and coins of the period Claudius–Nero.[100] At 54–58 Lombard Street burnt debris filled the top of a rubbish pit containing pottery and glass of the Claudian–Neronian period,[101] and it would seem that although the pit was partly filled before the revolt occurred in AD 60, the site itself was probably not occupied by a building.

BOUDICAN DESTRUCTION, AS 60

Since the burning, believed to be the result of the Boudican uprising in AD 60, seems to have been mainly restricted to the south-east part of the forum site, there is little that can be said of the general nature of the effects of the rebellion. A wider view of *Londinium* shows that the main region of burning lay to the south and west of the forum, between Lombard Street and Cannon Street (Fig. 14).[102]

In contrast to Colchester, where burnt buildings of AD 60 have been found still containing at least part of their stock of goods,[103] the burnt buildings of London are usually devoid of such objects, so that the grain discovery was exceptional.[104] The archaeological evidence therefore seems to reflect the recorded historical events by showing that unlike the inhabitants of *Camulodunum*[105] the occupants of *Londinium* had time to flee from the city taking most of their possessions with them.

POST-BOUDICAN PHASE

Although some pit groups of the Neronian-Vespasianic period have been found elsewhere in London, indicating urban redevelopment during the decade following the Boudican destruction, the forum site itself has revealed very little trace of occupation during this period. This may simply be due to the patchy quality of the archaeological investigations, though it is also possible that it reflects a period slow redevelopment following the revolt.

It has been suggested that an 'official' building (Fig. 15), perhaps associated with the Procurator, may have been constructed on the forum site during the 60s.[106] Although this is possible, and a close examination of the evidence suggests a possible phase of activity intermediate between the Boudican fire and the first forum, it is not now possible to define either the nature or date of that phase. However, pottery associated with the building at 54–58 Lombard Street[107] suggests a Flavian date perhaps even as late as the construction of the second forum *c* AD 100.[108]

The forum site, therefore, has provided no clear evidence of a speedy recovery from the effects of the Boudican revolt. The only certain evidence of activity was recovered from 168–170 Fenchurch Street and from 54–58 Lombard Street. On the first site the upper part of the burnt debris had been turned over, presumably as a result of levelling the ground, while on the latter the burnt debris from nearby buildings had been dumped, also probably to level the debris.

THE FIRST FORUM

As it is likely that the construction of the first basilica and forum followed the granting of a charter of self-government to the city of *Londinium*, it is particularly important to establish the date of its construction as closely as possible.

Until now the only detailed published account of part of the first forum has been by Brian Philp who excavated the site of 168–170 Fenchurch Street and found the south-east corner of a building which he termed a 'proto-forum'. He concluded that it was probably constructed during the decade AD 60–70, since associated samian ware was mainly of Neronian date and excluded late Flavian material. In addition he claimed that, after its construction, large dumps of rubbish of *c* AD 75–85 accumulated immediately east of the building.[109]

If Philp's suggested sequence of events is correct it would seem to mean that (1) the forum was built AD 60–70, (2) the rubbish was dumped close to the east side of that building *c* 75–85 AD, and (3) the street on the east side of the forum was therefore constructed twenty or thirty years after the forum was constructed.

However, in the light of evidence from earlier excavations which was not available to Philp, and which is published in this report for the first time, it is clear that his conclusions need revision. Moreover, the identification of the first forum as such now means that it is extremely unlikely that the Roman authorities, having undertaken at great cost the building of the basilica and forum, would have omitted the construction of the street on the east side until much later, and instead allowed a large dump of rubbish to accumulate beside the building.

The evidence from the earlier excavations not only enables the nature of the basilica and forum to be determined (p. 22), but also shows that it was built after AD 71. This date is derived from a coin minted in that year, which is said to have come from a rubbish pit cut by the south wall of the first basilica. Found by Frank Cottrill at 83–87 Gracechurch Street in 1934 (p. 119) the coin has recently been re-cleaned, and its original tentative identification confirmed. The associated Flavian pottery, also from the pit, was deposited in Guildhall Museum, but is now lost. Fortunately, the dating of Flavian pottery was well established by the 1930s, and there is no reason to doubt the dating of this group.

It is reasonable to expect that the street on the east side of the forum and basilica was contemporary with the construction of the forum itself, and that the offending rubbish dumps were earlier than the forum. There is no certain proof of this, however, since the street was not stratigraphically related to the forum building. Nevertheless, Philp's only reason for believing that the dumps were later than

the construction of the forum is that they seemed to stop short of the east side of the forum, as if the building was already standing (Fig. 20). In fact this is hardly a conclusive argument, for the east side of the forum followed an earlier pre-Boudican property boundary which marked the junction of the gravelled market place and the shops and dwellings to the east (Fig. 13). This pre-forum boundary was well defined by the western limit of the Boudican fire debris so positively described by Philp.[110] The boundary, therefore, marked the junction of public and private property before the Boudican destruction, and its continuing use evidently determined the eastern limit of the first forum and the western limit of the rubbish dumps.

In view of this it would seem that the sequence was (1) the dumping of rubbish immediately east of the gravelled market place, followed by (2) the construction of the first basilica and forum and its eastern street which partly overlay the rubbish dumps.

The date of the construction of the basilica and forum was evidently later than AD 71; but as the rubbish was being dumped during the period *c* AD 75–85,[111] it seems that the eastern street, and therefore the first forum, could hardly have been built earlier than AD 80–85. The crucial dating evidence from the dumps comprised fifty-seven samian ware sherds, twenty-two of which were found beneath the eastern road. Of these, one is dated *c* AD 70–85, and another is dated *c* AD 75–90.[112]

In view of the short life of the first forum, a date in the 70s might seem preferable to a date in the 80s, as Merrifield has so clearly pointed out,[113] but this would imply a pre-Agricolan granting of self-governing status to *Londinium*. On the other hand a completion date during the 80s would suggest that *Londinium* had been granted self-governing rights under Agricola, who was Governor from AD 78 to 84. The actual status of the city is unknown, but perhaps was that of *municipium*.

The care and symmetry with which the basilica and forum were planned is evident from their measurements (Fig. 18); the length of the whole complex being exactly twice the width. Similar proportions were used for the basilica itself, though the width of the forum left 'shoulders' where its north end abutted the basilica. The 2:1 proportion was clearly a determining factor in the design of the complex, though it can hardly have been the only reason for creating a short basilica. However, it is of value to note that the importance of creating the correct proportions in basilicas was stressed by Vitruvius.[114]

Why this was so in *Londinium* is not clear, though it would seem that a basic measurement, the north-south length of the whole complex, was established by two existing east-west Roman streets, those beneath Lombard Street and beside Corbet Court (see pp. 32 and 102).

The basic plan of the basilica-forum complex cannot be exactly paralleled, and the simple layout of the basilica without attendant offices is unusual in Britain, though well represented in Italy (eg *Velleia* and *Pompeii*) and in Gaul (eg Augst, to which in the 3rd century AD a *curia* was added; and *Glanum*, near Saint-Rémy-en-Province).[115] In London the *curia* and other essential municipal offices clearly lay elsewhere, perhaps in one wing of the forum or indeed in a nearby building. The elongated form of the London forum is perhaps somewhat paralleled by the fora at Leicester, Cirencester and Wroxeter,[116] but as there was much variety in forum architecture generally it is difficult to judge whether or not this has any real significance in any architectural typology.

The small temple, probably of classical type, which lay just outside the London forum seems to have been part of the civic centre complex (p. 108), and as such may generally be compared with the temples attached to the fora at *Verulamium* and Caerwent.[117] These associated temples would seem to indicate a modification of the 'Gallic type' of forum, in which the temple was sometimes placed in the courtyard actually inside the forum. It has been suggested that the absence of the temple precinct within British fora .might have been due in some measure to the effects of the Boudican revolt, and to disagreeable reminders of the siege of the temple of Claudius at Colchester in AD 60.[118] Usually, however, British fora do not seem to include temples, as opposed merely to shrines, as part of their architecture. The inclusion of the temple beside the first forum complex of London would thus underline the continental associations in the planning of the first basilica and forum of London.

REBUILDINGS OF THE FIRST FORUM

At some stage during its short life of about twenty years the forum was extensively rebuilt within the outermost walls of its east and west wings. That there was more than one phase of construction seems clear, but the detail remains uncertain (Fig. 22). The final effect is apparent, however, for the shops and other enclosed chambers were cleared away and replaced by rows of brick piers which presumably supported a new roof.

The reasons for the change cannot be defined though, at whatever stage it occurred, the considerable expenditure of labour and money implies that the city council could not have envisaged that within so short a time all would be swept away to create a new and much larger complex. The forum was small by any standards, and the enormous increase in the size of the second forum suggests that its predecessor

was inadequate for *Londinium*, and that this need might already have motivated the rebuilding with piers in the first forum. The piers supporting the roof probably gave a far greater flexibility in the use of the forum, for temporary partitions and stalls could be so placed as to allow the building to function more satisfactorily, without permanently impairing access.

The London forum was not alone in Britain in being rebuilt in this way, for the forum at Caistor by Norwich similarly had its three wings and the chambers that they contained, completely demolished and replaced by piers and walls.[119] On the Continent piers are also known, for example in the forum at *Glanum* in Gaul,[120] though the dating of the piers is not always clear.

THE SECOND FORUM AND BASILICA

The construction of a new basilica and forum, five times more extensive than the first complex, was a landmark in the history of Roman London (Figs. 25, 26, 28). Since this was by far the largest civic centre in Britain and one of the larger in the Roman world, it is likely that its construction marked a change in the status of *Londinium* (Fig. 59).[121] The date ·of its construction, therefore, is of special importance in understanding its historical significance.

The dating evidence so far recovered is rather limited, and has led to some differences in interpretation. Part of the problem is that all the evidence has been recovered from beneath the floors of the forum and basilica, so that there is merely a *terminus post quem* date for the construction of the buildings. In spite of this, the fact that the evidence has been recovered from seven sites, from six of which nothing has been found dating later than the end of the first century AD, makes it look likely that *c* AD 100 rubbish ceased to be deposited on the site, presumably because of the construction of the forum and basilica. The exceptional site, All Hallows, Lombard Street, produced pottery probably of the 2nd century. In consequence, Ralph Merrifield has proposed a date in the 90s for the construction of the new forum,[122] while Marsden has suggested a date in the 120s, perhaps associated with Hadrian's visit to Britain.[123]

The difficulty in accepting a construction date in the 90s is that it gives the first forum and basilica an extremely short life of twenty years, in the course of which a major rebuilding phase has also to be accommodated. The problem attaching to a construction date in 120s is that in that event more than one site would probably have produced pottery of the early 2nd century. A further difficulty is that the crucial dating evidence from the 2nd century was lost during the last war, and so cannot be checked. Indeed, dating evidence has only survived from three of the seven sites from which such evidence

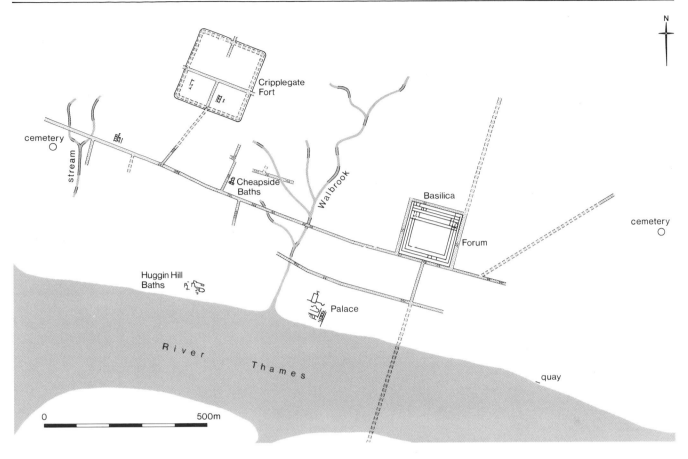

Fig. 59 Plan of Londinium in the early 2nd century AD, showing the location of the enormous second basilica and forum.

was found: 168–170 Fenchurch Street, 68 Cornhill and 54–58 Lombard Street.

The dating evidence from each site is as follows:

(1) At 168–170 Fenchurch Street there was a thick dump of clay that raised the ground level for the construction of the second forum. Flavian pottery found below the dump included a samian ware sherd of *c* AD 80–95.[124] From within the dump itself were fourteen samian ware sherds, mostly of Flavian date, the latest being of *c* AD 75–90.[125] The finds are in the Museum of London.

(2) At 19–21 Birchin Lane (see pp. 79, 82) a dump of rubbish, pre-dating the Roman street beside the west side of the forum, contained stamps of the following samian ware potters: FELIX, *c* AD 45–65; MVRRANVS, *c* AD 45–70; VITALIS, either *c* AD 50–65 or *c* 75–100; AQVITANVS *c* AD 50–65; and BASSVS, *c* AD 45–65.[126] Beneath the street itself were stamps of the potters ALBINVS, pre-Flavian; and QVARTVS, ? date. These finds are now lost.

(3) At 52 Cornhill (see pp. 84–85), rubbish pits were found underlying the basilica, with pottery said to be of the period *c* AD 65–80 and *c* AD 60–75. There was also a well which had been filled by about AD 80, and above it pottery from a rubbish layer which Gerald Dunning dated to *c* AD 80–90. Nothing definitely of 2nd century date was found beneath the basilica floor. Many of these finds are now lost though they were described by Gerald Dunning[127].

(4) At 68 Cornhill (see pp. 88–89), rubbish dating from the period *c* AD 85–120 was found beneath the east-west street along the north side of the basilica. No specifically 2nd century pottery types were found. The finds are in the Museum of London.

(5) At 15–18 Lime Street (see pp. 131–132), the Roman street on the east side of the forum overlay rubbish containing the samian ware potters' stamps of PONTVS, *c* AD 65–90; and PERRVS, *c* 55–75. There was also a coin of Nero, AD 64–68.

These finds are now lost.

(6)   At 54–58 Lombard Street, the clay dumped to raise the floor level of the forum was found to contain a little Flavian pottery (see pp. 145–146).
These finds are in the Museum of London.

(7)   At All Hallows Church, Lombard Street (see p. 136) the rubbish below the mortar floor of the second forum contained a samian ware potter's stamp said to be AVENT, on a form 18 dish. Adrian Oswald, who excavated the site, referred it to the *Index of Potters' Stamps on Terra Sigillata* by Felix Oswald, 1931, and identified the potter as AVENTINVS of Lezoux, dated Hadrian-Antonine. On this identification this stamp would be the latest known object from beneath the forum floor. However, more recent samian ware research suggests that this interpretation may be incorrect. Geoffrey Marsh of the Museum of London reports that the record of the stamp does not make sense, since dishes of form 18 made during the 2nd century are not otherwise recorded. Thus the sherd could be either a first century Dragendorf form 18 from South Gaul, or a stamp of the Lezoux potter AVENTINVS who worked during the Antonine period. Sadly, the object is lost and there is now no means of checking.

In addition from this site there were decorated fragments of samian ware, identified by Adrian Oswald as being in the style of the potters FRONTINVS (form 37) and MEDETVS (form 29). The former, if correct, dates from *c* AD 75–95, but the latter is less certain. Geoffrey Marsh reports of the latter that 'if this is a form 29 and the potter is incorrectly identified then the sherd should be of pre-*c* AD 85 date, when the manufacture of form 29 largely ceased. But if it is, as stated, a form 29 of MEDETVS, which is most uncommon, it would be of *c* AD 110–120'. This object too is lost.

Also, in the mortar of a pier (p. 137) apparently of the second forum, was found a *quadrans* of Hadrian (AD 117–138). There is nothing to suggest that this pier was part of the original structure of the forum, for it was apparently in an isolated position in the south wing. It may thus have been an addition to the forum, perhaps to support an internal monument. Hence the coin may have no significance in dating the forum.

In general, therefore, the evidence from this site is so uncertain that its significance cannot be positively interpreted. Of the sherds found beneath the forum floor two may be of 2nd century date, but as these later sherds, particularly that bearing the AVENT stamp which may be of Antonine date, are inconsistent with the remainder of the dating evidence, they could have been derived from a disturbance in the south wing, perhaps associated with the construction of the pier. Apart from these two sherds it seems most likely that the second forum and basilica complex was built about AD 100.

Having established that the new basilica – forum complex was probably built within a few years either side of AD 100, and therefore during the reign of Trajan rather than that of Hadrian, it is necessary to consider the possible significance of this new civic centre.

By the end of the Flavian period *Londinium* was probably the greatest centre of population in Britain, and also the largest port of entry and exit for goods in the province. Although the first forum may well have been considered unduly small, even when built as late as *c* AD 80, it does raise the question of whether or not the increasing size of *Londinium* during the following twenty years or so was such as to justify a five-fold increase in size of the civic centre. The difference seems too extreme to be explicable purely by practical considerations.

Part of the answer may be found in the probability that *Londinium* acquired another role during the Flavian period, as the seat of the provincial government. To judge from the Classicianus inscription[128] it seems that the *procurator* was already established here, perhaps even before the revolt of AD 60. It has been argued that during the Flavian period the Governor of the province probably took up residence in the city[129], an important part of the evidence being the remains of a large palatial residence in Cannon Street[130]. The Governor undoubtedly enhanced the importance of *Londinium*, and it may have been considered appropriate to elevate the status of the city to that of *colonia*. The result could then be the construction of a forum and basilica commensurate with its size, wealth and status.

This explanation, though based upon strong circumstantial evidence, lacks decisive confirmation: no inscriptions have been found which define the status of *Londinium* at this period. Nevertheless the hypothesis would explain the apparent inclusion in the second basilica of government tiles bearing some variation of the stamp P.P.BR.LON, believed to refer to the 'Procurator of the Province of Britain in Londinium', and suggests that the second basilica had been receiving at least some government support.[131]

The layout of the second forum and basilica complex was different from that of the first forum, in that it conformed to the '*principia*' type also evident at, for example, the fora of Silchester and Caerwent.[132] This type has been described as owing much of its architectural plan to the *principia* building found in legionary fortresses. If so, perhaps the plan of the second basilica and forum in *Londinium* may reflect some military (i.e. governmental) planning. However, this suggestion has been disputed[133] and the actual basis for this type is placed in doubt.

Nevertheless, a military involvement in the planning of some *fora* and *basilicae* in Britain is likely[134] and the London complex might provide a further case for the reasons given above. It would seem, in conclusion, that the weight of the evidence strongly suggests that the second basilica and forum complex was a colossal political statement of Roman civic authority at the hub of the provincial administration, producing a civic centre on a scale not matched by any other city in Britain.

FOOTNOTES AND REFERENCES

1   E. Loftus Brock in the *Journal of the British Archaeological Association*, 28, 1872, pp. 176–179.

2   P. Norman and F. Reader, 'Recent Discoveries in connexion with Roman London', *Archaeologia*, 60, 1906, pp. 224–5.

3   *Building News*, 60, 1891, p. 901.

4   P. Norman and F. Reader, 'Further Discoveries relating to Roman London, 1906–12', *Archaeologia* 63, 1912, pp. 317–9.

5   Ibid. in Note 2, pp. 223–4.

6   Ibid. in Note 21, map sites 214 and 226.

7   Ibid. in Note 21, map site 227.

8   A reference in *Britannia* XV, 1984, p. 308 mentions that some pre-Roman deposits were found at 79 Gracechurch Street. Subsequent study shows that there is now no reason to believe that they are pre-Roman.

9   Ibid. in Note 22, p. 7.

10 Ibid. in Note 22, p. 7.

11 Ibid. in Note 22, pp. 7–8.

12 Ibid. in Note 22, Fig. 22.

13 Ibid. in Note 22, pp. 8–9.

14 Ibid. in Note 22, p. 9.

15 Ibid. in Note 22, pp. 9–16.

16 S. Frere, *Verulamium Excavations I*, Report No. XXVIII of the Research Committee of the Society of Antiquaries of London, 1972, pp. 13–23.

17 Ibid. in Note 22, p. 14.

18 Ibid. in Note 22, p. 15.

19 Ibid. in Note 22, pp. 9–16.

20 Ibid. in Note 22, pp. 9–16.

21 Ibid. in Note 21, p. 90.

22 P. Marsden, *Roman London*, London, 1980, pp. 30–35.

23 Ibid. in Note 22, pp. 9–16.

24 R. Merrifield, *London City of the Romans*, London 1983, pp. 59–60.

25 S. Frere, 'Town planning in the Western provinces', in *Festschrift zum 75 Jährigen Bestehen der Romisch – Germanischen Kommission*, 1979, p. 101.

26 R. Merrifield, *The Roman City of London*, London, 1965, p. 320, 329.

27 B. Philp, 'The Forum of Roman London: Excavations of 1968–9', *Britannia* VIII, 1977, Fig. 23, section 3, extreme west end.

28 P. Marsden, 'The Excavation of a Roman palace site in London, 1961–72', *Transactions of the London and Middlesex Archaeological Society*, 26, 1975, pp. 36–41.

29 Ibid. in Note 27, p. 17.

30 Ibid. in Note 27, p. 18.

31 Ibid. in Note 4, p. 320.

32 Ibid. in Note 27, Fig. 23, section 2, layer 30.

33 S. Frere, 'The Forum and Baths at Caistor by Norwich'; *Britannia* II, 1971, p. 7, Fig. 3.

34 Ibid. in Note 27, pp. 23–24.

35 Ibid. in Note 27, pp. 22–23.

36 Ibid. in Note 26, map sites 222, 223.

37 Ibid. in Note 27, pp. 40–43.

38 Ibid. in Note 27, p. 41.

39 Ibid. in Note 27, p. 28.

40 Ibid. in Note 27, p. 25.

41 Ibid. in Note 27, p. 30, Fig. 22, feature F65.

42 Ibid. in Note 27, p. 28, Fig. 22.

43 Ibid. in Note 27, p. 28, piers 1–3.

44 W. Martin, 'Roman remains: Lombard Street – Gracechurch Street', *Transactions of the London and Middlesex Archaeological Society* V (NS), part 3, 1926, pp. 317–323.

45 Ibid. in Note 24, pp. 66–67.

46 Ibid. in Note 33, pp. 11–14.

47 Ibid. in Note 27, p. 30.

48 Ibid. in Note 27, pp. 22–23.

49 Ibid. in Note 27, pp. 22–23.

50 Ibid. in Note 26, map site 222.

51 Ibid. in Note 27, p. 24.

52 Ibid. in Note 27, p. 25.

53 Note by G. Dunning in the *Journal of Roman Studies* 21, 1931, p. 237.

54 Royal Commission on Historical Monuments, *Roman London*, 1928, p. 41.

55 Ibid. in Note 2, p. 223; report by J. Grover in the *Proceedings of the Society of Antiquaries*, 2nd series, vol. 14, 1891–93, pp. 6–8.

56 W. Martin and W. Edwards, 'Roman London: Cornhill', *Transactions of the London and Middlesex Archaeological Society*, (NS) V, part 2, pp. 189–194.

57 Ibid. in Note 55b.

58 Ibid. in Note 2, p. 223.

59 Ibid. in Note 54, p. 41; Ibid. in Note 53, p. 238.

60 *The Builder*, 1, 1881, p. 110.

61 Ibid. in Note 54, p. 127.

62 Ibid. in Note 53.

63 Ibid. in Note 55b.

64 Note in *Antiquaries Journal* 2, 1922, p. 260; *Journal of Roman Studies*, 11, 1921, pp. 219–20.

65 Note in *Antiquaries Journal* 2, 1922, pp. 140–141.

66 Ibid. in Note 27, p. 27.

67 Ibid. in Note 27, p. 27.

68 Ibid. in Note 27, p. 27.

69 Ibid. in Note 27, p. 25.

70 Ibid. in Note 27, Fig. 23, section 1, layer 39.

71 Ibid. in Note 27, pp. 28–29, piers 6 and 7.

72 D. Atkinson, *Report on the Excavations at Wroxeter in the County of Salop, 1923–7*, Oxford 1942, p. 88.

73 Notes by J. Price in *Proceedings of the Society of Antiquaries*, 2nd series, 10, 1883–5, pp. 92–93; and by S. Cuming in the

Journal of the British Archaeological Association, 24, 1868, p. 76, plate 7.

74   Ibid. in Note 27, p. 9, Fig. 4.

75   E. Ekwall, *Street Names of the City of London*, Oxford, 1954, pp. 54, 186–7.

76   Ibid. in Note 1, pp. 176–9.

77   C. Barron, *The Medieval Guildhall of London*, Corporation of London, 1974.

78   Eg. at Silchester, see G. Boon, *Silchester, the Roman city of Calleva*, Newton Abbot, 1974, p. 109; J. Wacher, *The Towns of Roman Britain*, London, 1976, p. 45.

79   Ibid. in Note 26, p. 78, note 60.

80   R.E.M. Wheeler, 'The Topography of Saxon London', *Antiquity* VIII, 1934, pp. 290–302; but see J.N.L. Myres, 'Some thoughts on the topography of Saxon London', *Antiquity* VIII, 1934, pp. 437–442; and R.E.M. Wheeler, 'Mr. Myres on Saxon London: a reply', *Antiquity* VIII, 1934, pp. 443–447; also see R. Whittington, 'St. Peter's Church, Cornhill', *Transactions of the London and Middlesex Archaeological Society* IV, 1875, pp. 301–312.

81   J. Bloe, 'Report of the visits made to the site of All Hallows, Lombard Street', *Transactions of the London and Middlesex Archaeological Society* (NS) IX, part 2, 1945, pp. 180–189.

82   M. Fitch, 'John Stow commemoration address, 1982', *Transactions of the London and Middlesex Archaeological Society* 34, 1983, p. 200. Since good quality ragstone is a true limestone there is no reason in principle why it could not have been burned to make lime. In later times chalk was preferred for lime burning because it was both more pure and easier to work. But in the 12th century builders using mortar would either have had to burn limestone robbed from the Roman ruins or import chalk, since chalk was not generally used by the Romans as a building material.

83   Ibid. in Note 75, pp. 75–76.

84   Ibid. in Note 27, pp. 31–32.

85   Eg. pottery of phases I and II at 168–170 Fenchurch Street. Ibid. in Note 27, p. 7.

86   Ibid. in note 27, p. 7.

87   M. Hammerson, 'The Coins', in *Southwark Excavations 1972–74*, Vol. 2, London, 1978, pp. 587–600; P. Marsden, *Roman London*, London 1980, pp. 28–29, 208 note 25.

88   T. Dyson and J. Schofield, 'Excavations in the City of London, Second interim report, 1974–1978', *Transactions of the London and Middlesex Archaeological Society* 32, 1981, p. 25.

89   Ibid. in Note 27, p. 7.

90   Ibid. in Note 24, pp. 35–6, 43–6.

91   J. Wacher, *The towns of Roman Britain*, London, 1976, p. 87.

92   B. Cunliffe, *Excavations at Fishbourne 1961–9*, Report of the Research Committee of the Society of Antiquaries of London XXVI, London, 1971, pp. 37–46, 72–74.

93   J. Kent, 'The London area in the late Iron Age: an interpretation of the earliest coins', *Collectanea Londiniensia: studies presented to Ralph Merrifield*, London and Middlesex Archaeological Society, Special Paper no. 2, 1978, pp. 53–58.

94   Ibid. in Note 27, p. 11, 45.

95   Tacitus, *Annals*, XIV, 33.

96   F. Haverfield, 'Roman London', *Journal of Roman Studies*, 1, 1911, p. 149; Ibid. in Note 54, pp. 1–2, 27; Ibid. in Note 22, pp. 30–37; Ibid. in Note 24, pp. 41–42.

97   Ibid. in Note 16, pp. 13–23.

98   Ibid. in Note 22, pp. 25–26.

99   G. Milne, *The port of Roman London*, London, 1985, pp. 25–27.

100   Ibid. in Note 27, pp. 44–45.

101   Museum of London, *Excavation Register* no. 639.

102   Ibid. in Note 22, pp. 30–37.

103   Ibid. in Note 91, p. 110.

104   Ibid. in Note 27, p. 15, 45 (nos. 8, 9), 55 (nos. 15, 16, 17).

105   G. Webster, *Boudica, the British Revolt against Rome A.D.60*, London, 1978, pp. 113–120.

106   Ibid. in Note 26, p. 145.

107   Ibid. in Note 101, nos. 623, 629.

108   Ibid. in Note 101, nos. 622, 676, 726.

109   Ibid. in Note 27, p. 19.

110   Ibid. in Note 27, Fig. 22.

111   Ibid. in Note 27, p. 19.

112   Ibid. in Note 27, p. 48, nos. 52, 53.

113   Ibid. in Note 24, pp. 61–67.

114   Vitruvius, *De Architectura*, Book V, ch. 1, 2–5.

115   J.B. Ward-Perkins, 'From Republic to Empire: reflections on the early provincial architecture of the Roman West', *Journal of Roman Studies*, 60, 1970, pp. 1–19.

116   Ibid. in Note 91, pp. 42–46.

117   J. Liversidge, *Britain in the Roman Empire*, London, 1973, p. 41.

118   R. Goodchild, 'The origins of the Romano-British Forum', *Antiquity*, 20, no. 77, 1946, p. 77.

119   Ibid. in Note 33, pp. 11–14.

120   Ibid. in Note 115.

121   Ibid. in Note 24, p. 68.

122   Ibid. in Note 24, p. 71.

123   Ibid. in Note 22, pp. 98–103.

124   Ibid. in Note 27, p. 50, no. 94.

125   Ibid. in Note 27, p. 50, no. 109.

126   Thanks are due to Geoffrey Marsh for dating the potters' stamps.

127   Drawings of the pottery were made by Gerald Dunning and are available for consultation in the Museum of London.

128   Collingwood R., Wright R., *The Roman inscriptions of Britain*, Oxford, 1965, no. 12.

129   Ibid. in Note 22, pp. 79–97; R. Merrifield, *London, city of the Romans*, London, 1983, pp. 72–83.

130   P. Marsden, 'Excavation of a Roman palace site in London, 1961–72'. *Transactions of the London and Middlesex Archaeological Society* 26, 1975, pp. 1–102.

131   T. Morgan, 'Inscription on Roman tiles found at Leadenhall', *Journal of the British Archaeological Association*, 39, 1883, p. 389; W. Martin and W. Edwards, 'Roman London: Cornhill', *Transactions of the London and Middlesex Archaeological Society*, V (NS), part II, 1925, p. 191; P. Marsden, 'The excavation of a Roman palace site in London, 1961–1972', *Transactions of the London and Middlesex Archaeological Society* 26, 1975, pp. 70–71.

132   Ibid. in Note 72, pp. 345–362.

133   Ibid. in Note 118.

134   P. Bidwell, *The Legionary bath-house and basilica and forum at Exeter*, Exeter, 1979, pp. 82–83.

5

Description of sites

Site 1.   19–21 Birchin Lane, 1935

Archaeological features exposed during the rebuilding of this site in 1935 were recorded by Mr F. Cottrill for the Society of Antiquaries, and it is from his records deposited with the Museum of London that this report is compiled. The pavement from which depth measurements were taken lies at 18.91m above OD.

The rebuilding seems to have required selective digging for the insertion of foundations, and although it was only possible to record the archaeological features by means of sketch sections with measurements, some general clearance of the eastern half of the site did enable a spread of Roman road metalling and a length of robbed Roman wall to be recorded (Fig. 60).

THE EARLIEST DEPOSITS

The natural subsoil of brickearth lay about 6m below pavement level, probably that of Bengal Court on the north side of the site though this is not specified in the excavation notes. In the western half of the site the brickearth was mostly overlaid by layers of dirty clay (Fig. 61, Sections 3 and 4), though in the north-west corner (Section 1) there was a thick layer of burnt debris presumably indicating the site of a building destroyed by fire, perhaps during the destruction by Boudica in AD 60 (Fig. 60). In the eastern half of the site the natural subsoil was overlaid by apparently dumped deposits of brickearth (Section 6) and rubbish (Section 7). Finds from the rubbish layers of Section 7 included samian ware sherds of forms 15, 18, 24/25, 27, 29, 30 and 35; while on sherds of forms 15, 18, 27 and 29 were stamps of the potters FELIX, MURRANVS, VITALIS, AQVI-TANVS and BASSVS. Also recovered was a ring-necked jug of early type. The dark occupation debris observed in Section 8 was also noted further north where it overlay the natural brickearth; while in this area parts of two shallow rubbish pits were observed, each having been dug into the natural subsoil. Pottery found in unspecified layers included sherds of mid first-century date, together with a

pillar-moulded glass bowl. Rubbish layers observed at about 5.8m below pavement level were found to include burnt clay showing the marks of laths, and also sherds (including bead-rim jars) of the mid first century AD.

This evidence suggests that the occupation on the site started at the beginning of the Roman period, accounting for the build-up of occupation debris and dumped clay. The thick deposit of burnt clay in the north-western corner of the site, so close to the natural subsoil, is probably best interpreted as a wattle and daub building which had been destroyed by Boudica.

LATER ROMAN FEATURES

In the eastern half of the site the early deposits increased in thickness, as if the land level had been deliberately raised in this area to provide a base for the substantial Roman road which overlay the deposits.

The road was built of superimposed layers of gravel, and it is clear that it was aligned roughly north-south. The eastern side of the road was not clearly defined, but gravel layers which appear in Sections 3 and 4 are likely to have been overspill dumps from the road proper. The main part of the road appeared in Sections 5, 6, 7 and 8 where the gravel deposits were at their greatest thickness. In Section 5 the road metalling was 1.5m thick, and was formed of hard gravel evidently rammed in layers, and a dark layer which probably indicated the dirty silting of the road surface. When the road was built it was evidently constructed over half filled rubbish pits, for on the east side of the trench in which Section 5 was revealed, the bottom of the gravel was found to be irregular and descended to a level of 6.4m below modern pavement level. Between the bottom of the gravel and the natural brickearth there was some slight occupation debris, and it was from this or the lower part of the gravel that samian sherds were found bearing potters stamps of ALBINVS (Form 30) and QVARTVS (Form 15).

An unrecorded section at the north end of this

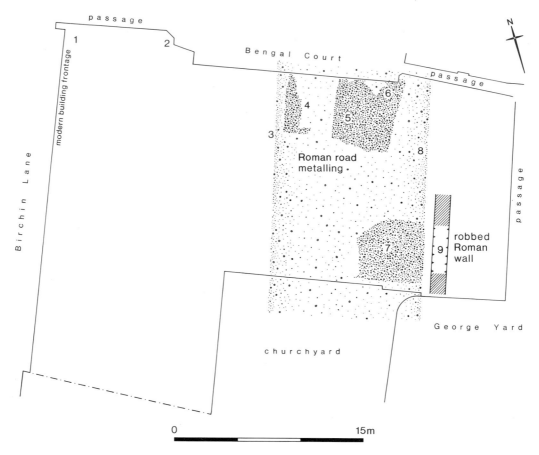

Fig. 60 19–21 Birchin Lane. Plan of a Roman street and wall forming the west side of the second forum. Heavy stippling indicates street metalling that was found. The numbers refer to sections in Fig. 61.

Fig. 61 19–21 Birchin Lane. Sections drawn relative to the pre-1935 basement level the depth of which is not known. The section numbers refer to the plan Fig. 60.

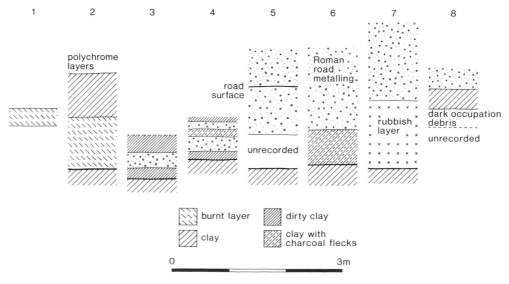

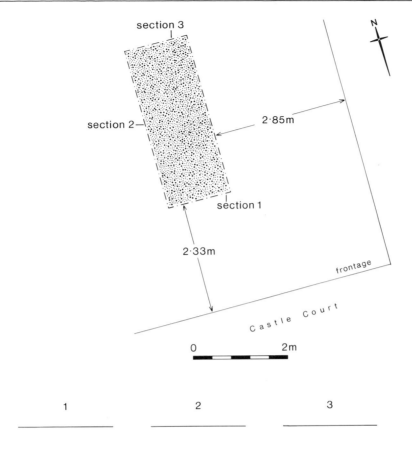

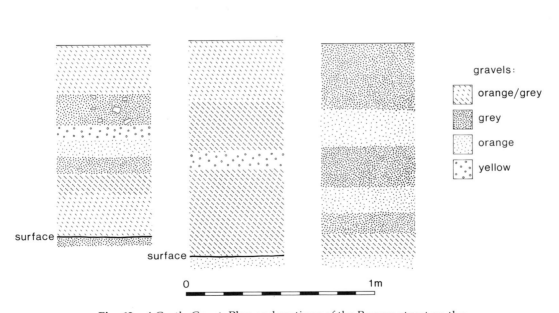

Fig. 62 4 Castle Court. Plan and sections of the Roman street on the west side of the second forum.

trench revealed part of a rubbish pit dug into the natural brickearth and partly filled with gravel, thus showing that it had been open when the road was constructed. Pottery believed to have come from the pit includes a flagon neck of the mid first century together with other sherds of the first century.

The date of the construction of the street is uncertain but on the evidence of the potters' stamps it cannot be earlier than Nero, while the proximity of the gravel layers to the natural surface, and the fact that the earliest deposits are at the same level as the possible Boudican deposits also suggest that the street may be of Neronian date. This view is supported by the fact that the earliest gravel layers are well below the level of the Forum floor, as found on other sites. However the upward slope of the land surface underlying the road, evidently caused by dumping on the eastern side of the site (Sections 7 and 8), does suggest that some of the gravel had been dumped to construct a level roadway, perhaps when the dumping occurred to elevate the land for the second Forum in the later first century.

The robbed Roman wall (Fig. 60, Feature 9) was roughly aligned north-south and was most likely the west wall of the second Forum, not only because the Forum walls on the other sites nearby had frequently been robbed, presumably in post-Roman times; but also because the robber trench was 1.2m wide, the usual thickness of many of the forum walls. The filling of the wall robber-trench no doubt reflected the construction of the wall foundation itself, for it primarily contained building debris, particularly powdered cement and numerous lumps of ragstone.

This wall helps to establish the width of the Roman street, for if it is assumed that the wall and roadway co-existed, as seems likely, the road would form the western boundary of the second Basilica and Forum. The west side of the street was not established with precision, but if the gravel layers in Section 4 are overspills of the road metalling then it may be concluded that the street itself was about 9m wide.

Site 2.   4 Castle Court, 1976

A trench dug during November 1976 in the cellar of this building exposed the extremely hard and compacted layers of gravel metalling of a Roman street (Fig. 62). Although the edges of the road were not revealed, discoveries on nearby sites show that this was part of the main north-south street which skirted the west side of the forum. The modern pavement lay at 17.855m above OD.

The surviving top of the gravel lay just beneath the modern concrete cellar floor, at 3.63m below the pavement level of the Castle Court, and it extended downwards to the bottom of the trench for more than 1.14m.

Although the gravel layers were extremely hard, and there was a tendency for deposits of clean orange gravel to alternate with dirty grey gravel, only one clear surface could be identified. The clean gravel presumably represented remetalling layers in the Roman street, while the dirty grey gravel layers probably mostly represented the disturbed road surface.

It was unfortunate that the trench was fairly small, and had been dug along the axis of the road, while also the sections in the sides of the trench had been seriously disturbed by post-Roman rubbish pits. As a result it was not possible to observe any camber. Nevertheless, the apparently almost horizontal layering of the gravel and the lack of silting on the road surfaces indicated that the trench had probably been dug near the middle of the Roman street.

Site 3.   52 Cornhill, 1930
by the late G. Dunning

INTRODUCTION

During the first half of 1930, the premises of No. 52 Cornhill, were demolished, and the whole site, with a frontage on Cornhill of 40ft (12.2m) and depth of 75ft (22.86m) was excavated down to gravel. In the process of this work, two Roman walls and several minor structures were discovered, and totally destroyed. The architects, Messrs. Easton and Robertson, readily granted me permission to watch the excavation, and I am further indebted to them for supplying a large-scale plan, which forms the basis of the detailed plan (Fig. 63).[1]

GEOLOGY

After the modern building had been demolished, the area was excavated below the basement level (about 10ft (3m) below the level of Cornhill), revealing the ancient land-surface of the brickearth at a depth of about 16ft (4.88m) below the surface of Cornhill. The brickearth was about 5ft (1.52m) thick and rested on the underlying river gravel.[2]

THE EARLY OCCUPATION

The former buildings had been carried down nearly to the surface of the brickearth over the southern end of the site, but on the northern and eastern sides the upper strata were undisturbed, and the description mainly refers to this part of the site (Fig. 64). The brickearth was covered by an occupation layer of dark earth and rubbish, about 12in (0.3m) deep, thinning out towards the south to a few centimetres in thickness. In the north-eastern corner of the site

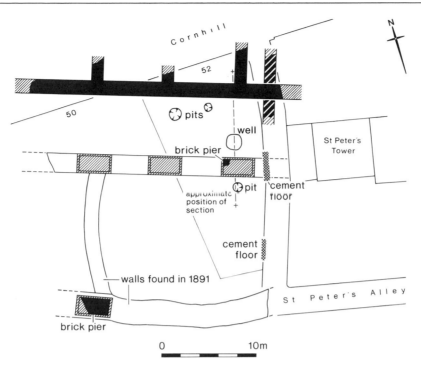

Fig. 63 52 Cornhill. Plan of the site, redrawn from an original by Gerald Dunning. The section is shown in Fig. 64.

Fig. 64 52 Cornhill. Section across part of the second basilica, redrawn from an original by G. Dunning. The position of the section is only approximately known and is shown on Fig. 63.

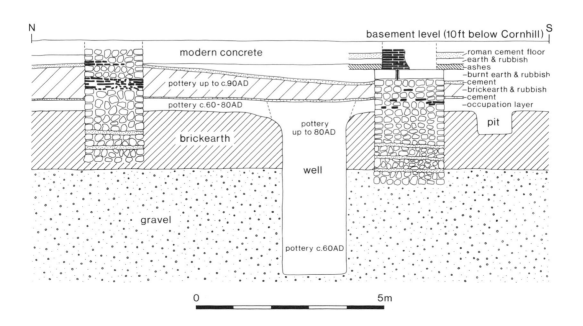

this layer increased to 3ft (0.91m) in depth and filled up a dip on the brickearth. Although some pre-Flavian sherds were found, most were of the early Flavian period, suggesting that the site was first sparsely settled in the Claudian period, and that the main occupation was from AD 60 to 80.

Three rubbish pits and a well belong to the latter period and a large piece of burnt clay daub, showing the marks of sticks, and a few fragments of painted wall-plaster, attest the presence of timbered buildings on or near the site in the pre-Flavian period. The three small rubbish pits had been dug into the brickearth during the early occupation of the site. All were filled with damp grey clayey material, containing streaks of charcoal and decayed vegetable matter. The pits were rich in broken coarse pottery and also samian ware. Pit 1 was 4ft (1.22m) in diameter, 3ft (0.9m) deep, and contained pottery of the period AD 65–80. Pit 2 was 2ft 6in (0.76m) in diameter, 1ft (0.3m) deep, and contained pottery of the period AD 60–75. Pit 3 was 3ft (0.9m) in diameter, 2ft (0.61m) deep and contained one piece of Neronian pottery, the base and lower frieze of a samian bowl, form 29; the upper part of the same vessel was found at the bottom of the well.

A well had been sunk through the brickearth into the gravel between pits 2 and 3. It was 14ft (4.27m) deep and 5ft 6ins (1.68m) in diameter, and at the bottom were a few oak planks, 3ft (0.9m) long and 1in (0.025m) thick, probably the remains of its lining. The filling consisted of soft wet earth mixed with brickearth, containing small pieces of charcoal and burnt earth. A large quantity of pottery was found in the well, and by keeping a close watch on the excavation, it was possible to separate the material into three groups, from the lower, middle, and upper thirds of the well filling respectively. A large fragment of a samian bowl was found at the bottom of the well, and fitted on to the base found in Pit 3, showing that the filling of the bottom of the well and of Pit 3 took place at about the same time. The well was completely filled up by about AD 80, and both well and pits were effectively sealed by the layers of rubbish subsequently deposited on the site. Pottery from the lower filling of the well is of the Neronian period, and included a complete coarse ware jug. Pottery from the middle filling of the well seemed to be a little later, and pottery from the upper filling dates from about AD 80.

THE BASILICA

The southern-most Roman wall, which crossed the middle of the site between the wall and pit 3, and passed eastwards under St. Peter's Alley opposite the southern side of the tower of St. Peter's church, was evidently part of the second basilica. The wall and its foundation was 6ft (1.83m) thick and 9ft (2.74m) high, built of rough blocks of rag set in hard yellow mortar. The lower 3ft 6ins (1.07m) consisted of three layers of loose rag bedded in 3in (0.076m) layers of mortar, with the foundations in the gravel at 12–13ft (about 3.9m) below the basement level. The wall was faced with ten or eleven courses of squared rag, and in the upper 2ft 6ins (0.76m) of its core were several broken red bricks, forming a rough bonding-course about 2ft (0.6m) below the top.

In addition, three complete segmental bricks were recovered from the core of the wall. The bricks are of two types: (1) with lateral lug for bonding into a wall, forming an engaged half-column, 33ins (0.84m) in diameter, similar lugged bricks, quadrant-shaped, having been found by Mr A.W.G. Lowther on the site of a Roman villa at Ashstead, Surrey;[3] (2) wedged-shaped, without lug, five to a half-circle of 33ins (0.84m) in diameter, identical bricks having been found on the site of the eastern part of the basilica under Leadenhall Market.[4] These bricks may be considered as re-used material[5] as nothing like them has been recorded as forming part of the reconstructed basilica.

The southern wall was a sleeper-wall only, and carried a series of solid brick piers, traces of two of which remained. The eastern pier was the better preserved, but had been largely destroyed in previous building operations. It rested on a footing of large blocks of dressed stone, forming a base 11ft 6ins (3.5m) thick. The western end of the base was well preserved and consisted of two blocks of Kentish rag, separated by a ½in (0.038m) red brick. The central part of the base had been previously cut away, but fortunately the eastern end was intact, and included a block of coarse oolitic limestone, probably derived from the Bath district.[6] One corner only of the brick pier remained, but it was possible to trace its original dimensions from mortar adhering to its stone footing. The pier was originally 10ft 6ins (3.2m) long and 4ft 8ins (1.42m) wide. Nine courses of red tiles survived to a height of 20ins (0.5m). The tiles measured 16½ins (0.42m) by 10½ins (0.27m) by 1½ins (0.038m) and were set in hard yellow mortar 1in (0.025m) thick, with joints 1cm wide. The rag footings of the western pier alone remained, close to the western side of the site, with a mortar joint-line 6ins (0.15m) from the edge, indicating the position of the brick pier.

The northern wall also part of the second basilica, passed from the north-western angle of the site to St. Peter's Alley, parallel to the sleeper-wall described above, and 21ft (6.4m) from its northern face. At both ends, the wall was well preserved to a height of 9ft 6ins (2.9m), but the middle portion had been previously destroyed down to the foundations. The wall was 5ft (1.52m) thick, and built of ragstone set in hard yellow mortar mixed with finely crushed chalk, and faced with dressed stones. The foundation consisted of two layers of loose rag between 3in (0.076m) layers of mortar, with the base near the bottom of the brickearth at 10ft 6ins (3.2m) below basement. Two bonding courses of red bricks crossed the wall, at about 6ft 6ins (2m) and 8ft 6ins (2.6m) respectively above the base. The lower course extended right through the wall and consisted of four courses, mostly of broken pieces of brick up to 8ins (0.2m) in length, but there were also a few complete bricks, measuring 17ins (0.43m) by 12ins (0.3m). The upper course consisted of two irregular courses of broken brick and appeared only on the northern face of the wall. On the north side of this wall, and of the same construction, were two cross-walls, 21ft (6.4m) apart, passing under the frontage on Cornhill (Plate 12). The walls were 4ft (1.2m) thick, with a bonding-course of four layers of brick, 9ins (0.23m) wide, about a foot (0.3m) higher than the similar course in the main northern wall. In the north-eastern angle of the site, the cross-wall survived to a height of 4ft (1.22m) above the bonding-course, and was faced with six courses of dressed stone, then a single bonding-course of bricks at 2ft 6ins (0.76m) high, topped by three courses of stone.

At some later date, two cross-walls were bonded into both faces of the main northern wall, near the eastern side of the site, under St. Peter's Alley. These walls, 4ft (1.22m) thick, were built of rag, broken bricks and a few black flints, loosely set in yellow mortar, without any bonding-courses. The base was in the brickearth at 7ft (2.1m) below basement level, and the walls survived up to 1ft (0.3m) below the level of St. Peter's Alley.

It will now be convenient to describe the make-up between the two walls described above, and the pottery found in these layers below the cement floor. Over the greater part of the site, the filling between the walls had been previously removed, or so disturbed as to render any stratigraphical observations useless. On the east side of the site, the layers were intact and it was possible by plotting a series of sections to obtain a complete section of all the layers between the walls (Fig. 64). The cement floor was revealed in two places, for a length of 10ft (3m) above the sleeper-wall and again, for a length of 7ft, (2.1m), 20ft (6.1m) to the south in the south-eastern corner of the site (see plan, Fig. 61). The floor, 6ins (0.15m) thick, was made of pink concrete mixed with crushed brick and chalk. Below the floor came a series of rubbish layers as follows, from the top: a 6in (0.15m) layer of dark earth with small debris; 5ins (0.13m) of black ashes and charcoal; 12ins (0.3m) of red earth and rubbish – broken tiles and pottery. Below this were 3ins (0.076m) of crumbling cement and stone chips above a layer of brickearth mixed with rubbish, 2ft 9ins (0.84m) thick near the northern wall, and thinning out to 12ins (0.3m) south of the sleeper-wall. This brickearth was probably derived from the trenches cut through the brickearth for the foundations of the walls. The lowest layer comprised 2ins (0.05m) of mason's debris immediately on top of the early occupation layer. It was not possible to allocate the pottery recovered from the make-up underneath the cement floor to individual layers of rubbish. It is certain, however, that all the fragments came from the make-up on the east side of the site, as the layers above the cement floor had been previously removed to make way for modern concrete, so that at the time this part of the site was being excavated, digging was not proceeding elsewhere. Although not abundant, there is sufficient pottery to give a reliable terminal date for the building of the walls and cement floor and hence for the constructed basilica of which they form part. The bulk of the samian is of Flavian date, the latest piece being not later than about AD 90; another fragment is pre-Flavian, and was probably derived from the early occupation layer when cutting the foundation trenches for the walls. The coarse pottery does not permit of such close dating as the samian, but is clearly of late 1st century date, and none of it need be of later date than the samian. The absence of any pottery of definitely early 2nd century type is notable.

Little remains to be said of the subsequent history of the site, owing to the almost entire removal of the strata above the Roman pavement. However, under the Cornhill frontage, in the filling between the two cross-walls, some pottery was found about 8ft (2.4m) below Cornhill, ie some 3ft (0.9m) above the floor of the Basilica. This pottery was all of 4th century type. Elsewhere, under Gracechurch Street and Leadenhall Market, remains of later pavements have been noticed above the original floor of the basilica. Nothing corresponding with these structures was observed at 52 Cornhill, but the late pottery at any rate serves to prolong the occupation of the site into the fourth century.

Site 4.   69–73 Cornhill, 1894, 1897, 1959 and 1982

The redevelopment of this site during 1894, or soon after, revealed massive Roman walls which clearly comprised part of the north range of the second basilica. This may have been the discovery that was reported in 1897 when a Roman wall was mentioned as being found on the site,[7] but no details were published. A drawing showing the location of the 1894 discoveries at 71 Cornhill was found in 1959 amongst the records of the Australia and New Zealand Bank, which occupied the site, and in addition the corner of two Roman walls was found to have been preserved in an inspection pit below the basement of the modern building. The redevelopment of the site in 1959 enabled some additional

Roman walls to be recorded by Mrs. E. Harris and P. Marsden (Fig. 65).

WALLS FOUND *c.* 1894

The walls comprised parts of three adjacent rooms, the central one of which was almost completely uncovered and, according to the plan, measured 6.7m E-W by 6.25m N-S, with walls about 1.52m thick. On the exterior of the north side of the room there was apparently a buttress, 1.37m wide, projecting 0.76m beyond the north face of the basilica wall.

The internal faces of the walls and foundations forming the NE corner of the central room had been preserved in a viewing chamber beneath 71 Cornhill, and were examined in 1982 (Fig. 66). The foundations of both north and east walls were bonded together, showing that they were of contemporary construction, and had been built of irregular lumps of ragstone set in hard buff mortar. The tops of the foundations formed an offset which made the foundations considerably wider than the walls above. The offset lay at exactly 13m OD, and the foundation extended below 11.62m OD. Only the superstructure of the east wall had survived, and comprised two courses of ragstone, above which lay four courses of red tiles, and then three courses of ragstone. The base of the wall facing, at about 13m OD, presumably indicates the level above which lay the floor of this room.

Although incompletely excavated, the room on the east side of this central chamber also apparently measured about 6.7m E-W by 6.25m N-S. Traces of a room on the west side were also found; much of this was discovered in 1959 on the site of 73 Cornhill.

WALLS FOUND IN 1959

The redevelopment of 73 Cornhill, immediately east of Newman's Court, enabled the continuation of the walls found *c* 1894 to be examined. Because the redevelopment of the site occurred without reducing the former basement level, the new foundations merely being concrete piles, only small portions of the Roman walls were encountered. In spite of this it is clear, as much from the absence as from the presence of the Roman walls, that another room of approximately the same size as the other two lay here.

There was some indication that the north-western corner of the room under 73 Cornhill had been robbed perhaps during the medieval period, and that only the ragstone and concrete core of the foundation remained.

In one pile hole, the foundation of the west wall of this room extended from a depth of about 3.5m to at least 7.3m OD below Newman's Court, at which level it was decided to abandon the pile hole due to the great difficulty of removing the massive and extremely hard Roman foundation. At one point, about

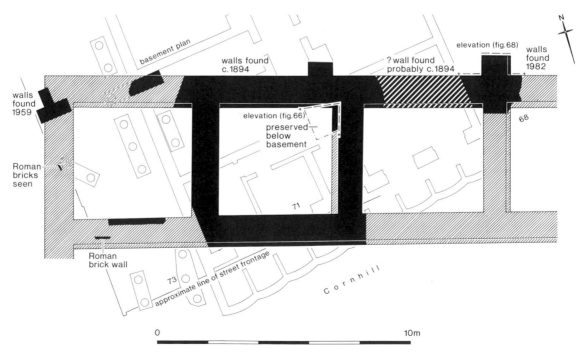

Fig. 65   69–73 Cornhill. Plan of Roman walls of the second basilica found on the site between 1894 and 1982.

the middle of the west wall, traces of red bricks, probably of Roman date, were noted in a trial hole, suggesting that the upper part of the wall had been built partly of bricks. This was confirmed when four courses of red bricks forming a wall face were found nearby at a depth of about 0.9m below the modern basement floor (*ie* about 3.5m below Newman's Court). This brick face apparently lay 0.9m south of the edge of the southern foundation of this room, suggesting the former existence of a recess in that wall.

Site 5.   68 Cornhill, 1981–2
A summary report by P.A. James

Redevelopment of 68 Cornhill in late 1981 and early 1982 provided the opportunity to examine a hitherto unrecorded part of the second basilica, which was revealed during building operations, and also to conduct a controlled excavation in an area immediately to the north of the basilica.

WALLS RECORDED DURING A 'WATCHING BRIEF'

The massive masonry remains uncovered by the mechanical excavator clearly form an eastern continuation of those previously recorded under 69–73 Cornhill. They comprised a 3.2m length of a rough-hewn ragstone and mortar foundation, at least 1.6m

wide, and on an E-W alignment (Fig. 65). Bonded into this foundation on its south side was another, of the same composition, which lay at 90° to it (i.e. on a N-S alignment) and which was at least 1.5m wide. This extended beyond the southern limit of the trench, and was evidently the foundation of another in the series of internal partition walls which lay within the north range of the basilica. Symmetrically opposite this partition wall, on the north side of the main E-W foundation, was the ragstone and mortar foundation of an external buttress, which measured 1.2m N-S, by 1.7m E-W. This foundation was bonded into the main E-W foundation only for the uppermost 0.8m, which suggests that the buttress was added at a time when the main foundation was nearing completion.

The tops of all three foundation elements lay at 13.0m OD. Above this point all three had four horizontal courses of red tiles, which are interpreted as the bases of the superstructure walls (Fig. 68). At the western edge of the trench the E-W wall survived to a height of 14.15m OD, where seven courses of ragstone in mortar, with squared facing stones, lay above the tile courses. The superstructural remains of both the partition wall and the buttress were narrower than the foundations on which they stood, being 1.2m and 1.45m wide respectively. The northern face of the main E-W wall lay flush with its foundation, but it was not possible to say whether this was also true of its southern face. The evidence from 69–73

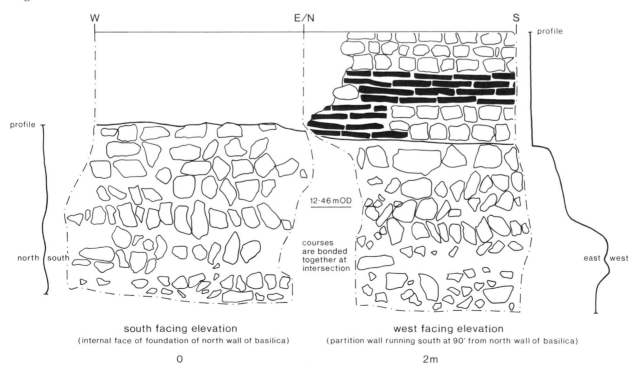

south facing elevation
(internal face of foundation of north wall of basilica)

west facing elevation
(partition wall running south at 90° from north wall of basilica)

0   2m

Fig. 66   71 Cornhill. Elevations of walls of the second basilica preserved in a small chamber beneath the basement of the modern building.

Cornhill, however, suggests that there was an offset here.

After they were recorded the remains were broken up and removed, leaving a section through them along the western edge of the trench. This revealed that the base of the foundation trench had been cut into natural gravels, at c. 10.65m OD, giving a total depth of foundation to the main E-W wall of 2.35m. (It was observed during its removal, however, that the base of the buttress foundation lay at 10.85m OD, some 0.2m higher). The section also revealed that a number of differently constituted mortars had been used in the construction of the foundations. These mortars lay in a series of horizontal bands which presumably reflect the deposition of successive loads during construction. The irregularity of the ragstones used in the foundations, together with the convex profiles displayed by the foundations visible in the viewing chamber under 69–73 Cornhill,

implies that they were 'trench-built'. This is supported by what was visible of the foundation trench in the section, where at its base, at least, it was vertically-sided and completely filled with construction materials.

EXCAVATIONS TO THE NORTH OF THE BASILICA: ROMAN STREET

Detailed excavation of an area immediately to the north of the line of the second basilica revealed for the first time a series of metalled street surfaces on an alignment parallel to the north side of the basilica (Fig. 67).[8] The first surface, of compacted gravel and pebbles, overlay a c. 0.2m deep deposit of ballast composed largely of used building materials (Fig. 69). The base of this street foundation lay at c. 13m OD, and the pottery from it dates from AD 85–120. Above this a total of four metalled surfaces

Fig. 67 68 Cornhill. Plan of the north wall of the second basilica and the adjacent street, excavated by P. James in 1982.

survived which, together with their respective make-up layers of sand and gravel, had a maximum depth of 0.4m. Above this the stratigraphy had been truncated by the floor of the late Victorian basement. The northern and southern edges of the street were defined by linear drainage ditches. At both edges new drains had been cut, in much the same positions, on numerous occasions, but it is not possible to say with any certainty which of the drains functioned with any one surface. It is clear, however, that the street, allowing for minor fluctuations on its northern side, was *c.* 5m wide. No dating evidence was recovered from the fourth and latest surviving surface, but the related strata immediately to the north of the street surfaces, where evidence for several phases of timber buildings was found, yielded pottery from the Trajanic and Hadrianic periods. Owing to the Victorian truncation of the deposits it could not be determined how long this

street continued in use, but an indication of a long history was provided by the base of a timber – lined ditch, on the same alignment and in the same position as earlier drains on the northern side of the street. This apparent street drain was filled with material which contained pottery of the late 3rd and early 4th centuries.

Site 6. St. Dionis Backchurch, Lime Street (after 1878)

In 1878 the church of St. Dionis Backchurch in Lime Street was demolished, and the site subsequently built upon. Henry Hodge recorded an elevation of the west wall of the church, and also various Roman features, which were published as a print. A copy of this was found by Charlotte Harding in the Maps and Prints Section of the Greater London Record

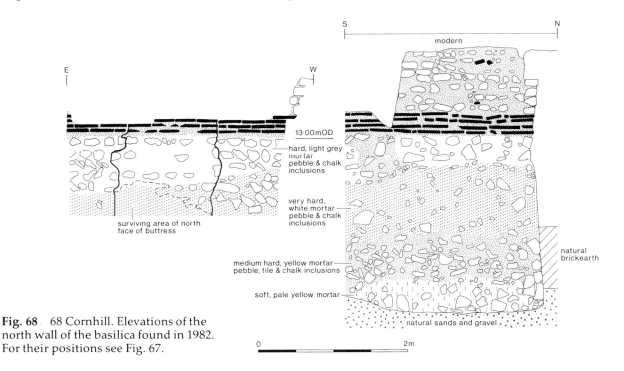

Fig. 68 68 Cornhill. Elevations of the north wall of the basilica found in 1982. For their positions see Fig. 67.

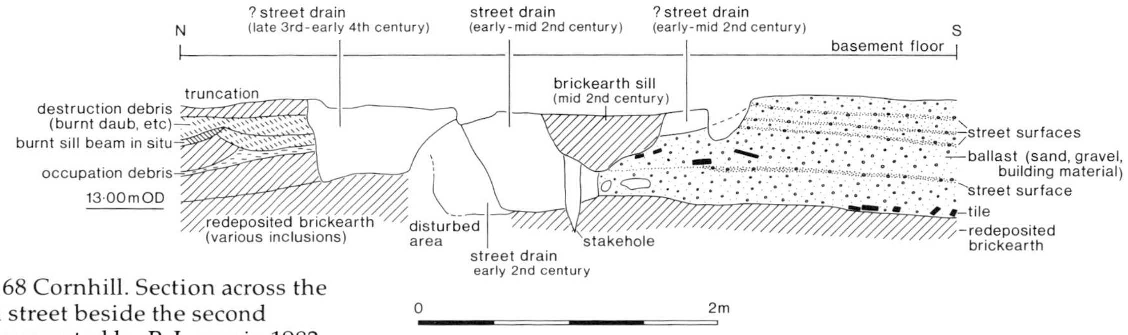

Fig. 69 68 Cornhill. Section across the northern street beside the second basilica, excavated by P. James in 1982. See Fig. 67 for its position.

Office and History Library (Accession no. 4785). The original drawings by Hodge were subsequently found in Guildhall Library. One of these is illustrated here (Plate 2) and shows a plan of the Roman walls on the site together with a section of the strata.

THE SECTION

This shows that the natural brickearth was overlaid by a 'black seam', which may be interpreted as occupation debris of the mid 1st century, for above it is a 'red seam' which was undoubtedly the Boudican fire debris of AD 60. This burnt layer was found all over the site of 160–162 Fenchurch Street (Site 7, p. 96) during the excavations by A. Boddington in 1976. The section by Hodge shows an important feature, a rubbish pit or well overlaid by the 'black seam' which must therefore date from the beginning of the occupation of Roman London. Hodge records that it was 'filled with gravel, chalk, red and buff brick, rag, oyster shells, brown and red mortar fragments – black colour filling in five round oaken stakes shaped to points'. The significance of the stakes is not clear.

THE RAGSTONE WALLS

Three ragstone walls were recorded by Hodge, but only one of them is ascribed to the Roman period. It is clear from subsequent excavations, however, that they were all part of the second forum.

The westernmost wall was partly preserved below the foundation of the west wall of the church, and was correctly described by Hodge as being of Roman date. Three courses of squared ragstone blocks of the facing of the wall had survived above a foundation described as a 'rough rag wall'. It would seem from the scale of the plan that this wall was about 2m thick.

The central 'rag wall' was only seen at the north end of the site, and the plan suggests that it was 3.43m wide.

The easternmost 'rag wall' extended across the site from south to north, and was about 1.6m thick. It is shown in the section as extending down through the natural brickearth to the top of the underlying natural gravel, at a depth of 6.78m below the level of Lime Street. It is described as being built of 'small stones, pieces of red brick and chalk, brown mortar. The brick and chalk very scarce'. It would seem that only the foundation had survived.

CONCLUSION

On the evidence of this record, it seems that after some initial Roman occupation before AD 60, a building on the site was destroyed in the Boudican revolt. Since the bottom of the wall facing of the Roman forum lay above the burnt layer, it is clear that the forum was built later than the fire. These conclusions are fully supported by the excavations on the site in 1976 (see Site 7, p. 97).

Site 6A.   22 Lime Street, immediately north of St. Dionis Backchurch Site, 1969

During the rebuilding of the site for Barclays Bank in 1969, it was possible for the author to record some archaeological deposits and structures, and some additional observations were made by B. Philp (Figs. 70, 71).

Fig. 70   Site north of St. Dionis Backchurch, Lime Street. Plan to show the location of walls of the east wing of the second forum, recorded by B. Philp and P. Marsden.

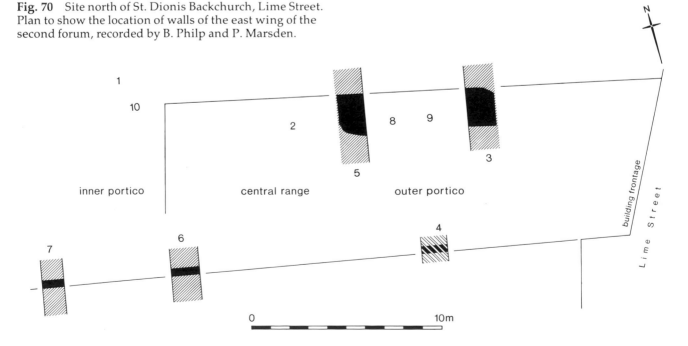

The earliest features were traces of gravel metalling, perhaps part of an east-west Roman street, that was overlaid by burnt debris, probably from the Boudican fire of AD 60. Subsequently the east wing of the second forum was built across the site and there was evidence of at least three or four superimposed floors in its outer portico.

PRE-SECOND FORUM FEATURES

Section at 1 (Fig. 70). The earliest feature recorded on this site was a layer of gravel about 0.15m thick, whose surface lay at about 12m OD. Possibly part of a road or courtyard, it had evidently lain adjacent to buildings for it was covered by red burnt debris, which at this level was probably of Boudican date, about 0.1m–0.15m thick. The debris was clay burnt to a violet rather than a red colour. A western limit to the burnt debris was observed.

Section at 2. This section revealed a Roman floor of buff-coloured mortar 0.04m thick at about 12.6m OD, overlying a deposit of brickearth 0.38m thick, below which there was a layer of hard gravel resembling road metalling. Above the floor was a deposit of dark occupation debris 0.08m thick. The mortar floor is unlikely to have been part of the second forum since it lay below the level of the faced stonework of the forum wall nearby (wall at 5). The surface of the gravel metalling lay at 12.27m OD, and may therefore have been an eastward continuation of the metalling observed in the Section at 1.

SECOND FORUM

Wall at 3. The dark filling of a trench more than 1.55m wide, probably indicated the location of a robber trench of the outer wall of the outer portico of the east wing of the second forum. The east side was not recorded, but the west side was found to lie 5.46m west of the frontage of Lime Street.

Wall at 4. This wall was noted by B. Philp who was unable to record its construction because it lay in the side of a deep and dangerous modern excavation. He stated that it appeared as a shapeless mass of ragstone about 1.22m wide and at least 0.91m high.[9] Philp also noted that the east side of this wall lay about 7m west of Lime Street, but in section 9, a short distance to the north, the author could find no trace of the wall, and it seems most likely that the wall was a pier situated in the centre of the outer portico of the east wing of the forum.

Wall at 5. The surviving top of this wall, apparently only 0.74m wide, lay at a depth of 14.1m OD, and was covered by a thick dark burnt deposit. Below this

were successively: four courses of faced ragstone wall, set in buff-yellow mortar, with an offset in the middle at 13.87m OD; two courses of tiles, the bottom course at 13.5m OD; two more courses of facing stone, their bottom level, at 13.3m OD, indicated by a small offset; and the foundation of ragstone and mortar which descended to an unknown depth below 12.45m OD. An adjacent section to the east showed that the courses of tiles probably marked the level of an early mortar floor. The east face of this wall lay 10.77m west of Lime Street.

Wall at 6. The wall was recorded by B. Philp[10] (Fig. 71, 'west centre foundation') and P. Marsden. Both describe its foundation as 1.47m wide, and as built of ragstone set in whitish mortar. Only the east face of the upper part of the wall had survived, and here there were four courses of faced stonework overlying the foundation. Above were four courses of tiles, with an offset above the lowest tile course. Philp records the upper part of this wall as a 'brick pier', but nowhere in the text of his report is it described as such. The published drawing[11] shows it as having an east-west face lying across the north-south axis of the wall, but as this face is neither shown in the photograph nor recorded by P. Marsden,[12] it seems likely that this is an error, and that the elevation of stones facing the lower part of the wall had been drawn in the wrong position. The east face of this wall lay 20.27m west of Lime Street.

Fig. 71 Site north of St. Dionis Backchurch, Lime Street. Sections by B. Philp across walls 6 (west centre foundation) and 7 (west foundation) shown on Fig. 70.

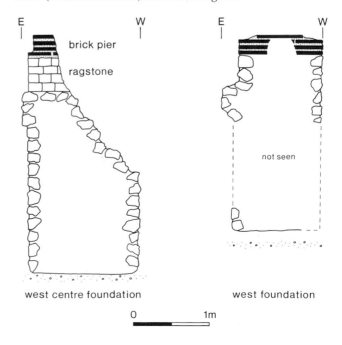

west centre foundation

west foundation

0   1m

Wall at 7. This wall was recorded by B. Philp[13] (Fig. 71, 'west foundation'). Its foundation was built of ragstone set in yellow mortar, above which it was 1.1m wide and was constructed of four courses of tile. The east face of this wall lay 27.6m west of Lime Street (recorded by P. Marsden).

FLOORS AT 8

A section within the outer portico revealed three of its mortar floors. The earliest, of pink mortar, was 0.1m thick, and its surface lay at 13.25m OD. It overlay a deposit of gravel at least 0.18m thick. Another layer of sandy gravel overlay this floor, and was presumably a levelling deposit for the second floor, of buff mortar, 0.064m thick. The surface of the second floor, which lay at 13.47m OD, seemed to be burnt, but as it was not covered by burnt debris the fire was probably of minimal proportions. A deposit of brown sandy earth overlay the buff mortar floor, and may have been laid in preparation for the next floor, of pink and buff mortar 0.18m thick. The surface of this latest floor lay at 13.74m OD, and was overlaid by dark grey occupation debris, and by a dump of clay.

FLOORS AT 9

A series of mortar floors was recorded immediately adjacent to the inner wall of the outer portico (the wall at 5). The lowest floor seems to have been of *opus signinum*, the surface of which lay about 13.53m above OD. This was apparently replaced by a buff mortar floor with a burnt surface, at about the same level. Rubble formed the foundation for the next floor, of mixed pink and buff mortar, at about 13.87m, and this floor was overlaid by black occupation debris. Two dumps of yellow clay (brickearth), separated by a deposit of dark grey (? occupation) soil, may represent subsequent floors, and these were succeeded by a deposit of light grey clay and a buff mortar floor whose surface lay at about 14.32m OD.

FLOORS AT 10

Two floors were recorded in the inner portico. The lower floor, whose surface lay at about 13.4m OD, was of mortar and had a burnt surface with a layer of burnt debris above. The upper floor, whose surface lay at about 13.87m OD, was of chalk and was overlaid by a layer 0.61m thick of ragstone rubble and Roman tiles.

CONCLUSIONS

Only slight traces of the Roman occupation preceding the second forum were found, but these suggest the existence of a gravelled street, and also a timber-framed building with clay walls which had been burnt probably during the Boudican revolt of AD 60.

This extremely valuable but brief opportunity of examining the east wing of the second forum has provided the most detailed record so far obtained of that wing. The outer portico 5.31m wide was found to have three or four mortar floors, upon which occupation debris and traces of burning suggests fairly intensive use. One of the floors of the inner portico, overlooking the forum courtyard, also exhibited traces of burning, suggesting similar use. The floors of the central range of rooms, where the shops were no doubt originally located, were unfortunately not recorded, and no dating evidence for the forum was recovered.

Site 7.   160–162 Fenchurch Street, 1976
by A. Boddington and P. Marsden

Six major Roman phases were identified: Phase 1 comprised the initial occupation of the site, represented by gravel and brickearth surfaces, occupation layers and a small gully. In Phase 2 these features were levelled and an extensive building or buildings with mud brick walls was constructed. During Phase 3 these were destroyed in the Boudican fire of AD 60. This was followed in Phase 4 by the construction of gravel and brickearth surfaces with little evidence of associated structures; and subsequently in Phase 5 a series of levelling deposits were laid down which apparently preceded the construction of the walls and floor surfaces of the second Forum during Phase 6. A Phase (7) during which the Forum walls were robbed was followed by the construction of the church of St. Dionys Backchurch, whose earliest known reference is *c.* 1100.

INTRODUCTION

The site is located on the west corner of Lime Street and Fenchurch Street and was redeveloped as the second phase of the Limebank building. Archaeological work on the first phase had been carried out by B. Philp in 1968 and by P. Marsden in 1969, both for the Guildhall Museum. During redevelopment the site was investigated early in 1976 by A. Boddington for the Museum of London.

Prior to permission being obtained to work on the site, the contractors excavated Trench A along the west side of the site. Once permission had been obtained, the section on the east side of the trench was drawn, and three trenches (Fig. 75, trenches B, C and D) were excavated, partly under controlled archaeological conditions. Simultaneously the destruction of deposits elsewhere on the site was watched throughout.

The greater part of the site was occupied by a large basement, originally a bank vault, some 3m deep below the present pavement level; under most of this 1.2 to 1.6m of archaeological deposits remained. To the south lay a narrow strip, 6m wide, along Fenchurch Street, which contained only a few shallow basements and where some 5.2m of deposits survived from just below modern street level to natural brickearth. In this area were found grave deposits associated with the church of St. Dionys Backchurch, which had stood on the site from at least the 12th century until 1878. These burials were carefully removed by the London Necropolis Co. Ltd. in collaboration with the archaeological excavation.

GEOLOGY

The natural subsoil of the site comprised a layer of brickearth overlying the sand and gravel of a former river terrace. At the north end of the site the undisturbed brickearth was 1m thick and the top lay at 11.4m OD, but at the south end it was 0.2m thick, the top being at 10.5m OD.

PHASE 1 *(Fig. 72)*

Little evidence of this period was recovered since it was represented only by gravel and brickearth

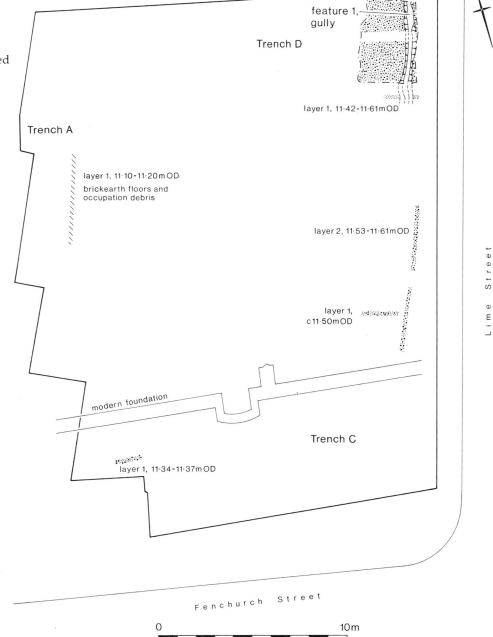

Fig. 72 160–162 Fenchurch Street. The earliest Roman features, *c.* AD 50–55, recorded on the site.

surfaces and a single gully. In Trenches B, C and D it appeared as a gravel surface up to 0.13m thick, though it is uncertain whether these areas of gravel formed a single surface. In Trench A there was a more complex build-up of brickearth and silt surfaces.

The gully was located in Trench D. It was found to cut through the gravel surface, and to be aligned roughly north-south, with irregular sides so that it varied in width from 0.28m–0.60m. The sides had slumped in places, and the bottom was irregular. The gully sloped down both to the north and to the south from a ridge in the middle of the exposed length. The depth of the gully was 0.35m at the south end of Trench D and 0.43m at the north end, and it was filled with light grey sandy silt containing many oyster shells and occasional tile fragments.

Except for the few tile fragments in the fill of the gully there was a complete absence of tile, chalk, ragstone, mortar and wall plaster in the Phase 1 deposits. Consequently little can be deduced about the nature of the occupation, except that it was perhaps of short duration as suggested by the lack of accumulated surfaces.

PHASE 2 *(Fig. 73)*

There was clear evidence from Trench A for a phase of levelling by the dumping of brickearth, clay and some gravel, whose total thickness was 0.15–0.31m. This was probably represented in Trenches B, C and D by a single layer forming a deposit 0.10–0.29m thick.

In the southern half of the site a building with mud-brick walls was constructed during this phase. Fortunately its destruction by fire, no doubt in AD 60, preserved elements of its construction that would otherwise have been difficult to interpret. Walls 1 and 2 were constructed on deep foundations of flint nodules and light brown mortar. The foundations were just over 1m deep, about 0.60m wide, and were each overlaid by a plank 0.04m thick, the plank in Wall 2 being 0.48m wide. Above the planks the walls were built of clay, Wall 2 being 0.48m wide and Wall 1 probably similar, though its western face had been destroyed by a later construction. The flint foundations of Wall 2 protruded about 0.14m above the top of the probably contemporary surface, and those of Wall 1 protruded 0.11m above the level to the east. Little of the mud-brick of Wall 2 survived, but in Wall 1 it stood to a height of 0.35m. There were clear traces of a brickearth rendering, which bore an impressed herring-bone pattern surviving in a small area on the east-side. The north end of Wall 1 was located in Trench B, but due to a later disturbance its presumed return to the west could not be traced.

Wall 3 was 0.49m wide and was constructed with a central core of mud bricks 0.44m wide. On either side was a brickearth rendering 25mm thick, which had an impressed herring-bone pattern identical to that of Wall 1. The foundation of this wall was slight, consisting of a layer of mud-brick fragments, some 0.15m thick, laid on the bottom of the construction trench. The mud-brick and brickearth rendering continued down for 0.25m below the top of the associated layers of occupation debris, and it is clear that the brickearth floor must have been laid up against the wall after its construction (Fig. 74. Plate 1).

Wall 4 only survived as a very short length, 0.43m wide and 0.02m long. Nothing is known of its structure.

Wall 5 was apparently aligned east-west and its foundation was set in a construction trench 0.15m deep and at least 0.41m wide. The trench was lined with wood, 0.02m thick, on the bottom and north side, though the south side was not seen. It was not clear whether the fill of the trench was of broken or laid mud bricks.

The herring-bone pattern on Walls 1 and 3 was evenly applied, suggesting that it had been stamped or rouletted rather than incised, but an insufficient length was exposed to determine which of these methods was used.

There were clearly two types of wall in this building, one on a deep foundation, obviously designed for load-bearing, and the other set in a shallow construction trench, which, in at least one case, was filled with broken mud-brick. No evidence of wattle-and-daub construction was discovered.

The mud-bricks were apparently of varying size. One complete brick from the burnt rubble to the east of Wall 1 measured 0.18 × 0.08m. At the top of the surviving south end of this wall the bricks were seen to be narrower, though they may have been set on their narrow sides. They were laid in a header bond and, as in Wall 3, were 'mortared' with brickearth.

Fig. 74   160–162 Fenchurch Street. Section across wall 3 of the building shown in Fig. 73.

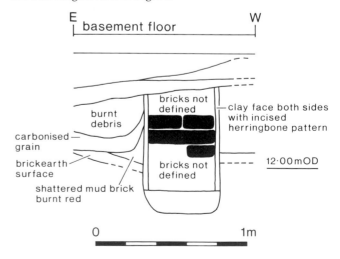

Fig. 73 160–162 Fenchurch Street. Plan of part of a building destroyed in AD 60. The carbonised grain was at its greatest thickness just east of wall 3.

Wall 3 was constructed partially of bricks which were the width of the core of the wall itself, *ie* 0.44m long and *c* 0.25m wide, (the width is estimated as it was not possible to recover a complete brick).

Regardless of size, the bricks were all made of the same material. From the unburnt bricks in the destruction rubble and the less severely burnt areas of wall, it was possible to show that these bricks were originally of unfired brickearth (presumably sun-dried). The burnt bricks indicated that a straw and coarse sand-temper had been used, and that they were crudely finished with rounded corners.

Eventually these bricks and their brickearth bonding must have merged to become indistinguishable, though this stage had not been reached with the Phase 2 walls, where the individual bricks could be clearly distinguished.

The reason why the foundations of the load-bearing walls protruded above the associated surfaces may have been the need to protect the base of the wall from erosion. Keying for plaster is the most obvious interpretation for the herring-bone impressions on the brickearth rendering, although there was a complete absence of wall-plaster on the walls in the Phase 2 deposits. Indeed the earliest evidence of wall plaster occurring on the site is in Phase 6. Thus the pattern should probably be regarded as decorative.

No definitive evidence of roofing materials was discovered, tiles being absent except for occasional fragments in the levelling deposits, but this could well have been imported onto the site. In Phase 2 the only deposit with fragments of tile (and here they were only occasional) was the surface in Trench D (Fig. 73). It is likely therefore that the roof was thatched.

Since the mud bricks were so insubstantial it is to be expected that the building was timber framed, but at no point were traces of timber uprights found, and there were certainly none at the junctions of Walls 3 and 4. However, the conditions under which this site was investigated were such that traces of timbers could have been easily missed. The surfaces adjacent to the walls were of brickearth, but there was no evidence of gravelling or of timber flooring to indicate whether they were external or internal. To judge from their deeper foundations Walls 1 and 2 were load bearing, perhaps forming external walls on the south and east sides of the building. Thus the possibility should be considered of a corridor on one or other side of Wall 2. The drain and the slope of the brickearth surface east of Wall 1 rules out a corridor on the north and east sides. Indeed, the top of the brickearth here was unburnt, and the burnt mud-brick debris thinned out abruptly within a short distance of Wall 1, confirming that this area was outside the building. However, the probability of a corridor on the south side of Wall 2 was suggested by

the burnt mud-brick debris which continued to the southern edge of the site at an even thickness, and also by the burnt occupation debris on the brickearth floor. The absence, immediately south of Wall 2, of any trace of the main east-west street which ran through the Roman city along the south side of the area from the mid-first century strengthens the likelihood of the existence of an intervening corridor between the road and wall.

Wall 5 may have represented the north wall on the west side of the site. If projected eastwards parallel with Wall 2 it would lie 1.7m north of the north end of Wall 1. Its foundations, however, were insubstantial, somewhat similar to those of the internal Wall 3. No evidence of a wall north of this was seen in Section 1, though 3.3m of the middle of the section had been destroyed by modern intrusions. The burnt mud-brick debris continued at an even thickness up to this modern disturbance, suggesting that the building had extended to this point, and thinned out to the north of it. This is in contrast to Trench B where the mud-brick debris thinned out dramatically within one metre of Wall 1, just north of which there lay a timber-lined box-like drain which ran from west to east with a gradient of about 1:17. It is probable, therefore, that the drain lay outside the building. It had been constructed of planks on its sides, bottom and top, its internal dimensions being 0.54m across and 0.12m high. The planks survived as a soft brown amorphous peat 0.01–0.02m thick.

Summarized, the evidence is of a single building with a minimum of three rooms, and probably with a corridor or verandah along the south side. The east room, bounded by Walls 1, 2, 3 and 6 had a north-south external dimension of *c*. 8.2m, and an east-west internal dimension of *c*. 7.2m, but as Wall 3 was only approximately positioned this measurement is somewhat tentative.

If Wall 5 formed the north side of the west room, and Wall 2 its south side, then the room was about 11m across externally and about 10m internally north-south. Walls 3 and 4 may have formed a north-south corridor approximately 3.3m wide internally, but so little of Wall 4 was uncovered that this suggestion must remain tentative. There is some evidence for a corridor along the south side of the building south of Wall 2, and for another room to the north of the west room. To the north of the building, on the east side, ran the west-east box drain which presumably carried waste water to a point beyond the east side of the building.

PHASE 3

Covering the entire excavation, except where removed by later disturbances, was a layer of burnt mud-brick up to 0.65m thick in the area of the building, but which thinned out to the north and east. To the east in Trench B, and to the north in Trench A, it was levelled up with tips of brickearth, grey silt and burnt mud-brick, to a total thickness of 0.5–0.6m. Although it is not certain that the levelling was of this Phase, it is here considered primarily as a consequence of the Phase 3 destruction rather than as a foundation for the Phase 4 levels and structures.

The catastrophic fire fortuitously preserved the fine details of the Phase 2 walls, which were all burnt to an orange-red varying to purple-black. Particularly important was the nearly pure carbonised grain layer (see Appendix, p. 151), which at one point just east of Wall 3 was 0.12m thick, though elsewhere in the room it was up to 1m thick. The grain mainly occurred in the zone between 1.5m and 2m from the east face of Wall 3, indicating the location of what was the main store of grain, which was perhaps contained in sacks.

The grain was found fairly densely spread over an area of some 9 square metres, and it seems that the fire had scattered it beyond the main deposit. No evidence of sacking was seen, though the intense heat may have caused this to disintegrate completely, as had the grain itself in some areas. The grain was also mixed with the overlying burnt and fragmented mud-bricks, this having obviously occurred during the levelling after the fire. In extent the pure grain and brick mixture was contained mostly within the east room, though the mixture also spread beyond the east wall. The only other occurrence of grain (which was again mixed into the burnt mud-brick layer) was in the extreme north-west corner of the site. There was no evidence of any structure in this area, and its occurrence at this point may be the result of general site levelling.

PHASE 4

This phase was represented by brickearth and gravel surfaces, which had associated layers of occupation debris. In some areas the occupation debris lay immediately on top of the burnt rubble, the top of which had become compacted and even. In each trench except D there was a layer of grey silty occupation debris with horizontal streaks of brown vegetation debris which may have represented straw. These were variably built-up on layers of brickearth, burnt mud-brick rubble, and dark grey silt. The gravel surfaces in the area of Trench A (Fig. 75) may represent a road presumably orientated north-south in common with some other linear features of the Roman period, since it was not seen immediately east of the section.

Only three features were discovered: a small possibly clay-lined gully, a pit and a possible timber foundation slot (Fig. 75). The north-south oriented slot was found in Trench B and contained fragments of ragstone in its fill, the only ragstone occurring in the Phase 4 deposits. No tile, chalk, wall plaster or

mortar occurred throughout. Thus, the evidence for structures of this phase is scant, though much may have been missed.

PHASE 5

A phase of dumping of large quantities of dark grey silt, brickearth, sand, gravel and ragstone rubble occurred next, and raised the land level presumably to prepare the site for the construction of the second Forum. The dumps no doubt covered the whole site, but only survived to their full thickness of about 1m in Trench C, though there were traces of dumping in Trench A.

PHASE 6 *(Fig. 76)*

Foundations of walls forming the south-east corner of the second Forum were located on various parts of the site, together with traces of some floor surfaces. In particular the walls of the outer porticos of both the east and south wings were identified.

The foundations had been constructed in trenches dug to the top of the natural gravel, and, to judge from the level of the lowest tile course in the overlying wall, the foundations were originally about 2.6m deep. They were constructed of ragstone and a hard light grey-brown mortar which contained an aggregate of chalk and small pebbles.

Although the inner, or western, wall of the east wing portico was found, its position on the site was not exactly established. It was 0.83m thick, and it seems that the portico was about 7.25m wide. The foundation of the outer or easternmost wall of this portico was exposed in Trenches B, C and D, and in Trench C a little of the wall above had survived to a height of about 1m. The wall itself, 1.15m wide, was constructed of ragstone and courses of broken tiles, the ragstone having been roughly squared where it was used in the face. Above the foundation the courses were, from bottom to top: two courses of tile, four courses of ragstone and two courses of tile. To the south the construction was slightly different in that there were more courses of tiles (Plate 18). A crack separating these two areas was obviously the result of subsidence since there was no evidence for separate phases of construction. There was no straight joint and the mortar used was the same. Since the many tiles lay only 2–3m north of the south-east corner of the Forum it is likely that the corner itself was constructed largely of tiles, and that the great weight of the superstructure had caused it to subside. The corner itself had been robbed, as had parts of the south wall of the portico. The width of this eastern portico foundation was not determined throughout, though its western edge was flush with the wall face, suggesting that the foundation was about 1.15m thick.

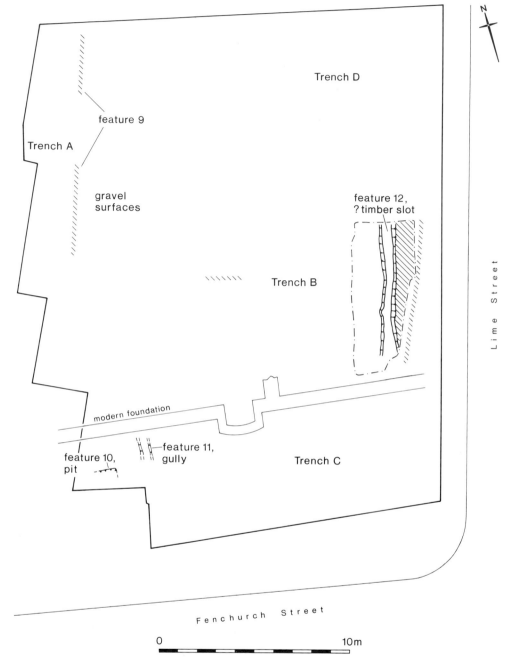

Fig. 75   160–162 Fenchurch Street. Plan of features of phase 4. The hatching represents occupation surfaces and debris.

Because the inner wall of the east portico did not extend to the south end of the site it may be presumed to have turned westwards to form the inner wall of the outer portico of the south wing. However, no trace of this south wing inner portico wall was observed in the difficult recording conditions. The outer wall of the south portico was located, however, but it had been largely robbed during the medieval period (Phase 7). Another forum foundation of similar construction was found in the north-

west corner of the site, but it was not possible to record its position. This was evidently the south-east corner of the inner portico that was recorded by Henry Hodge *c.* 1878 (see p. 90. Plate 2).

The floors of the south portico had survived and comprised many sand, gravel and white mortar surfaces which clearly represented a long period of use, for they eventually accumulated to a depth of 1.15m. The sand layers were particularly striking. Generally lacking in pottery, bone and charcoal, most

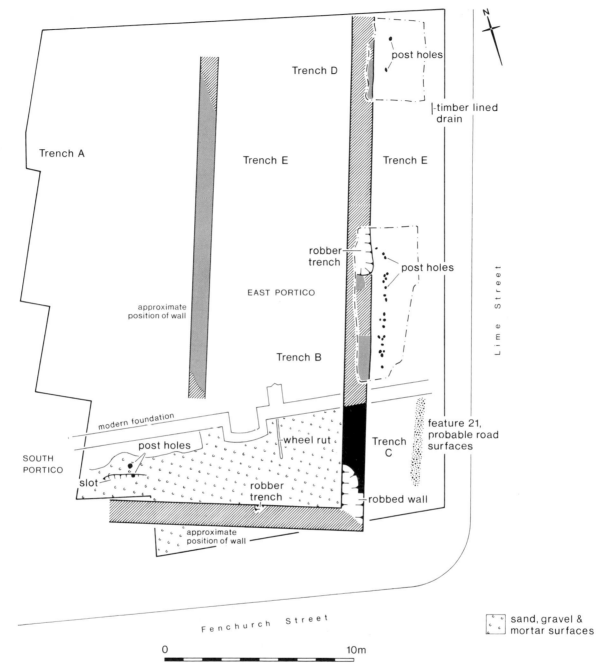

Fig. 76 160–162 Fenchurch Street. Plan of features of the second forum.

of the layers had firm compacted tops. Some had a laminated nature, peeling off in a series of small surfaces, indicating that they had built up gradually on mortar and gravel surfaces.

A small east-west slot, 0.36m deep, in one of the floors was found close to the south side of the southern portico, and just north of it were found two post holes. This puzzling feature in the portico was fairly extensive for the slot was traced for a distance of 4.6m and its ends were not found. The fill of the slot was composed of horizontal layers and lenses of crumbly mortar and grey silt, suggesting a slow accumulation. One of the post holes, oval shaped and measuring 0.27m × 0.14m × 0.32m deep, had been set into the slot and packed around with broken tiles. The second post-hole, 0.50m to the north, was 0.28m square and 0.28m deep, and was packed around with sandstone blocks.

A longer narrow hollow, clearly a wheel-rut, was traced for a length of 2.16m across the floor at the east end of the portico. It was 0.11–0.13m wide and 0.13m deep, with parallel edges and a U-shaped profile. A layer of very hard packed gravel and green-brown sand in its bottom was evidently a repair. This rut was particularly important for not only does it reflect the vehicular use of the portico, but it also suggests that there was an entrance through the south wall of the portico just west of the south-east corner of the Forum.

No trace of the main east-west street of London was found immediately south of the portico, for the mortar and sand surfaces continued for at least 1.8m beyond the south portico wall. It is clear that there was a narrow area around the Forum, separating it from the edge of the main streets, which on the east side of the site was about 3m wide. In this zone immediately beyond the eastern outer portico wall was found an irregular row of post holes, ranging in diameter from 0.08–0.2m, and in depth from 0.16–1.12m (the average depth being 0.38m). These were roughly parallel to the Forum wall and had been driven through the destruction debris of the Boudican fire, Phase 3, and were possibly for scaffolding associated with the construction of the outer portico wall.

A timber-lined drain, aligned north-south and found about 3m beyond the eastern outer portico wall, was probably for draining the side of the main street which bounded that side of the Forum. The width of the drain could not be established since it partly lay beyond the limit of excavation. The timber lining had been constructed in a ditch *c.* 1m deep, which had been partly back-filled with brickearth, sand and gravel. The timber lining of the drain had survived as a thin wood stain, indicating that the channel had been plank-lined on its sides and bottom. The drain was filled with lenses of sand and sandy silt.

PHASE 7

No evidence for the destruction of the forum was found, but instead during the 12th or 13th centuries parts of the forum walls were robbed. A rubbish pit was also dug during this period. The fragmentary remains of the church itself will be published in a subsequent report.

Site 8.   GPO Tunnel along Gracechurch Street, 1977

During 1977 the GPO excavated a tunnel for cables beneath the centre of Gracechurch Street, extending from Eastcheap to Threadneedle Street, and thus traversing the whole basilica – forum complex. Because the tunnel, about 1.92m wide and 1.4m high, was generally between 3.7 and 5.1m below the

present street (*ie* at about 12m OD), important parts of the first and second basilica – forum buildings were disclosed (Fig. 48). Various modern obstructions, particularly sewers, were met with, especially at the intersections of Gracechurch Street with Lombard and Fenchurch Streets, and with Cornhill. These caused the tunnel to be diverted to a lower level, and also Ordnance Datum levelling was not usually possible within these confines. Nevertheless, excellent facilities were given for archaeological recording at crucial points where sections were cleaned up, photographed, measured and drawn. In spite of the physical difficulties it was possible for the main phases of the forum to be identified, and this enabled many previous archaeological records to be amplified and checked, and an over-view obtained of the building sequence and plans.

This note includes only those Roman structures which were revealed on the site of the south wings of the first forum building, and also, the south wall of the first basilica. Features related to the second basilica and forum are described in the synthesis of this report.

Grateful thanks are due to those who worked in the dark narrow confines of this tunnel, and in particular to John Maloney.

EAST-WEST STREET

The tunnel was dug through the gravel metalling of the main east-west Roman street which partly underlies Lombard and Fenchurch Streets. The earliest street surface, which is known from neighbouring sites to lie on the natural brickearth, was not found because the natural subsoil was not reached at this point. The floor of the tunnel lay at about 11.53m OD, while the natural brickearth at the neighbouring site of 168–170 Fenchurch Street lay at 11.28m OD.

Some of the later layers of road metalling were recorded. Near the central axis of the street the gravel metalling attained its greatest thickness of more than 1.4m, the height of the tunnel, above 5.12m below street level (*ie* above 11.53m OD). Six layers of clean hard-rammed gravel metalling were recorded together with two thin dark silty deposits which were sandwiched between the gravel layers. These presumably represent worn muddy surfaces before remetalling.

THE EARLY GRAVELLED AREA

A spread of hard gravel metalling, 0.1m thick and overlying the natural brickearth, was traced in the tunnel between 11 and 13m north of the north face of the southernmost foundation of the south wing of the second forum. A little above this was a remetalling deposit which extended from 11m to a little over 42m north of the same foundation. The original Roman limits of these layers were not revealed in the tunnel, those recorded being merely a result of its upward incline through the deposits from south to north.

There is no doubt that these hard gravelled layers formed part of the large area of metalling of pre-Boudican date, which was recorded both at 168–170 Fenchurch Street[14], and in a shaft dug into the pavement of Gracechurch Street just south of Ship Tavern passage (Site 9, p. 101). There was no trace of the Boudican fire.

THE FIRST FORUM AND BASILICA

In its northward course along Gracechurch Street, the tunnel was forced below the sewers beneath the intersection of Gracechurch Street and Fenchurch Street, and thus penetrated the natural brickearth. Beyond the intersection the tunnel gradually inclined upwards and cut through the foundations of the south wings of the first and second forum buildings.

Three foundations of the first forum were encountered, each aligned roughly east-west, and each constructed of flints which had been quarried from chalk, set in brownish mortar. This distinctive construction is characteristic of the foundations of the first forum, and, moreover, the foundations can be related fairly accurately to other portions of walls of the south wing of the first forum, of which it is clear that they were continuations. From south to north the widths of the three foundations were 0.77m, 0.55m and 0.8m spaced at intervals of 5.28m and 5.85m respectively.

THE FIRST BASILICA

An east-west wall, discovered at the bottom of a tunnel access shaft opposite the southern boundary of 85 Gracechurch Street, included an eastern door jamb. From its location the wall was evidently a continuation of the south wall of the first basilica in which, on the site of 85 Gracechurch Street, another doorway had been found (p. 126). The door jamb found in the tunnel shaft was apparently part of a central entrance into the basilica from the forum courtyard (Figs. 17, 19).

The masonry which supported the door jamb continued across the shaft, and comprised at least three courses of tiles overlaid by three courses of ragstone, all set in the brownish buff-coloured mortar characteristic of the first basilica and forum.

The top of the masonry door sill lay at 4.44m below Gracechurch Street (*ie* at 13.2m OD), and was marked by a single course of tiles set in white mortar. This white mortar thickened up against the west face of the door jamb suggesting that it was a floor surface.

The wall forming the door jamb, above the sill, had been mostly robbed away, the subsequent filling comprising loose ragstone and broken tiles. However, the north face of the wall and the face of the jamb had survived in sections, from which it was clear that the wall was standing here to a height of 0.33m. Above the white mortar, the wall comprised a course of ragstone overlaid by three courses of tiles, all set in pink mortar.

Site 9. Gracechurch Street, south of Ship Tavern Passage, 1978

A shaft 3.4m in diameter was dug in the newly pavemented area of Gracechurch Street just south of Ship Tavern Passage. Deposits associated with the origin of Roman London were revealed and were recorded by Peter Marsden. The modern pavement level lies at 17.45m OD.

THE GRAVELLED AREA

The natural brickearth surface was revealed at a depth of 5.68m below the pavement of Gracechurch Street (*ie* at 11.77m OD). This was overlaid by gravel metalling 0.216m thick (Fig. 12, layer 1), which seems to have been part of the large early Roman metalled area found on the site of 168–170 Fenchurch Street immediately east of this shaft.[15] There was no grey 'trampled' soil surface to the brickearth as is normally found on other sites, indicating that the brickearth had been de-turfed before the gravel was laid.

A thin dirty deposit (layer 2) lay upon the surface of the gravel metalling indicating a period of use, and this was in turn overlaid by 0.13m of grey earth (layer 3), apparently dumped and containing flecks of charcoal, broken red tiles, oyster shells and pieces of ragstone and flint. This may have been in preparation for the re-metalling, represented by layers of orange gravel and clean sand 0.114m thick (layers 4 and 5). The sandy surface was overlaid by a dark grey ashy soil 0.025m thick (layer 6), which appeared to have been derived from a nearby site of a fire. Since the re-metalled area of gravel found adjacent to this site (see Fig. 13) was in use at the time of the Boudican fire, it is reasonable to assume that the ash was blown, burnt debris from nearby buildings destroyed in AD 60.

The ash was overlaid by a deposit of yellow clay (layer 7) containing some grey ash, which may have been dumped in preparation for a new floor of mortary sand and gravel (layer 8) 0.28m thick, which on the east side of the shaft was seen as a mortar layer 0.025m thick. This surface may have been a re-instatement of the open area after the Boudican fire but before the first forum was built *c* AD 80.

Site 10. 3–6 Gracechurch Street, 1964, 1966

SUMMARY

Gravel metalling, possibly representing an east-west Roman street, and probably of about the middle of the 1st century, was an early feature of this site. To the south were traces of two phases of early Roman buildings, probably timber-framed and with clay walls. It is likely that these were of pre-Boudican date even though there was no trace of the Boudican fire of AD 60. The north aisle of the first basilica was subsequently constructed on this site, and, on the evidence of other sites, was replaced after its demolition by the second basilica of which the south sleeper wall of the nave was also found on the site. Unfortunately these two basilica buildings were not stratigraphically related to each other due to deep modern foundations and cellars.

INTRODUCTION

The importance of this site was known since the discovery here of a wall of the second basilica in 1881–2. The rebuilding of the site in 1964 and in 1966 gave an excellent opportunity for the Roman structure to be further recorded by Peter Marsden, particularly as much of the digging for rebuilding was carried out manually. It is unfortunate, however, that all the archaeological features were destroyed during the rebuilding operations (Figs. 77–80).

GEOLOGY

The natural subsoil was brickearth, the undisturbed surface of which lay at about 12.1m OD.

THE EARLIEST ROMAN PHASES

The earliest Roman deposits survived only in the western half of the site where it was unfortunately not possible to make a detailed study of the strata. Traces of three possible phases were found: (1), a possible east-west road with a building on its south side; (2), a second building with mortar floors; and (3), a probable north-south road, perhaps contemporary with the first basilica. It must be stressed, however, that these interpretations are very tentative, though as all the archaeological deposits have been destroyed it is unlikely that any additional evidence of activity on this site will be found, except, perhaps, beneath St. Peter's Alley and the adjoining churchyard.

PHASE 1

A considerable thickness of layers of gravel metalling was located just south of St. Peter's Alley, possibly indicating the former presence of an east-west street of the 1st century (Fig. 77). The metalling was more than 1.8m wide, and was noted in three sections over an east-west distance of 7.6m. In the westernmost section the layers of gravel metalling were 0.9m thick, and their lowest layer occurred at 0.15m above the natural brickearth, showing that the metalling was one of the earliest features on the site. In the central section the layers of gravel metalling were 0.53m thick, but included a deposit of carbonised material

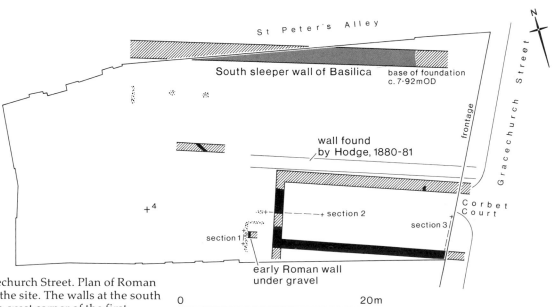

Fig. 77 3–6 Gracechurch Street. Plan of Roman features found on the site. The walls at the south end form the north-west corner of the first basilica, with traces of gravel metalling to the north which possibly represent part of an east-west street. At the north end of the site is the southern sleeper wall of the second basilica.

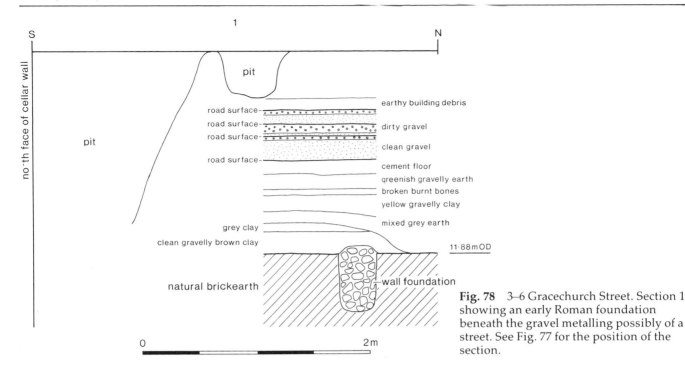

Fig. 78 3–6 Gracechurch Street. Section 1 showing an early Roman foundation beneath the gravel metalling possibly of a street. See Fig. 77 for the position of the section.

0.025m thick. The upper part of the gravel metalling here may have been removed later, for in the easternmost section it was 0.79m thick, although including a black deposit of carbonised material 0.22m thick. It is possible, though no dating evidence was recovered, that this black deposit was debris from the Boudican fire, but, if so, it could not have been derived from a building to the south for no trace of any fire was found there. R. Merrifield, who recorded the central and eastern sections, suggested that the carbonised layers in both sections may have been the same deposit. In both sections the gravel metalling overlay a deposit of dirty brickearth about 0.076m thick, which in turn overlay the natural brickearth, whose surface here lay at about 12.24m OD.

There was evidence of occupation to the south of the possible road. In one section the grey trampled natural brickearth surface was overlaid by a deposit of clean brickearth 0.15m thick, and above this were dark grey deposits of occupation debris 0.28m thick. Further east, at Section 1, the natural brickearth was overlaid by a thin ash layer, and then by deposits of dumped clay containing a little pottery and bones. Since the foundation of a Roman wall was recorded in Section 1 (Fig. 78), it is likely that some of the clay layers south of the conjectured street could have been the floors and collapsed clay brick walls of this building. The foundation itself was aligned roughly east-west, and was constructed of ragstone and gray clay deposited in a trench 0.33m wide and 0.48m deep, dug into the natural brickearth. Since a thin ash layer overlying the natural brickearth also over-

lay the rounded top of the foundation it seems likely that the wall was an early feature of occupation, perhaps pre-dating the possible road which in contrast did not lie immediately above the natural brickearth.

PHASE 2

A hard white mortar floor 0.13m thick, with a foundation of broken tiles, was recorded in Section 1, and as this overlay the dumped clay, occupation debris and the early wall foundation of Phase 1, it shows that a subsequent phase of reconstruction had occurred. The floor lay 0.8m above the natural subsoil, and was seen in a number of sections, (*eg* Fig. 79, Section 2), and apparently extended over a considerable part of the site west of the first basilica at about this level. In one Section (Fig. 77, no. 4), for example, a similar mortar floor 0.15m thick was noted 0.96m above the natural subsoil. Two mortarium rims,[16] found beneath the floor in Section 1, have been dated to the 1st century. It was not possible to record the extent of the mortar layer, but presumably it served as the floor of a building on the south side of the conjectured street. The apparent absence of stone walls suggests that the walls of the building were timber framed and built of clay. However, the mortar floor in Section 2 extended up to the west wall of the first basilica, and although it is likely that it was earlier than the basilica there is no definite evidence of this. The reasons why this was probably the case are: (1) that the basilica is known to have been dug into the earlier deposits and that this

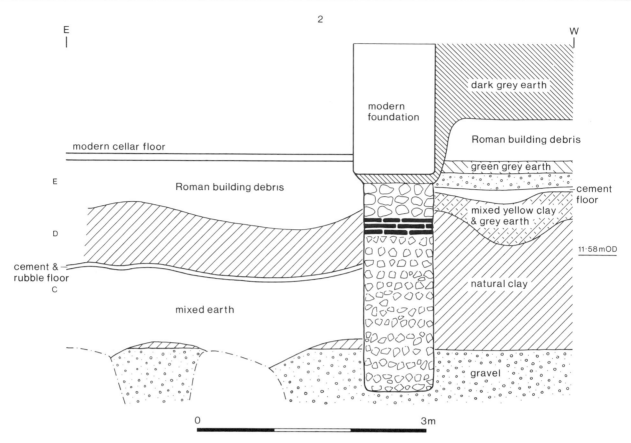

Fig. 79 3–6 Gracechurch Street. Section 2 across the west end of the
first basilica. For the position of the section see Fig. 77.

would create a deceptive association between the
wall and the floor; (2) that it is unlikely that there was
a large area of mortar floor west of the basilica, in a
location where in other Roman cases there is usually
an adjacent street. In fact there is evidence in Phase 3
to suggest the existence of such a street.

PHASE 3

Six layers of gravel metalling, with a total thickness
of 0.43m, were recorded in Section 1 just west of the
first basilica. The gravel was also recorded in Section
2, but here was thinning out as if at the edge of the
deposits. It is likely that these layers represent
repeated re-surfacings of a north-south street flanking the west side of the first basilica. The gravel
metalling overlay the mortar floor of Phase 2, but did
not extend as far west as Section 4, indicating that the
gravelled area was less than 9.75m wide. The fact that
its apparent eastern edge lay just west of the first
basilica suggests that it was contemporary with that
building.

THE FIRST BASILICA

The north-western part of the first basilica was
extremely well preserved on this site, and comprised
the west end of the north aisle, a compartment 5.94m
wide and more than 17.7m long.

The south wall, presumably a sleeper wall or
foundation separating the nave from the north aisle,
was 0.9m thick, and was built of ragstone and brown
mortar, and had two triple courses of red bonding
tiles; the upper at about 11.9m and the lower at about
10.7m OD. Two courses of ragstone were recorded
above the upper triple course. The foundation of the
wall was constructed of layers of flint set in brown
mortar, with its base at 8.8m OD and laid in the
natural gravel (Fig. 80. Plate 3).

The west wall was also 0.9m thick and of similar
construction, except that it contained only one triple
course of bonding tiles, a continuation of the upper
course in the south wall, below which was the flint
and brown mortar foundation whose base lay at
9.75m OD. The east face of the ragstone upper part of
the wall was coated with brown mortar to give it a

rough rendering, and on this were slight white traces, possibly though not certainly, of paint.

Of the north wall of the compartment, only a small portion of the foundation of layered flints and brown mortar was recorded, but its construction was exactly as in the south and west walls and quite different from the ragstone foundation of the second basilica, further to the north on this site (see below). This difference is important, for a Roman wall not quite parallel with that of the second basilica, was recorded by Henry Hodge on this site in 1881–2. It lay approximately in the same position as the north wall of the first basilica and on the same alignment (Fig. 77), but is unlikely to represent it for there was an important difference from the structure of the basilica found on the opposite side of Gracechurch Street (at Nos. 83–87) in 1934. In the latter case the wall was 0.9m wide with buttresses on its north side projecting 0.9m from the wall, whereas, according to Hodge, the wall in the former case was 1.2m wide and had no buttresses. It may be significant that Hodge recorded the wall as having extended for some distance to the west of what is now regarded as the first basilica, suggesting that he may have found both the north wall of the first basilica and the south wall of the second basilica, which here lay immediately adjacent to each other, and that, believing that they were parts of the same wall, he mistakenly conflated their attributes.

At some stage during the Roman period the area within the north aisle was apparently excavated to a level below the top of the flint foundations, and was subsequently filled with various deposits. It is likely that this excavation was to construct a basement, a view supported by the fact that the ragstone facing and lowest triple course of bonding tiles in the south wall lay 1.4m below the surface of the natural brickearth (Fig. 80). It is true that at the west end of the chamber the surface of the natural gravel was uneven (Fig. 79), though in fact the bottom of the ragstone facing and the lowest course of tiles in the west wall of the chamber lay at a higher level, corresponding with the level of the natural brickearth and suggesting that the basement may not have extended that far. Moreover, the existence of a basement would explain not only the exceptional depth of the south wall (Fig. 80, Section 3), but also the purpose of the dumped gravelly yellow clay deposit A (Section 3) which probably served as the basement floor. In its turn this overlay a cement layer 0.025m thick which covered the natural gravel. The thick deposits of black 'occupation debris', level B, which covered the clay 'floor' and which were piled high against the south wall, therefore, presumably represented the actual use of the basement. A few sherds were recovered from this deposit[17] and have been dated to the period *c* AD 70.

The filling-in of the 'basement' preceded the

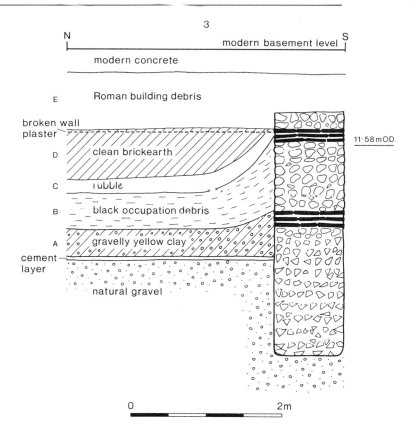

Fig. 80 3–6 Gracechurch Street. Section 3 across the north aisle of the first basilica. For the position of the section see Fig. 77.

demolition of the first basilica. At the west end of the chamber the natural gravel and brickearth was overlaid by a mixed earth with no stratification, which was presumably dumped (Fig. 79, Section 2). A few sherds were recovered of the (?early) Flavian period. Above the lowest filling already described there was a succession of deposits which occurred throughout all parts of the compartment that were seen. The lowest of these was a thin layer of loose mortar, hardly compact enough to have been a floor. Above was a thick deposit of dumped brickearth, Level D, the upper part of which contained many fragments of wall plaster. Above this was Level E, a thick deposit of building rubble containing stones, tiles and mortar exactly similar to the material used in the walls. It is reasonable to conclude that this was derived from the demolition of the building. The fact that this rubble did not extend beyond the west wall of the chamber suggests that the wall had been left standing to limit the spread of the rubble. It is significant that this wall alone had been robbed, so that it was evidently visible and accessible after demolition. The demolition rubble, however, overlay the south wall of this chamber as if to confirm that it was merely a sleeper wall for a row of columns or piers.

THE SECOND BASILICA

The base of the east-west foundation of the southern sleeper wall of the second basilica was recorded in the northern part of the site, below the modern sub-basement which lay at 7.92m below the level of Gracechurch Street (Fig. 77). The Roman foundation was 1.82m wide, and its base lay in the natural gravel at a depth of 9.75m below the modern street pavement (*ie* at about 7.92m OD). It was constructed of ragstone and extremely hard white mortar, and included a few large pieces of broken red Roman bricks.

This foundation was also recorded by Henry Hodge in 1881–2, when he drew a section across it. This section is confirmed by the 1964 observations, except that Hodge recorded the bottom of the foundation as varying in depth from 6.93m to 9.14m below modern street level. But the 1964 observations that the base lay at a depth of 9.75m and that the foundation width was 1.82m merely confirms Hodge's impression that the basilica foundation was of varying size. In fact the level of its base varied by up to 3m on this small site. Hodge also recorded the upper part of the foundation, and showed that it supported a wall 1.37m thick, probably made of

bricks. No certain trace of the south or outer wall of the south aisle of the second basilica was found, though part of a foundation of ragstone and buff mortar was found in approximately the correct position. This, seen only in section, seemed to be aligned roughly east-west, and to be about 0.91m thick: there is no evidence to date it to the Roman period.

Site 11.   17–19 Gracechurch Street, 1934–5

INTRODUCTION

The site was investigated by the late Frank Cottrill for the Society of Antiquaries during 1934–35, at which time the redevelopment of the site apparently destroyed all the archaeological deposits (Fig. 81). The manuscript records by Frank Cottrill have been deposited in the Museum of London together with a few of the finds, but unfortunately the objects that

Fig. 81   17–19 Gracechurch Street. Plan of Roman structures found on the site. The west wing of the first forum lies on the east side of the site, and a temple, apparently contemporary with that forum, lies to the west.

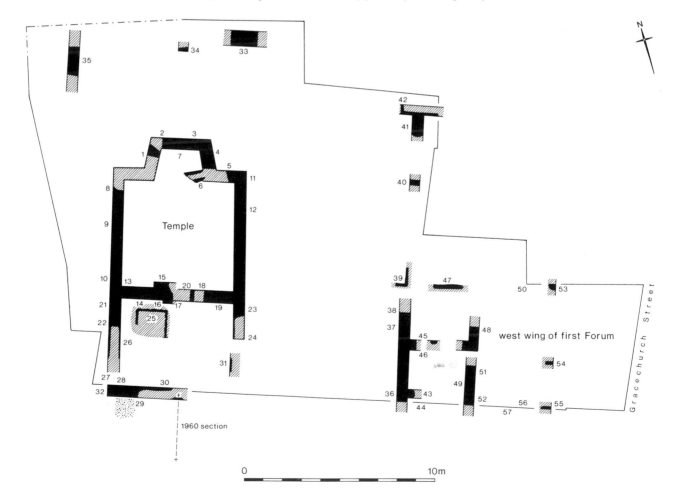

were deposited in the former Guildhall Museum in 1934–35 are now lost.

A short note about the Roman temple on the site was published by Frank Cottrill in the *Journal of Roman Studies*,[18] and subsequently Ralph Merrifield briefly described the site.[19]

The records of the archaeological features recorded during the rebuilding are mostly in the form of sketched and written descriptions of sections, some of which have been redrawn in a diagrammatic form for publication here. Thus although the relative levels of features and construction details can easily be compared, it must be stressed that the sections were originally merely sketched during brief pauses in the rebuilding operations, and that they should not be interpreted too literally.

The levels of the features described in the manuscript notes mostly relate to their depth below the site basement, but although the depth of the basement below pavement level was recorded it was not specified which pavements were used. The basement just north of the temple apse was 9ft 6in (2.9m) below pavement level, presumably of Bell Inn Yard nearby; while above the forum walls towards the east end of the site the basement lay at a depth of 7ft (2.1m) below pavement level, presumably that of the neighbouring Gracechurch Street. These two depths might imply that the basement lay at two different levels, but since the surface of the natural gravel lay at about 10ft (3.04m) below the basement over most of the site, it is clear that the variations in basement depth below the pavements must be due to the relative differences in level between the pavements of Bell Inn Yard and Gracechurch Street. In view of the uncertainty of the relationship of the old basement of the pre-1934 office building to the modern Ordnance Datum level, all depth measurements will be related to the old basement. However, it seems most likely that these basement levels were related to the pavement of Gracechurch Street, which lay at 17.435m OD. If this is correct then the basement lay at 15.335m OD.

SUMMARY

The sequence of events on this site is not completely clear. It seems that after an initial occupation of some form which did not result in any fire debris from the Boudican destruction of AD 60, the site was occupied by part of the west wing of the first forum. Initially this may have comprised simply a range of rooms with flint foundations, but a ragstone foundation to the east of the wing suggests that an inner portico may have been added subsequently. Just outside the forum lay a small classical temple, around which there was probably a walled enclosure. Various small sections were recorded by F. Cottrill in 1934–5 which led him to the opinion that the temple 'appears to

have been deliberately dismantled and the level of its site raised, and it is a fair assumption that this took place when the Forum and Basilica were constructed'.[20] This interpretation is also indicated by a section examined by P. Marsden in 1960 (Fig. 85), immediately south of the temple, in which the dumped building debris overlying the temple wall was itself found to be overlaid by mortar floors believed to be part of the courtyard of the second forum. No significant dating evidence was found (see p. 113).

GEOLOGY

The surface of the natural brickearth lay between 2.89m and 3.35m below the basement, the average of ten recorded depth measurements being 3.17m.

The natural gravel which underlay the brickearth was observed and recorded on five occasions, its depth being exactly 4.88m below the modern basement.

THE EARLIEST DEPOSITS

There is little information about the earliest deposits on this site, and no dating evidence. The earliest deposits overlying the natural brickearth were observed in six sections, and since it seems that the floor levels of the temple and of the first forum, both buildings dateable from other sites to the Flavian period, lay at approximately 2.48m below the basement, or at about 0.70m above the natural surface, it is clear that the deposits below this must relate to the earliest phases of London's occupation.

It is not clear what form of occupation and land use occurred on the site during the middle of the first century. The sections suggest some occupation which resulted in a limited accumulation of debris, including a cement layer, possibly a floor, overlying the natural subsoil. These sections, however, primarily comprise substantial dumps of brickearth, presumably deposited to help prepare the site for occupation. It may be significant that nowhere on this site was there found any trace of the Boudican fire of AD 60, suggesting that it was not built upon at that time. Any buildings in this area might be expected to have caught fire from those which were found burnt on the site of All Hallows church, immediately to the south. Whatever the form of occupation, it is possible that there was an open space, perhaps a street, in the western part of this site, for in one section the natural brickearth was overlaid by gravel 0.6m thick, and in another the natural surface was overlaid by mixed gravel.

THE TEMPLE *(Figs 81, 82, 84, 85)*

The walls and foundations of a small temple of the architectural style called *distyle in antis* were recorded in the western half of the site. Its overall dimensions were 10.66m wide and 20.7m long, and it was orientated approximately north-south (Fig. 82).

It comprised a *cella* with an angular apse in its north wall, and a doorway in its south wall, while to the south was a rectangular area mostly enclosed by walls with shallow foundations. The portico on the south side of the *cella* was flanked by two projecting *antae*, between which was situated a substantial foundation which possibly once supported pillars. The shallow walls of the rectangular enclosure to the south of the *antae* were clearly never intended to support a heavy superstructure, and it is likely that they enclosed a staircase leading to a podium floor level within the *cella*. This would account for the absence of any trace of a floor within the *cella* at the contemporary ground level. Alternatively, it has been suggested that the shallow walls may have formed a small courtyard or anteroom in front of the entrance, but this view creates certain problems of interpretation.

Traces of a possible walled enclosure or *temenos* were found to the west and north of the temple, with some architectural feature projecting internally from the north wall exactly on the central north-south axis of the temple. A gravelled area was found on the building site immediately south of the temple in 1960–61, suggesting that the temple precinct extended beyond the south side of the site of 17 Gracechurch Street and onto the site formerly occupied by the church of All Hallows, Lombard Street.

NORTH WALL AND APSE OF CELLA *(Figs. 81, 82)*

Section at 1. Only part of the foundation of this west wall of the apse was recorded, between 2.6m and 3.8m below the basement floor. The foundation was 0.99m wide, and was built of flint rubble and yellor mortar, with roof tile fragments in the surviving top few centimetres. This means that the junction of the tile wall and its flint foundation lay at about 2.66m below basement level. The bottom of the flint rubble foundation was not recorded.

Section at 2 (Fig. 83). The surviving top of this north wall of the apse lay at 1.83m below the basement, and below this the wall of tiles survived to a height of 0.91m above the flint rubble foundation. The wall was 0.91m thick, but the outer or northern face of the tile wall had been demolished to a lower level than that of the inner face. The tile wall was built with roof tiles, some with their flanges, presumably forming the facing, laid irregularly. The bottom of the tiles lay at 2.74m below the basement,

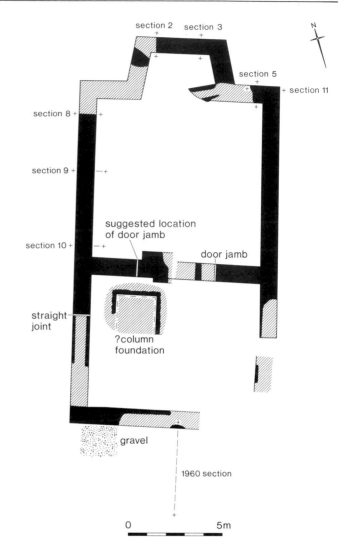

Fig. 82 17–19 Gracechurch Street. Detailed plan of the small Roman temple. The sections are shown in Fig. 83, and the 1960 section is shown in Fig. 85.

and about 0.30m above the natural brickearth. The bottom of the flint rubble foundation lay at 4.88m below the basement.

Section at 3 (Fig. 83). The surviving top of this north wall of the apse lay at 2.28m below the basement, and beneath this the wall was tiled to a height of 0.91m. The roof tiles forming the wall comprised at least six courses, and although already broken when built into the wall, those on the faces were so placed that their flanges were turned upwards. The tiles were set into a yellowish brown sandy cement, which was in such poor condition that the tiles could be dislodged by hand. The brick wall was 0.81m thick, and the foundation of flint rubble below was 0.91m thick. The bottom of the tile wall lay at 3.2m below the basement. The level of the bottom of the flint foundation was not established.

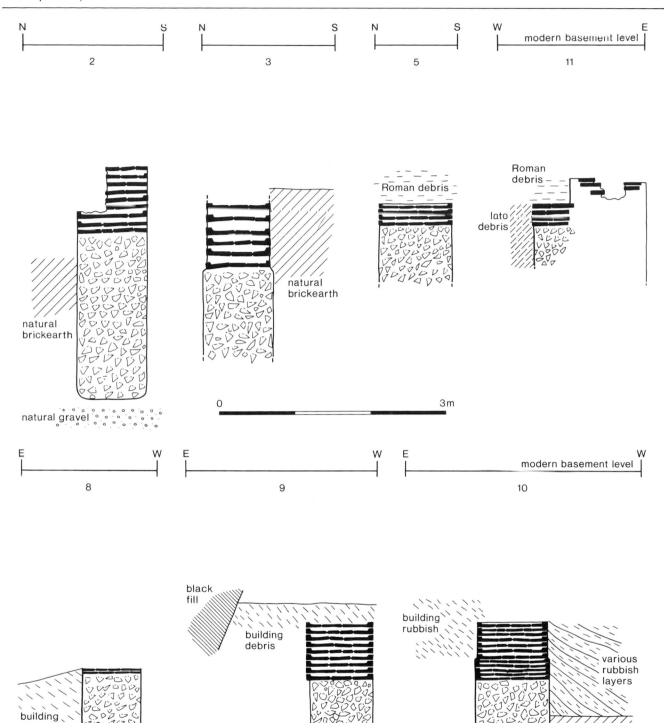

Fig. 83   17–19 Gracechurch Street. Sections of features in the Roman temple, the positions of which are shown in Fig. 82.

Section at 4.   The foundation of flint rubble, set in yellowish-brown cement with white particles, was located immediately below the base of the tile wall at a depth of 3.2m. The tile wall may have been robbed at this section since its plan was exactly occupied by a pit filled with a stony material. The section had been cut obliquely across this wall so that the foundation measured 1.04m thick, but towards the bottom of the trench the true thickness was found to be 0.86m. The bottom of the foundation lay at a depth of 4.88m.

Section at 5 (Fig. 83).   At this section close to the north-east corner of the *cella*, the top of the brick wall lay at a depth of 2.34m. The wall lay 0.35m below the top of the brickwork forming the north-east corner of the room, and as the raised part terminated in a vertical face Frank Cottrill suggested that it had perhaps not been intended to build the north wall of the room any higher than 2.34m below the modern basement. The north wall immediately west of the vertical face was built of roof tiles with upturned flanges on the faces of the wall. The facing survived to a height of 0.28m above the flint rubble foundation, and comprised four courses of tiles. The top of the flint rubble foundation lay at 2.44m below basement level, but its bottom was not recorded.

Section at 6.   The lowest part of a foundation of an internal wall of the apse was traced for a distance of 1.52m from the east wall of the apse. It was built of flint rubble, and its greatest recorded width was 0.84m, its south face being unlocated. The bottom of the foundation lay in the natural brickearth above the natural gravel at a depth of 4.04m below the modern basement. Since the purpose of this foundation was presumably to help support the apse opening, its alignment is puzzling.

Feature at 7.   This, possibly an internal foundation, was located within the apse. It comprised rough walling material, flints, fragments of tile, and yellow cement which, in Cottrill's opinion, had probably been disturbed. The feature rose to a higher level than the observed west wall of the apse (Fig. 81, section at 1), that is above 2.6m below the modern basement floor.

THE WEST WALL OF THE CELLA

Section at 8 (Fig. 83).   The top of the wall was noted at about 2.74m below the modern basement, though this was not necessarily the surviving top of the wall. The upper part of the wall, 0.76m wide, was built of roof tiles roughly coursed, the tile flanges being 0.02m thick. The flint and cement foundation was also 0.76m wide, and its bottom lay at 4.27m below

basement level, in the natural brickearth and at about 0.3m above the ballast. The lowest 0.9m of the foundation was of flint rubble and yellowish brown cement, laid alternately in rough courses.

Section at 9 (Fig. 83).   The east face of this wall was exposed over a length of 3.35m. The top of the wall lay at 2m below the basement beneath which level was 0.74m of tilework, and the tiles, already broken, were laid in regular courses set in yellowish-brown cement. The wall face was formed of the upturned flanges of the tiles, three courses comprising a depth of 0.23m. The tile wall was 0.89m wide, and its east face oversailed the flint foundation below by 0.13m, suggesting either faulty construction or perhaps some rebuilding.

Section at 10 (Fig. 83).   A section across the wall just north of the south-west corner of the *cella* revealed the top of the tilework at 2m below basement level. At 0.48m below the top was an offset of about 0.02m in the tile courses on the east and west faces of the wall, and the tiles extended 0.26m below this to the top of the flint foundation. The tile wall above the offset was 0.91m wide, but unfortunately the width of the flint foundation was not recorded, though elsewhere it was 0.76m wide (*cf.* section at 8). On the east face of the wall were traces of a rendering in buff cement.

EAST WALL OF CELLA

Wall at 11 (Fig. 83).   At the north-east corner of the *cella* the wall was built of ordinary Roman bricks instead of broken roof tiles. The surviving top of the corner lay at 2m below the basement.

Wall at 12.   The top of this wall lay at 1.93m below basement level, and beneath this was 0.6m of tile wall constructed as recorded elsewhere in the building, with the flanges used as wall facing. On the east face eight courses of tiles, 0.53m high, were recorded. On the west face was an offset of 0.025m immediately above the lowest course of tiles, but there was no corresponding offset on the east side. The actual location of the offset was not recorded. Below the tile wall, the foundation of flint rubble extended to a depth of 4.88m below the basement. The natural brickearth was recorded at a depth of 3.2m below the basement, on the east side of the wall and roughly opposite the middle of the *cella*. The natural brickearth deposit was about 1.75m thick, overlying the natural gravel upon which the bottom of the adjacent wall foundation rested.

SOUTH WALL OF THE CELLA *(Figs. 81, 84)*

The south wall of the *cella* was of somewhat more complex construction, with two projecting foundations and a doorway.

The wall at 13. The south wall of the *cella* had been bonded into the west wall of the chamber, and both walls had a level top at 2m below the modern basement floor (Plate 6). The upper part of the surviving wall was built of eight courses of tiles with the flanges forming the faces, but 0.48m below the top (*ie* at 2.48m below the basement) was an offset of 0.025m on both the south and north faces, and below this were three more courses of tiles for a depth of 0.23m. The top of the flint foundation lay at 2.71m.

The wall at 14. The tile wall here was 0.91m wide, and continued the offsets at the same level as at 13. The bottom of the flint rubble foundation lay at a depth of 4.88m, of which the lowest 0.23m was of unmortared flints extending slightly into the natural gravel. The flint rubble foundation was 2.13m deep below the tiles, the top of the flints lying at 2.75m below the modern basement. A foundation trench up to 0.3m wide was observed in a section on the north side of the foundation. It was dug into the natural brickearth, and was filled with brickearth with some charcoal and some red burnt clay.

Wall at 15. This was a projection on the north side of what was presumably a door sill. The projection was 0.46m wide and more than 1.07m long, its east end having been destroyed by a medieval pit. The projection was of one build with the main south wall of the *cella*, but was built of bricks, not tiles, and with a foundation of flints and cement. Two courses of bricks occurred in a depth of 0.1m, and the flints had a level bottom at 3.05m below the basement, and a vertical north face.

Wall at 16. A small projection was noted on the south side of the main foundation of the south wall of the *cella*. It was only 0.2m wide (N-S), and was absent 0.3m further to the east. It was built of bricks, and apparently had a shallow foundation of flints similar to the northern projection, 15.

Fig. 84 17–19 Gracechurch Street. Details of the doorway of the temple.

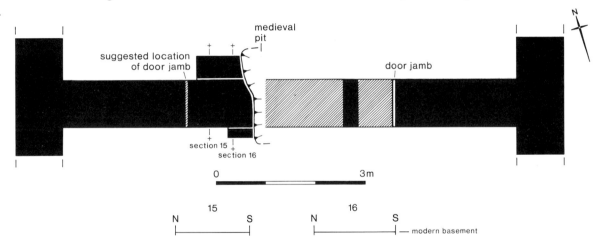

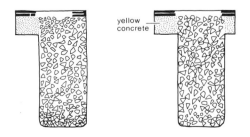

Wall at 17. The wall at this point was found to be 1.37m wide, and apparently included the northern projection. The top of the wall lay at a depth of 2.6m below the basement, and its south side was faced with flanged tiles, two courses amounting to 0.11m in depth.

Wall at 18. The sill of the doorway was preserved just west of the door jamb, and was formed of broken tiles set in yellow cement. The sill lay at 2.41m below the modern basement and, only 0.15m below the top of the sill, lay the flint foundation, copiously mortared throughout except for the lowest few 'inches' which was of flints only. The door sill was only 0.91m wide.

Wall at 19. The door jamb was of brickwork, not tiles, stood to a height above the sill of 0.28m, and comprised four courses of bricks. The wall had a level top at 2.13m below the basement, and was 0.91m wide.

Pit at 20. The doorway was damaged by a medieval pit whose black earth fill contained charcoal, a 'Norman' pot and other medieval sherds.

WESTERN ANTA *(Fig. 81)*

Wall at 21. The top of the wall lay at 2.35m below the basement, and comprised yellow cement with some tile fragments for a depth of 0.38m. Below this was a foundation of flint rubble, the top of which lay at about 2.73m below the basement. The wall was 0.99m wide in section, which, being wider than usual, suggests that the section may have been a little oblique to the line of the wall.

Wall at 22. The flint rubble foundation only had survived; the upper part of the wall with its tile construction having been destroyed. The bottom of the foundation extended about 0.3m into the ballast, the lowest 0.15m being of unmortared whole flints, patinated white by the chalk from which they had been quarried.

EASTERN ANTA *(Fig. 81)*

Wall at 23. Only the foundation of this *anta* was recorded. It was 0.91m thick, and had a flint rubble foundatin of the usual character, extending below the top of the natural brickearth, whose surface lay at about 2.90m below the basement.

Wall at 24. The bottom of this foundation lay at 5.03m below the basement, the construction being of flint rubble with yellowish-brown mortar with white

particles. The foundation ended at the south end with a vertical termination.

PORTICO *(Fig. 81)*

Wall at 25. A foundation was recorded in section at 2.74m below the basement. It was broadly spread, extending for over 2.1m in an east-west section, and over 2.29m in a north-south section. It was of yellowish-brown flint pebble cement resting on a layer of unmortared ragstone blocks at a depth of 3.2m. Below this, occupation debris extended to more than 0.6m, showing that the natural subsoil here lay below 3.8m from the modern basement. Since the surface of the natural subsoil lay at a depth of 2.9m only 4.8m away to the east, it is clear that the occupation debris was the filling of a hollow or pit dug into the natural brickearth. It is possible that this foundation supported one of a pair of pillars in front of the temple entrance.

SOUTH END OF THE TEMPLE *(Fig. 81)*

WEST WALL:

Wall at 26. South of the *anta* the north-south wall line was continued by a shallow wall with one or two courses of brick set in pebble concrete. The top of the wall lay at 2.74m below basement level, and the bottom at 3.35m.

Wall at 27. At a distance of 1.83m north of the internal south-west corner of this chamber the foundation of the north-south wall is not shown in the section, and was presumably absent.

Wall at 28. The south end of this wall was 0.91m wide.

SOUTH WALL:

Wall at 29. The top of this wall was found at a depth of 2.26m–2.41m below the modern basement, below which was 0.48m of brickwork (only two flanged tiles were noticed) set in yellow mortar. The wall was about 0.9m thick, and the bricks were of uneven thickness, one as much as 0.06m thick, and not always laid horizontally, one joint being 0.08m deep. At one point the south face preserved five courses in a depth of 0.38m. The top of the underlying foundation lay between 2.74 and 2.9m below the basement and comprised flint rubble mixed with much reddish gravel and occasional fragments of tile. The bottom of the foundation lay at a depth of 3.2m below the basement, and clearly it was not as deep as the foundations in the main part of the temple to the north.

Wall at 30. At the south end of a trench at this point a workman reported the discovery of a wall of Roman bricks above a foundation of flint.

EAST WALL

Wall at 31. The top of a wall consisting of three courses of brickwork was found at a depth of 1.98m below the modern basement. The three courses of brickwork were 0.18m high and were set in yellow cement levelled at the top. The foundation was of compact gravel 0.3m deep, at which level it apparently rested on the natural brickearth. However, since the total depth of the foundation appears to have been 2.46m, it is difficult to reconcile this with the natural brickearth surface nearby which lay at 2.9m below the basement.

WALLS PROBABLY ASSOCIATED WITH THE TEMPLE

Wall at 32. A rubble wall or foundation aligned approximately east-west was found abutting (*ie* not bonded into) the external south-west corner of the temple. It was built of large undressed blocks of ragstone and yellow mortar with flint pebbles. A length of only 0.53m had survived, the rest having been destroyed by a modern trench, and the wall or foundation had an irregular stone face. Its top was level with the top of the brick wall nearby (*ie* about 2.30m below the modern basement).

WALLS NORTH OF THE TEMPLE

Walls at 33. An 1.83m length of wall was exposed close to the northern edge of the site. It was 0.84m wide, and built of ragstone and yellowish-brown cement containing flint pebbles. The south face was built of undressed ragstone blocks, the largest measuring 0.28m long and 0.13m high, laid in five courses with a total height of 0.68m. Below these courses was a slight foundation only 'a few inches' deep. The top of the wall was level, perhaps for a tile course or as a sleeper wall, at 2.13m below the modern basement level.

Wall at 34. A pier, buttress or wall termination of ragstone and mortar, of similar construction to 33, was found 3.5m to the west of 33. Its south face was 0.76m long, and the block extended northwards for at least 0.46m. The top of the wall lay at 2.74m below the modern basement, but this low level was no doubt due to the destruction of its upper part at a later

period, since a pit full of black soil and with sloping sides was found immediately above it. A depth of 0.46m of wall structure was exposed.

Wall at 35. A trench 0.91m wide and aligned roughly north-south, was found filled with wall debris, including lumps of ragstone, flints, cement, tile fragments, and mud. It was evidently the location of a robbed wall. The trench was recorded in a section through the natural brickearth between 3.35 and 4.27m below basement level. The trench had been observed further south.

FEATURES SOUTH OF THE TEMPLE

A north-south section (Fig. 85), recorded by P. Marsden on the site of Barclay's Bank, Lombard Street, in November 1960, exposed an area immediately south of the temple. Part of a Roman brick wall set in brown cement was recorded (feature 1), and since this was on the line of the south wall of the temple (Wall at 29, 30) it was evidently a continuation of it. It was not possible to record the section fully, but further south the stratigraphy was more accessible and it was clear that there were two superimposed hard rammed gravel layers, each with a thin surface of grey or white cement (features 2 and 3). It is likely that these comprised the surface of the court immediately south of the temple, where the altar presumably lay.

The section revealed about 0.71m of debris (layers 4, 5 and 6) overlying both the wall and the gravel surface. The dumping may be interpreted as debris from the demolition of the temple, the first forum, and from adjacent timber-framed buildings with clay walls.

FEATURES IN THE SECTION

1 A Roman wall constructed of courses of brick in brown cement.

2 A floor of hard rammed gravel with a thin white cement surface.

3 A subsequent floor of hard rammed gravel with a grey cement surface.

4 Dump of Roman building rubble (ragstone and broken tiles) in a pink cement dust. A layer of red burnt clay lay within the dump.

5 A dump of brickearth containing fragments of painted wall plaster,[21] suggesting that the clay was the debris from demolished timber-framed buildings with clay walls.

6 Several dumped deposits of building debris: a layer of brown cement debris 0.15m thick, overlaid by light grey clay 0.051m thick, and covered

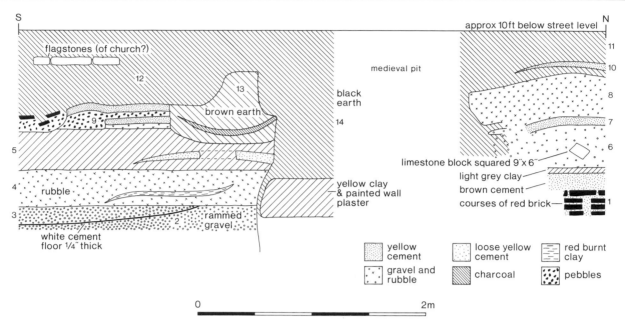

Fig. 85 54–58 Lombard Street (extreme north end). A section recorded in 1960 across the south wall (1) of the temple, and beyond it hard gravelled surfaces (2, 3) which lay immediately south of the temple. These features were overlaid by dumped debris (4, 5, 6) probably associated with the second forum. For the position of the section see Fig. 82. The 'black earth' (11, 12 and 14) was not charcoal (see key) but represents mostly the post-Roman periods.

by a deposit of building rubble and gravel 0.38m thick, in which was found a tooled, squared, limestone block measuring 0.23m by 0.15m.

7 A floor of yellow cement about 0.05m thick, presumably a floor in the courtyard of the second forum. This is likely to equate with the lower floor (9).

8 A dump of mixed Roman rubble and earth 0.35m thick, comprising clay, grey earth, pink mortar, wall plaster, bricks and ragstone.

9 Two Roman floors, each constructed of identical yellow mortar, and each 0.05m thick. The lower overlay a foundation of loose *opus signinum* 0.05m thick. The upper overlay a layer of gravel, and both floors had been cut by shallow pits or gullies which were filled with pebbles, the later pit also containing fragments of Roman brick.

10 A yellow cement floor 0.04m thick, probably of Roman date, with dark earth below.

11 A deposit of dark earth overlying the yellow cement floor (10).

12 Dark earth overlay the Roman floors (9), but as human bones were found at the bottom of the deposit it is likely that the earth comprised the fill of the churchyard of All Hallows, Lombard Street. At a higher level were flagstones, also probably associated with the church.

13 A pit containing brown earth and a layer of burnt wood. Undated.

14 A rubbish pit from which a medieval pot base[22] was recovered. The pit was filled with dark earth, but below this were layers of Roman yellow clay and building debris indicating that part of the side of the pit had collapsed at some stage.

THE FIRST FORUM *(Fig. 86)*

A range of chambers forming part of the west wing of the first forum was traced for a length of 23.57m in the eastern part of the site. The wing was 6.1m wide externally, aligned roughly north-south, and had foundations of flint and mortar. It also had two buttresses projecting from its west side, a characteristic of the exterior of the building. Portions of ragstone wall (Fig. 81, nos. 53, 54, 55), or series of foundations aligned parallel to the forum, were noted at a distance of 5.33m beyond the east side of the wing, and may have comprised an addition to the original structure, perhaps a portico.

WEST WALL OF FORUM *(Fig. 81)*

Wall at 36. The lower 0.65m of a brick and cement wall was still standing above a foundation of flint rubble. The bottom of the lowest three brick courses lay at 2.6m below the modern basement (*ie* 12.735m OD), and 0.19m above this was an offset of 0.04m on the exterior west face. Above this were four more courses of brickwork for a height of 0.46m. A vertical joint within the core of the lower part of the brick wall suggests that there may have been two phases of wall construction. The east side of the upper part of the wall had been destroyed during the Roman period, leaving much demolition debris including 'white wall plaster'. At a depth of 3.96m below the modern basement, the wall foundation was 0.86m wide.

Wall at 37. The lowest three courses of a brick wall, only 0.18m high, lay at a depth of 2.6m below the modern basement (12.735m OD), below which was a foundation 0.89m wide, composed of roughly coursed flint rubble in a hard yellow pebbly concrete. A pit-like feature overlay the top of the wall, and since it was filled with building rubbish, mostly 'red wall plaster' with some potsherds, it was possibly a robber trench.

Wall at 38. Three tile courses were located at 2.74m below the modern basement. Below that was a foundation, at least 0.84m wide, of flint rubble set in cement. The bottom of the foundation lay in the natural sand at a depth of 4.72m.

Wall at 39. The foundation of both the main wall and of a buttress were built of flint rubble and yellow cement. They were observed at a depth of 4.27m below the modern basement and in the natural brickearth. The buttress projected 0.84m from the west face of the main wall, the angle between the wall and the buttress being of more than 90°. The bottom of the foundation protruded into the natural sand to a depth of about 6.1m below the basement.

Wall at 40. The lowest *c.* 0.46m of the foundation was noted in the natural brickearth. The foundation was constructed of flint and yellow cement, and its bottom lay at 4.57m below modern basement level. The foundation trench was noted, containing building rubbish.

Wall at 41. The foundation of this wall, of flint set in yellow cement, was found dug into the brickearth. The foundation was 0.86m wide, and had a rounded bottom at 4.57m below basement level; just above the top of the ballast.

Wall at 42. The lowest 0.96m of this buttress was constructed of flints set in yellow cement. The buttress was 0.74m wide, and projected at least 0.63m. A foundation trench for the wall was found cut into the natural brickearth, and was filled with building debris (pebbles and crumbled cement). The

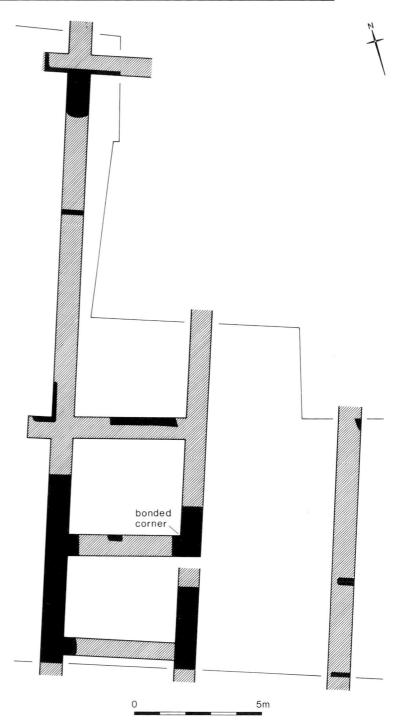

Fig. 86 17–19 Gracechurch Street. The west wing of the first forum.

bottom of the foundation lay at 4.57m below the modern basement.

INTERNAL WALLS AND FLOORS OF FORUM

Wall at 43. A flint rubble foundation with a level top at about 3m below the basement, above which was 0.53m of brickearth. The wall was 0.79m wide, but F. Cottrill seems to have thought that this was a 'projection' and not necessarily a cross-wall – probably because it was found early in the rebuilding and he was uncertain of its significance.

Floor at 44.   A floor of yellow cement was found at about 3m below basement level. The floor was 0.10m thick, and above it was brickearth 0.61m thick, and then a cement layer (? floor) up to 0.02m thick, this latter level lying at 2.39m below the basement.

Wall at 45.   A foundation of coursed flint rubble and yellow sandy cement was aligned roughly east-west. The bottom of the foundation rested in brickearth at a depth of 4.65m below the basement.

Pit at 46.   A rubbish pit, probably of post-Roman date, contained a filling of black earth, and had been cut through the Roman wall 45. The pit was 1.07m in diameter, and had been dug to a depth of 6.1m below the basement.

Wall at 47.   A wall aligned east-west was found and reported by a workman. Apparently about 0.6m of tilework, comprised of flanged roofing tiles, remained above a foundation of flint rubble.

EAST WALL OF THE FORUM *(Fig. 81)*

Wall at 48.   This was a wall aligned north-south, and 0.81m thick, of which only the foundation had survived at this point, the upper part having been robbed. The bottom 1.62m of the foundation was built of roughly coursed flint rubble, above which lay about 0.3m of ragstone rubble. Above this was the black earth filling of the robber trench. The bottom of the foundation lay on the natural gravel at a depth of 4.67m below the basement, and the surviving top of the wall lay at 3m below the basment. At a depth of 3.35m below the basement there was an opportunity to trace a little of the length of the Roman foundation, which was found to turn a corner to join the wall 45. Curiously, there was no southward continuation to join the wall 49.

Two cement layers, presumably floors, were found immediately east of the north-south wall. The lower cement layer abutted the wall a few cms above the bottom of the ragstone rubble, and the upper cement layer abutted the robbed part of the wall.

Wall at 49.   A foundation of flint rubble and hard light brown or cream coloured mortar was found aligned north-south, continuing the line of wall 48. The foundation was about 0.76m wide, and its lowest 0.11m was of unmortared flints resting in the natural brickearth at a depth of 5m below the basement. The

foundation stood only 1.75m high, but this may have been due to demolition in antiquity. At the south end of this length of wall the bottom of two courses of tiles was found at a depth of 3.3m (ie at 12.035m OD), overlying the flint foundation. Floors of cement were found overlying the forum wall at depths of 2.3m and 2.87m below the basement, and presumably these were of a later Roman date. It is possible, however, that they constituted the flooring of an opening in the wall, and that the corner of the wall at 48 was a door jamb. The south side of the putative doorway may have been in line with the cross-wall 43, for at its surviving south end a wall, 49, stood to a greater height, and the bottom of two courses of tiles was found at a depth of 3.3m.

FEATURES EAST OF THE WALL 48, 49

Floora at 51.   On the east side of the foundation at 49 there were two cement 'floors' at depths of 3.17m and 3.45m below the basement, but their level suggests that the latter at least was probably of earlier date than the foundation. The relationship of the 'floors' and the strata to the Roman wall is uncertain.

Pit at 52.   A rectangular rubbish pit filled with Roman building debris was found adjacent to the wall at 49. Its contents were all Roman, with pieces of ragstone, and fragments of brick, tile (*tegula* and *imbrex*), pink cement flooring and red painted wall plaster. The bottom of the pit lay at a depth of 4.39m below the basement.

Wall at 53, 54 and 55.   Three sections revealed a wall aligned north-south, and more than 0.74m wide. It was constructed of ragstone rubble and hard buff coloured cement, and was observed standing to a level of 3.15m below the modern basement, while its flat bottom was found at a depth of 3.66m (*ie* at 11.675m OD). Only the east side was found, but its facing was not recorded, and so it is not known if it was merely the foundation of a wall, or if it included any of the wall superstructure.

Gravel surface at 56.   A section revealed a gravel surface at a depth of 1.9m below the basement, and clay surfaces at 1.52m.

Floors at 57.   A cement floor 0.12m thick was uncovered at a depth of 3.05m below the basement, and a later cement floor was revealed at a depth of 1.37m.

Site 12.   77 Gracechurch Street, 1984
by Brian Pye

Prior to the demolition of 77 Gracechurch Street an excavation was carried out by the Department of Urban Archaeology, of the Museum of London, during July, 1984. The excavation of a trench 20m long and 1m wide was funded by Land Securities Management Ltd.

The archaeological sequence started with natural brickearth at about 11.5m OD, which was overlaid by redeposited brickearth. Above were compacted gravel surfaces about 0.25m thick. Dug into these surfaces were several pits, stakeholes and postholes, whose pottery finds gave a provisional date of about AD 55–80.

THE FIRST FORUM *(Figs. 87, 88)*

Cutting through these surfaces in the eastern part of the site were two Roman foundations aligned roughly north-south. They were similar in construction (flint nodules set in mortar, capped by tile courses), but varied in width from 0.8–1.0m and were 4.5m apart. In between was a truncated mortar floor at about 12.3m OD.

A third foundation, constructed about 4m to the west, was built of different material (ragstone and mortar) and was 1.8m wide on the north-south alignment. On its top surface in the eastern half were impressions left where a course of tiles had been removed at about 12.35m OD.

The west wall of the earlier structure had been demolished down to foundation level leaving vestiges of a mortar floor linking the two remaining foundations.

THE SECOND FORUM

The site was subsequently covered by dumps of sandy-gravels to a depth of 0.7m (Fig. 88), and the two remaining foundations were dismantled with demolition cuts through the gravels. Above the gravels were a series of mortar and silt surfaces. Very little pottery came from the gravel dumps or the surfaces above them, but what little was recovered suggested a date of between *c* AD 100–150 for their deposition.

CONCLUSIONS

This building sequence represents the east wing of the first forum built above an open gravel-surfaced area. The wing was later doubled in width by the addition of a new wall built to the west, in what was presumably the courtyard of the first forum. The walls were then demolished and the site became part of the interior of the much larger second forum.

Site 13.   79 Gracechurch Street, 1983
by A. Upson and B. Pye

An excavation by Miss A. Upson of the Department of Urban Archaeology, of the Museum of London, was funded by Land Securities Management Ltd., and was carried out during January–April, 1983.

Early Roman activity was represented by brickearth dumps overlying the natural brickearth deposits at about 11.7m OD. These dumps were superseded by isolated structural features: postholes, hearths and surfaces which were bounded to the east by a ditch. Beyond the ditch was a sequence of well-surfaced gravel metallings, perhaps a north-south street. This sequence was provisionally dated *c* AD 55–80 by pottery evidence and by a coin of AD 64–66 from one of the later surfaces.

THE FIRST FORUM *(Fig. 87. Plates 4, 5)*

The alignment established by these early features was not respected by the subsequent east wing of the forum. Two foundations of flint and mortar were found. One was aligned north-south and was *c* 0.8m wide, and was topped by two tile courses with a maximum surviving height to 12.3m OD. The other, aligned east-west, was found on the southern limit of the excavation. Between the two was a badly truncated mortar floor surface.

About 4m to the west of the north-south wall was a larger foundation also aligned roughly north-south. It was about 1.8m wide and was constructed of ragstone and mortar. At a height of 12.35m OD, the top surface of the eastern half bore mortar impressions of a tile course which had been removed.

At some time the eastern north-south wall was demolished and a pier was built upon its foundation. This pier seems to have co-existed with the western north-south wall for there was a substantial mortar floor between them.

THE SECOND FORUM

All the walls were eventually demolished and the site was covered with a dump of sandy gravels about one metre thick (Plate 5). It is not clear whether the dumping or the demolition took place first. On top of the gravels was a series of mortar and silt surfaces but their relationship to the pier is not known for the pier had been robbed at some stage, the robber pit having been dug through the dumped gravels.

CONCLUSIONS

This building sequence indicates that the east wing of the first forum was widened to the west, and that at some stage it was partly demolished and a pier

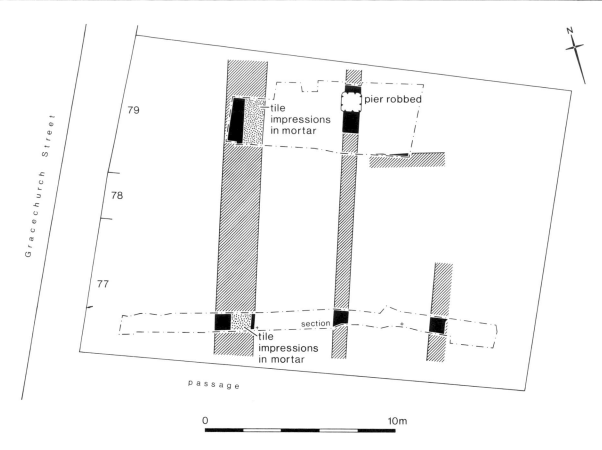

Fig. 87   77–79 Gracechurch Street. Plan of the east wing of the first forum.

Fig. 88   77–79 Gracechurch Street. Section across part of the east wing of the first forum showing the overlying gravel dumps associated with the second forum. The position of the section is shown in Fig. 87.

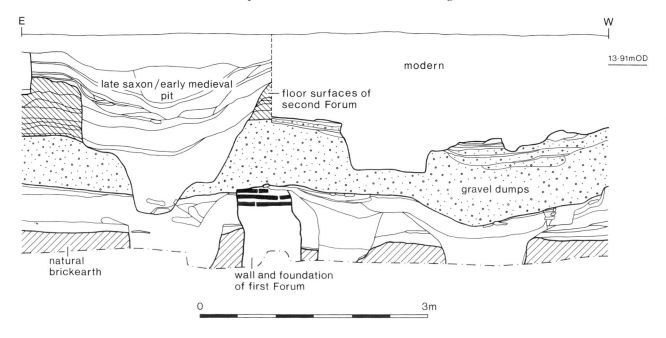

was inserted. Eventually, the building was demolished and dumps of gravel raised the ground surface about 1m, presumably for the courtyard of the much larger second forum.

Site 14.   83–87 Gracechurch Street, 1934

INTRODUCTION

The recording of archaeological features on this site was undertaken by Frank Cottrill between 10 March and 20 July, 1934, when he watched the digging of many trenches for the construction of new building foundations (Fig. 89). More than half of the archaeological deposits still remain, and should be carefully excavated when the opportunity arises, since only then will the history of the site be elucidated. The finds from the 1934 investigation were mostly deposited in the Guildhall Museum and, although some were accessioned, most have since been lost. All depths are measured from the old cellar floor of the pre-1934 building, which lay 3.69m below the level of Gracechurch Street. The pavement of Gracechurch Street in the middle of the building frontage lies at 17.76m OD, so the basement lay at about 14.07 OD.

GEOLOGY

The natural brickearth surface generally lay at a depth of about 2.74m below the then modern basement floor, which lay at 3.69m below Gracechurch Street. In several instances brickearth was observed at depths in excess of this – at 3.2m, 3.43m, and 4.04m – and it seems likely that these represent areas of disturbance in the natural subsoil. The top of the gravel which underlay the brickearth was also observed at varying depths, suggesting that it too had a uneven surface level, generally at depths of 3m–3.35m below the modern basement.

THE EARLIEST OCCUPATION

The earliest occupation on this site was presumably Roman, though this is not specifically stated by Cottrill. It was represented by deposits, up to 0.61m thick, of dark occupation debris. These dark deposits contrasted with the thick overlying deposits which were mostly of fairly clean brickearth which had presumably been dumped.

In trench 47 the presumably natural brickearth was overlaid by a few centimetres of brickearth, stones and tile fragments; above that was 0.23m of black occupation debris which contained charcoal, oyster shells and pottery fragments, including part of a mortarium; and above that again were the apparently dumped deposits of gravel, cement and fairly clean brickearth.

In trench 59 was also observed a layer of black occupation debris 0.68m thick in which were found oyster shells. This was at a depth of 2.9m, and again lay under a deposit of brickearth that had presumably been dumped. In several other holes (*ie* trenches 4, 11, 51, 59) the natural brickearth was seen to be covered by a thin dark deposit, perhaps a trampled surface, over which there was a further layer of brickearth, presumably dumped.

The only feature that was dated, however, was described by Cottrill as 'a large rubbish-pit containing Flavian and earlier pottery'.[23] The pit was found in trench 61 but had extended into nearby holes, and was important since not only did it help date the earlier occupation on the site, but it was also earlier than the construction of the first basilica, a foundation of which had been cut across the pit. The top of the pit was found at a depth of 2.6m, and its lower part had been dug into the natural gravel to a depth of about 4m below the basement floor. It was filled with black rubbish deposits, including charcoal, oyster shells and pottery which included samian ware. None of the pottery from this pit has survived, but there is no reason to doubt the Flavian dating which was well established at the time. A bronze coin is also believed to have been found in the pit: it was 'said by a navvy to have been found in rubbish filling against s. side of wall [*ie* of the Roman first basilica] 3.6–4.00m down'. This has been identified as of Vespasian (*Securitas Augusti* type) and was minted in AD 71. To judge from the date on which it was found, and its depth in the hole, it is very likely that the coin indeed came from this pit, the only one then being dug out – as long as what the navvy reported was true. This pit also helps to date the dumped deposits, since it was sealed by sand and gravel at least 1.07m thick.

In conclusion, the earliest occupation deposits clearly varied from place to place on this site, and there were traces of pits. The pit in trench 61, however, indicates that this phase of pre-forum occupation continued into the Flavian period. It is not possible to hazard a guess as to the form of this early occupation on the present evidence, though it is likely that the absence of red burnt deposits means that the site was not included in the area of burning by Boudica in AD 60, and therefore was not already built up.

RELATIONSHIP OF DUMPED DEPOSITS TO THE FIRST BASILICA

Dumped deposits overlay the early occupation layers and clearly represent a phase or phases in the subsequent modification of the site. The relationship of those deposits to the walls of the first basilica is not so clearly defined, however, though Cottrill believed that the dumping was later than the construction of the walls, since the deposits in several instances appeared to be piled up against the basilica walls.

The interpretation placed upon this by Cottrill was that the building, now identified as the first basilica and forum, had been constructed in the courtyard of the 'great' (second) forum, and that the clay and gravel dumps and their interleaved cement layers represented successive make-ups and surfaces of the (second) forum courtyard around the building.[24] In his actual site notes Cottrill did not offer an interpretation of what he had found, but the difficulty of interpreting the various features was clearly stated in the article in the *Morning Post*. At that time the purpose of only the great (second) basilica and forum had been identified:

'Inside the forum, however, and almost adjoining the basilica, there has been discovered another Roman building, of apparently the same date. This is completely baffling the experts at present.

'No other forum in the Empire . . . has a building inside it, unless the temple of Claudius, which occupies the central position in the forum at Colchester, be counted.

'Unfortunately the intruder into London's forum occupies what appears to be an entirely haphazard position, except that one wall is parallel to the outer wall of the basilica and almost as close to it as it would be possible to build separately.

'An attempt has been made to "turn it into a temple", but what has been discovered of the building gives little encouragement. From its position it can only be assumed that it was a public building of some kind and one which had somehow failed to get itself reconciled with the town-planning scheme.

'On the same site successive layers of cement floor have been discovered. These layers represent the surface of the open forum at various periods in its history. They are below the level of the unexplained walls so that any possibility that the "mystery" building might have been pulled down to make room for the forum is at once removed.

'The part of the building which has been discovered covers an area measuring 44ft (13.4m) by 80ft (24.38m); but it is evident from the ground-plan that the whole must have been very much larger.

'From a discovery of pottery beneath one wall it is concluded that the building cannot be earlier than the reign of Vespasian, who became Emperor in AD 70; and the general character of the building is stated to be consistent with an origin in the First Century AD.'

Fig. 89   83–87 Gracechurch Street. Plan of Roman features on the site. On the west side was recorded the east end of the first basilica, and at the east end was a wall of the east wing of the second forum.

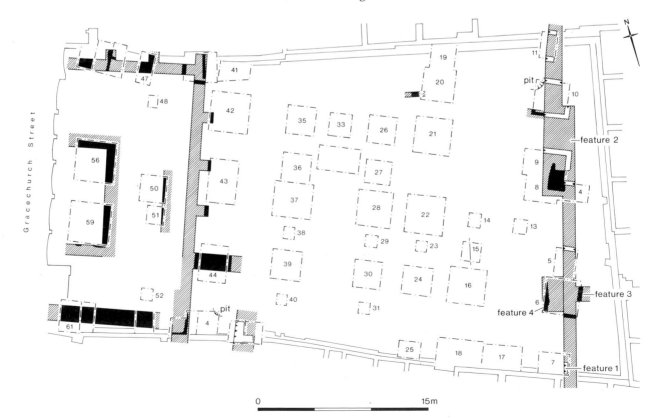

0   15m

However, B. Philp's excavations in 1968–9 on the site of 168 Fenchurch Street not only confirmed the existence of the first forum, but also showed that it had been demolished when the second was completed.[25] Consequently the interpretation of the relationship of the dumped deposits in and around the first basilica must be revised.

The re-assessment of the walls of the first forum, its floors and the dumped deposits will depend upon their relationship to each other. To judge from Cottrill's site records, there is no reason to doubt that the dumped deposits and the floors are later than the construction of the walls of the first forum at the west end of the site, since the deposits seem to have been piled up against the walls.

The dumping was approximately 0.9m thick, and the construction of the rough wall faces covered by these deposits suggested that they had not originally been intended to be seen at that level, and that the dumping was make-up for a raised floor level in the new basilica. The courses of bonding tiles in the zone of dumping were somewhat random and inconsistent in the way in which they were laid; a triple course in one place, and a single course, or even no tiles at all, a little further along the same wall (eg Fig. 91). Also, although the walls were built of ragstone between the bonding courses, Cottrill specifically mentions that the facing stones were undressed and only roughly coursed. Particularly important was the sill of a wide doorway or opening in the south wall of the first basilica, for this was level with the top of the dumped deposits, again indicating that the floor level was intended to lie at the top of the dumping (Fig. 92, sections 2–12). Cottrill actually found the Roman floor overlying both the sill and the dumping, and he also found that the south wall of the first basilica stood above this floor level. This floor, therefore, belonged to the first basilica – forum complex and not to the second. About a metre of tile-work comprising the western door jamb, however, lay beneath the level of the door sill, and this may indicate that the sill was originally lower at the base of the dumped deposits, and had subsequently been raised (Fig. 91). But no trace of this suggested lower sill was noted by Cottrill, and it is unlikely to have existed as a permanent feature, for the walls on either side of the doorway were only roughly faced.

The sequence of occupation and construction on this site is clearly complex, and needs checking, clarification and dating by further excavation. Nevertheless, at this stage it seems likely that the sequence of construction and dumping in the western half of the site was as follows:

(i) Occupation up to the Flavian period, leaving an accumulation of approximately 0.6m of debris overlying the natural brickearth.

(ii) The construction of the first basilica foundations of flint and mortar, with a layer of bonding tiles at the level of the natural brickearth surface.

(iii) The construction on these foundations of a ragstone wall 1.5m high, with undressed stone faces, and some courses of bonding tiles, this height being intended to serve as an additional part of the foundation.

(iv) Since the base of the ragstone wall lay below the 0.6m accumulation of earlier occupation debris, it was necessary to dump a thickness of only 0.9m of clay and gravel to build up the land level for the floor of the first basilica. The building of the basilica seems to have continued while the dumping took place, and resulted in mortar 'floors' at many levels, but primarily at 1.5m and 0.9m below the modern basement floor. The former level overlay the top of the early occupation layers, and the latter was intermediate in the dumping. In a hole dug between trenches 41 and 20 there was found at a depth of 1.2m or 1.5m 'a mass of white material, lime?, with some stones – a place for making cement?'.

(v) Finally a concrete floor was laid over the dumped deposits inside the basilica at a depth of about 0.3m below the modern basement floor.

The First Basilica and Forum

PLAN OF THE BUILDING

The east end of the buttressed building, identified as the first basilica, and the north end of the east wing of the first forum, were recorded on this site (Figs. 89, 90). Their deep foundations gave a fairly complete plan, but unfortunately very little of the superstructure had survived to help with their reconstruction. Nevertheless the basic plan on this site is so similar to basilica buildings excavated in other Roman towns that it may be interpreted with a reasonable degree of confidence.

The basilica was essentially a hall 20.42m wide internally, which had been subdivided by long foundations into a nave and side aisles. Presumably the foundations originally carried stone columns or brick piers to support the roof, forming a nave 8.38m wide, a north aisle 5.64m wide, and a south aisle 4.42m wide. A *tribunal*, which elsewhere was normally a raised dais, probably existed at the east end of the nave, and Wall 9 was probably its front retaining wall.

Since the top of the *basilica* foundations lay at a depth of merely 0.3m below the modern basement little trace of any superstructure had survived. Fortunately the south wall did preserve traces of a doorway about 4.88m wide at the east end of the wall (Figs. 91, 92). This evidently gave access to the basilica from the forum courtyard. The only other evidence of the building that would have been visible to its users were its floors of which few traces remained. In the north aisle and the nave the floor lay at a depth of 0.3m below the modern basement, corresponding with the top of the foundations, and was constructed of cream coloured concrete between 0.18m and 0.23m thick (Fig. 93); and in the doorway beside the south aisle there was an original floor of pink and white cement over a foundation of ragstone and mortar, and subsequently a floor of white cement 0.05m thick. No trace of the superstructure of the forum had survived, except that the top of Wall 3,

the north wall of the east wing, was found to have a course of tiles overlaid by at least 0.025m of pink cement, which was probably the floor in a doorway since cement of this colour was not generally used in the walls of this building.

CONSTRUCTION OF THE FIRST BASILICA AND FORUM

In general the walls of the buildings were of similar construction. Their upper parts were built of roughly faced ragstone, and included courses of bonding tiles; and the foundations, from the level of the natural brickearth downwards for a depth of 2.13m, were built of flints in mortar.

Wall 1 (Figs. 90, 93). The north wall of the basilica was about 1m thick, and was aligned approximately east-west. It survived up to 1.37m below the modern basement floor, at which level there was a course of

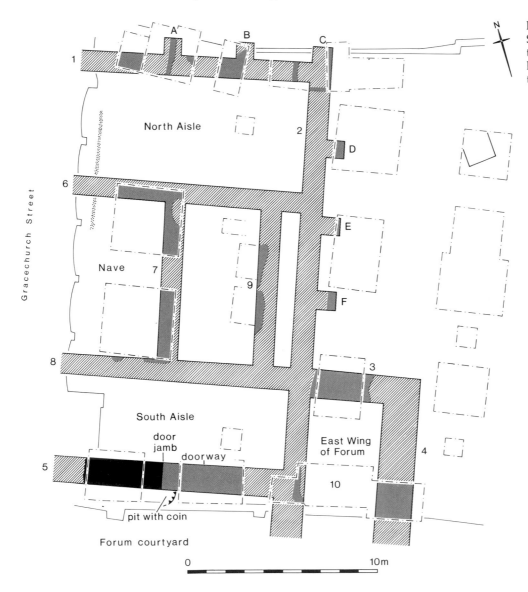

Fig. 90 83–87 Gracechurch Street. Plan of the east end of the first basilica, the walls having been numbered and the buttresses lettered.

bonding tiles. Below this the wall was built of ragstone and buff mortar mixed with flint and chalk. A triple course of bonding tiles, 0.23m in depth, was found between 2.08m and 2.31m below the modern basement, though the construction of the wall was not consistent, for at one point the top of a course of tiles was found at a depth of 1m.

The lowest course of tiles was level with the natural brickearth, and below this the foundation, comprising flint rubble in yellow mortar, extended down to 4.42m below the modern basement.

Buttresses A, B. Two buttresses (A and B), each about 0.91m square, projected from the north wall, and from the level of the natural brickearth upwards were constructed of courses of brickwork set in yellow cement. Below this their foundations, of coursed flint rubble and mortar, were bonded into the wall foundation and extended down to a similar depth (*ie* 4.42m) below the modern cellar floor. The top of Buttress A immediately underlay a modern foundation at a depth of 1.37m below the modern basement level. Beneath this were ten courses of

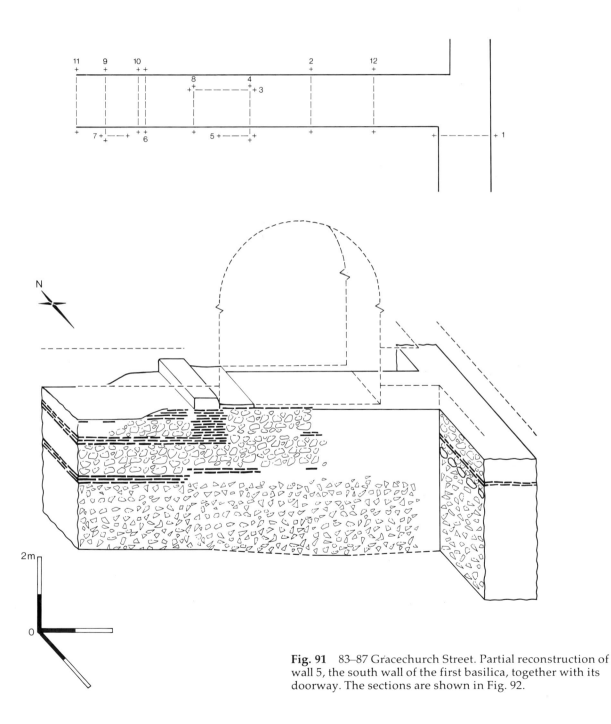

Fig. 91 83–87 Gracechurch Street. Partial reconstruction of wall 5, the south wall of the first basilica, together with its doorway. The sections are shown in Fig. 92.

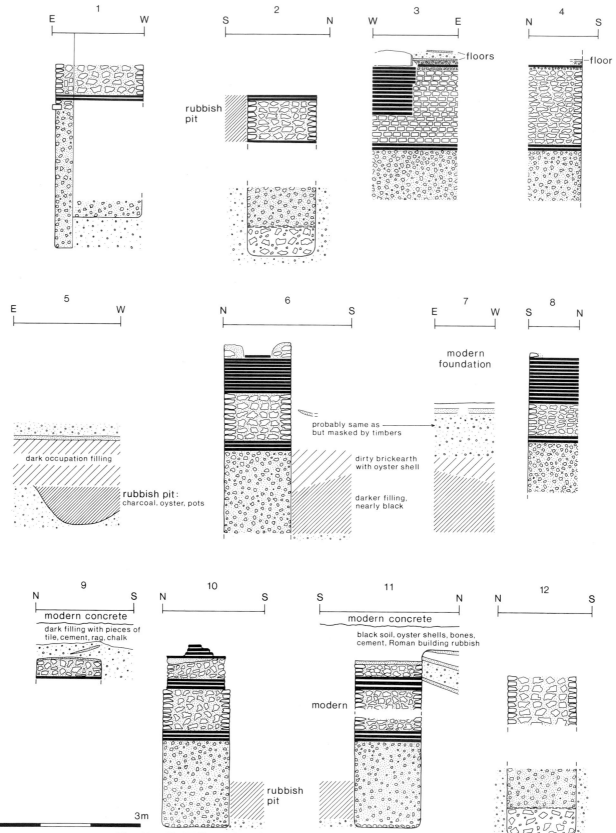

Fig. 92 83–87 Gracechurch Street. Sections associated with wall 5, shown in Fig. 91, all drawn below the same datum, the basement floor of the former office block on the site.

Roman bricks. The top of Buttress B lay at a depth of 1.78m below the modern basement floor, and contained six courses of brickwork.

Wall 2 and Buttress C (Fig. 94).   Only the north end of Wall 2 was examined, and as this included a buttress (C), at the north-east corner of the Roman building, its construction was somewhat different from that of the rest of the building. The east face of the wall survived to a depth of 1.32m below the modern basement floor, and below this, to a depth of 1.57m, were four courses of brick. Ragstone rubble lay between 1.57m and 1.78m beneath which were three courses of bricks from 1.78m to 1.98m. The coursed flint rubble foundation underlay the bricks. A section across the wall immediately south of this showed flint and ragstone rubble at a depth of between 1.68m and 2.05m, below which there was a triple course of tiles from 2.05m to 2.26m, underlain by the flint rubble foundation. There may have been some confusion in the recording at this point since the triple course of tiles does not correspond in the two adjacent sections which were recorded on different occasions. Only the lower part of the foundation of Buttress C had survived, and this was built of roughly coursed flint and mortar.

Buttresses D, E and F (Fig. 94).   These buttresses were about 3m apart, and each was about 0.9m square, projecting from the east wall of the basilica. The top of buttress D lay at 1.52m below the modern basement, below which there were at least seven courses of red tiles in yellow mortar. The bottom of the tiles occurred between 1.83m and 2.2m below the bsaement, though the actual junction between the tiles and the underlying foundation of coursed flint rubble and yellow mortar was not seen. The top of Buttress E was not observed, but its foundation was recorded at a depth of 1.52m below the basement floor. Between a depth of 1.52m and *c* 1.83m were only four courses of tiles, set in yellow mortar; and below this approximate level there existed the flint foundation which extended down to a depth of 4.8m Only the flint and mortar foundation of Buttress F was recorded, and it was of exactly similar construction to the other buttresses on the east wall of the basilica.

Wall 3 (Fig. 94).   This wall was 1.37m thick, and was built of ragstone with courses of bonding tiles above a deep foundation of flints and mortar. The top of the wall lay at 0.46m below the modern basement floor, at which level there was a single course of bonding tiles. Immediately above this was a layer of pink mortar 0.025m thick, perhaps the remnant of a floor overlying the wall. Between 0.46m and 1.22m below the modern basement, the wall was built of roughly coursed ragstone rubble and yellow mortar. Between 1.22m and 1.42m or 1.47m there was a triple course of

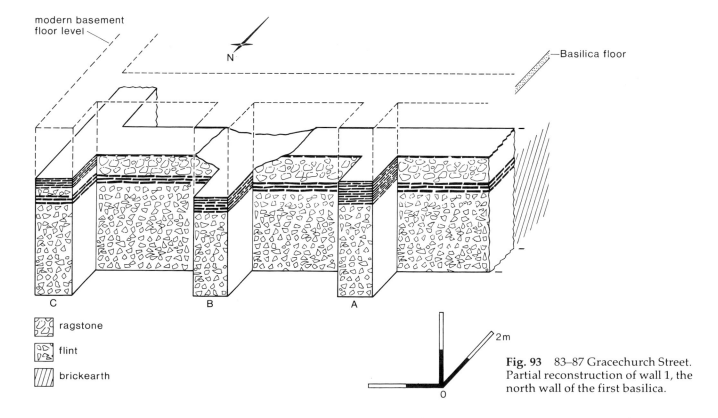

modern basement
floor level

N

Basilica floor

C   B   A

ragstone

flint

brickearth

2m

0

Fig. 93   83–87 Gracechurch Street. Partial reconstruction of wall 1, the north wall of the first basilica.

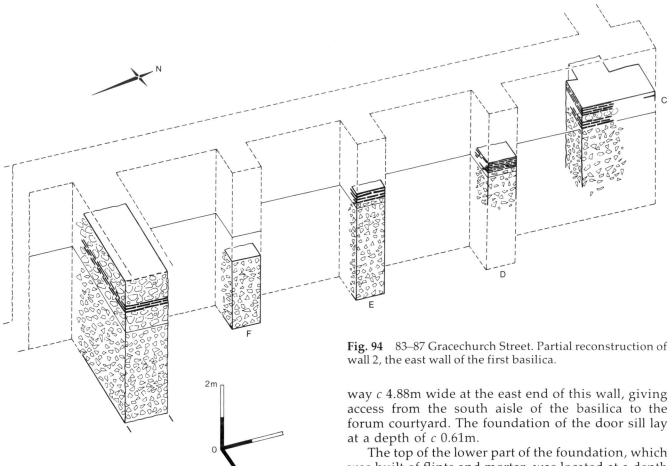

Fig. 94 83–87 Gracechurch Street. Partial reconstruction of wall 2, the east wall of the first basilica.

bonding tiles set in yellow mortar. Between 1.42m and 2.03m the wall was built of more roughly coursed ragstone rubble with some flint chips, set in yellow mortar. The top of the flint foundation lay at 2.03m and extended down to a depth of 4.88m.

Wall 4 (Fig. 90).   At a depth of between 1.68m and 2.9m was exposed a robbed wall, the robber trench at one point being 1.8m wide. The trench had been cut vertically through brickearth, and its filling comprised loose building materials, mostly a loose yellow crumbling cement, some flints and Roman tiles, and also small patches of brickearth. This was presumably the debris of a wall which had been thrown back into the robber trench. There was no indication of the date at which the robbing occurred.

Wall 5 (Figs 91, 92)   formed the south frontage of the first basilica, and overlooked the forum courtyard. Fortunately it was particularly well preserved up to, and slightly above, the floor level of the basilica which here lay at a depth of 0.46m below the modern basement. Originally there was an opening or door-

way *c* 4.88m wide at the east end of this wall, giving access from the south aisle of the basilica to the forum courtyard. The foundation of the door sill lay at a depth of *c* 0.61m.

The top of the lower part of the foundation, which was built of flints and mortar, was located at a depth of between 2.29m and 2.54m, and the foundation descended to a depth of 4.27m or 4.42m. Above this, the foundation was constructed of ragstone, tiles and mortar, except beneath the original doorway sill where there were very few tiles.

The top of the flint foundation was capped by a triple course of tiles at the west end of the wall. But as the wall was traced eastwards towards the area beneath the former door sill the tile course was reduced first to a double, then to a single course, and finally disappeared altogether. Roughly faced ragstone overlay this and supported the most striking feature of the foundation – the thirteen courses of tiles which formerly lay beneath the western door jamb. This mass of tiles extended down from 0.61m the level of the door sill, to 1.52m. The foundation of the wall at this level to the west of the doorway contained a great quantity of tiles and a relatively small amount of ragstone, particularly compared with what lay below the door sill.

A small portion of the western door jamb was found standing to a height of 0.15m above the surface of the Roman mortar floor overlying the door sill. Its core was built with yellowish or pinkish-buff mortar with white particles, but it is not clear if the wall at this level was built of tiles or ragstone. The former seems more likely, though it is curious that no tiles were seen in the section across the core of the wall. A block of ragstone was seen forming part of the south face of the wall close to the jamb. The actual face of the door jamb was seen as a transverse north-south face crossing the east-west wall foundation, and the plaster rendering of pinkish buff mortar with white particles, had a white and slightly uneven surface.

A single course of tiles set in mortar formed the top of the foundation of the door sill at a depth of 0.58m below the modern basement floor. Above this was a layer of mortar and ragstone chips 0.1m thick, serving as a foundation for the floor surface which was of pink and white cement about 0.013m thick. The floor was overlaid by a deposit of sand and gravel 0.13m thick which supported a white cement floor 0.038m thick. The surface of this later floor lay at a depth of 0.3m below the modern basement.

The east side of the doorway was not recorded, but presumably this too contained a mass of tiles in its foundation. Allowing for this it would seem that the doorway was about 4.88m wide.

Wall 6 (Fig. 95) was perhaps intended to be a foundation or sleeper wall for a row of columns supporting the north aisle from the nave. The surviving top of the wall was not observed, so that there is no indication of the form of its upper construction. It had a triple course of bonding tiles at a depth of 2.74m below the modern basement, above which it was built of ragstone rubble, faced, with a few flints. Below the tiles the wall descended to a depth of more than 3.66m. The wall was recorded as being more than 0.74m thick, but a gap for the wall in the Roman basilica floor, at a depth of 0.3m below the modern basement was 1.02m wide, suggesting the original thickness of Wall 6.

Wall 7 (Fig. 95) was located at a depth of 1.52m and also may be interpreted as a foundation wall. At a depth of 1.52m there was a triple course of tiles 0.18m thick, and in the 1.07m below there were nine courses of undressed ragstone which formed a rough face. The core of the wall behind this rough face was flint rubble with some ragstone. At a depth of 2.72m

Fig. 95 83–87 Gracechurch Street. Composite sections across the first basilica.

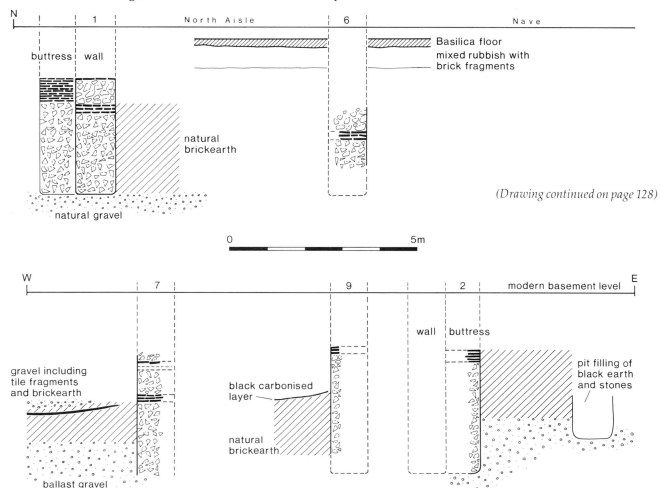

(Drawing continued on page 128)

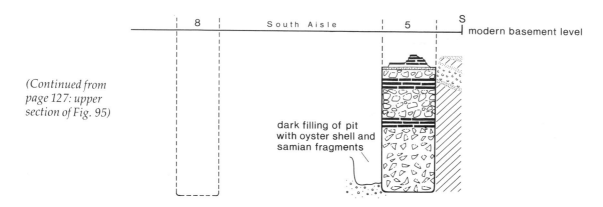

(Continued from
page 127: upper
section of Fig. 95)

dark filling of pit
with oyster shell and
samian fragments

was the top of another triple course of bonding tiles, below which there was a foundation of coursed flint rubble to a depth of 4.88m. This wall was more than 0.71m thick.

Wall 8 (Fig. 90)   was not uncovered, but was located in two places by probing into the side of a contractor's excavation. This too was perhaps a foundation or sleeper wall supporting columns which may have separated the nave from the south aisle of the building.

Wall 9 (Fig. 95)   was uncovered at a depth of 1.42m at which level was the top of a triple course of bonding tiles. Ragstone rubble underlay this down to a depth of about 1.83m below the modern basement floor. The foundation of flint rubble and yellow mortar lay beneath this and extended down to a depth of 4.27m.

The purpose of this wall may be interpreted as a front retaining wall for the *tribunal* at this east end of the basilica.

Wall 10 (Fig. 90).   Within the north end of the east wing of the first forum was found an 'irregular mass of rubble masonry' comprising flints and fragments of Roman bricks. It lay at a depth of 1.3m, and was about 1.2m wide (E-W). It did not extend into nearby trenches, and therefore may have been a pier, perhaps the base of a monument of some kind.

FLOORS IN THE FIRST BASILICA AND FORUM

Traces of cement layers inside the basilica were mostly indistinct, and since they occurred between individual dumps of clay they were probably temporary surfaces associated with the construction of the building. For example, in one section just south of Buttress A a 'pebble cement floor' was observed at a depth of 0.91m; and 'a trace of cement' was observed at a depth of between 1.37m and 2m between a thick dump of almost clean brickearth and a deposit of black occupation debris.

In contrast, the basilica floor was a much more solid structure, and was observed on this site at the extreme west end of the north aisle, at a depth of 0.3m (Fig. 95). A north-south section across the north aisle revealed the floor, of cream coloured cement with occasional Roman brick fragments and between 0.178m and 0.228m thick. The surface of the floor lay only 0.3m below the modern basement, and beneath it was mixed rubbish containing fragments of Roman bricks.

This floor was traced across the northern part of the nave at the same level; and although the wall separating the nave from the north aisle had been robbed (Wall 6), its position was indicated by a gap in the floor 1.02m wide in which there was a recent filling. The basilica floor in the north aisle extended up to this trench and finished on a vertical line.

The only other piece of the basilica floor was found in the doorway in the south wall of the south aisle (Wall 5). Immediately overlying the ragstone and concrete door sill was a floor of pink and white cement 0.013m thick overlying a layer of mortar and ragstone chips 0.1m thick (Fig. 92, Section 3). The surface of the floor lay at a depth of 0.46m below the modern basement, and above it was a subsequent floor of white cement 0.05m thick, whose surface lay at a depth of 0.3m below the modern basement. Between the two Roman floors was a layer of sand and gravel 0.13m thick.

A doorway may have existed at the north wall of the east wing of the forum (Wall 3), for above a course of tiles 0.46m below the modern basement was a layer of pink cement 0.025m thick, possibly a floor.

CENTRAL AND EASTERN PARTS OF THE SITE

A number of Roman structures, mostly walls, were found in the central and eastern parts of the site, but unfortunately none was either related to the associated stratigraphy or dated by any objects (Fig. 89). Although the archaeological record was fragmentary, the difficulty of correlating the features was increased both by the method of digging in small holes, and by the fact that some of the Roman walls had been robbed of building materials, probably in medieval times. Nevertheless it is clear that a masonry building or buildings had existed in the central and eastern parts of the site, perhaps contemporary with the first basilica, and that part of the east wing of the second forum had been built there too. In general the structures by themselves make little sense because their plan is too fragmentary, but the wall of the second forum is identified because it fits so well into what is known of the plan and construction of that building as found on adjoining sites.

Feature 1. A wall identified as part of the inner portico of the second forum, and which once probably supported a colonnade or arcade overlooking the forum courtyard. This wall was aligned roughly north-south and was 1.0m wide. It had been mostly robbed and the trench filled with dark stony rubbish. The lower part of its foundation had survived in places, and was built of ragstone and yellow mortar. Its base lay at a depth of about 3m below the modern basement, and had been dug through the natural brickearth to the top of the underlying natural gravel.

Feature 2. This was another wall aligned approximately north-south, but although no straight joint was noted between it and Feature 1, it is likely to have been a separate construction as occurred in other parts of the forum. There are several reasons for suspecting this: firstly because it had been built immediately beside the wall Feature 1; secondly because it was 1.24m wide, which is much broader than Feature 1; and thirdly because the level of the bottom of its robbed foundation was not quite as deep as the bottom of Feature 1. Its construction, of ragstone and soft yellow mortar, is somewhat similar to Feature 1, and there is no clue to which was the earlier wall. It too had been mostly robbed, probably during the Middle Ages.

Feature 3. This wall was aligned roughly east-west, and was seen in the side of a builders' trench. It was 1.32m wide, and was recorded between depths of 2.4m and 3.8m the latter depth being the level of its base. The foundation was built of ragstone and yellow mortar and the upper part of the wall had been robbed. This wall was originally located in the portico area, and if contemporary with the second forum is likely to have been the base of a monument of some kind.

Feature 4. A massive Roman foundation without any vertical faces was observed close to the wall, Feature 1. It was recorded between depths of 1.2m and its base at 2.9m. The upper part was built of

undressed ragstone, yellow mortar and occasional tiles, and overlay a single course of bonding tiles at a depth of 1.93m. Below this the foundation was built of ragstone 'with interstices completely filled with pinkish-buff mortar'. A pit had been dug into the upper part of the foundation, suggesting that it might have been robbed. There is no reason to think that this was a buttress-like projection of the forum foundation, Feature 1.

Feature 5. A ragstone foundation more than 0.29m thick was disclosed in the south-west corner of trench 10 (Fig. 89). It seemed to form the corner of a wall or pier, and was recorded at a depth of 2.28m, its base lying at 2.7m below the modern basement, on top of the natural gravel. It was overlaid by a later disturbance.

Feature 6. This was a wall of ragstone rubble and yellow mortar with flint pebbles, which was aligned approximately east-west. It was found in the south-west corner of trench 10 and may have been a continuation of Feature 5. The wall was 0.43m thick and was exposed from a depth of 0.3m to 0.6m below the modern basement. On its south side and at a depth of 0.68m was a cement floor containing Roman brick fragments. Since the level of this floor was so shallow it is likely that it was contemporary with the first basilica.

Feature 7. In an underpinning hole at the northern edge of the site north of trench 33, was found a rough pier of Roman brickwork laid irregularly in light-red cement. Its depth was probably at about 1.3m.

Feature 8. A 'rectangular cavity' was recorded in the brickearth at a depth of between 2.13m and 3m in trench 35. Its purpose is not known, but it was filled with black soil and was probably originally wood-lined. The rectangular feature measured 1.47m wide and more than 1.83m long, and cannot be assumed to have been a well since wells in London were usually not more than 1.20m square.

Site 15.   15–18 Lime Street, 1932

SUMMARY *(Fig. 96)*

There was evidence of 1st century occupation continuing into the Flavian period, after which a major north-south road and, apparently, the second forum were built. Traces of an undated building were found to the east of the road, and a sunken room suggests that this could have been a bath. A major fire swept across the site subsequently, after which a building with a plain mosaic floor was built.

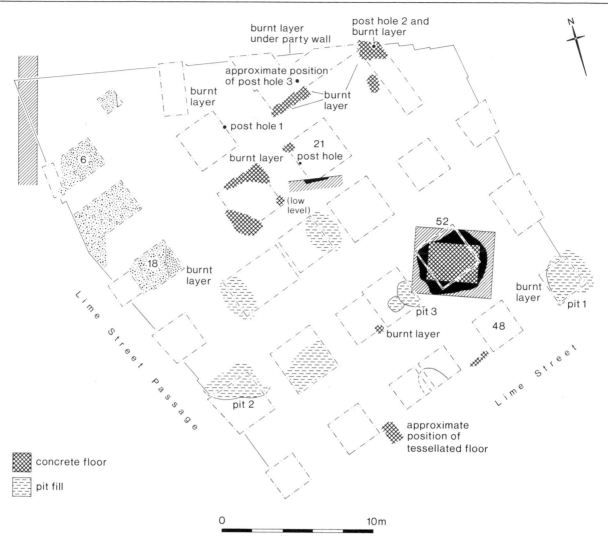

Fig. 96 15–18 Lime Street. Plan of all of the Roman features recorded. Only small portions of the forum wall in the N.W. corner of the site were found (Fig. 97), and are here shown as conjectured.

INTRODUCTION

This site was investigated in 1932 by Frank Cottrill, whose records are now deposited in the Museum of London. Although the recovered pottery was held at the Guildhall Museum it has since been lost. Fortunately the coins were stored with the site notes and are now at the Museum of London, together with Cottrill's drawings of significant pottery sherds. All depths of deposits on the site were recorded in relation to the then basement of the building which had just been demolished, and which apparently lay at 4.88m below street level.[26] The pavement level at the south end of the site lay at 17.44m OD and at the north-west corner of the site at 17.79m OD. The basement therefore lay roughly at 17.62m OD. A short note about this site was published in the *Journal of Roman Studies*.[27]

GEOLOGY

The natural surface of the site was brickearth which in places had been much disturbed by rubbish pits. In general, however, it lay at about 1.8m below the basement floor, but in many places was at 2.1–2.4m. The brickearth overlay the natural sand and gravel whose top lay at about 2.9m below the modern basement.

THE EARLIEST OCCUPATION

Little trace of the earliest occupation was recorded, but, at least in the northern half of the site, the natural brickearth was apparently covered by up to 0.6m of occupation debris – black carbonised deposits, dirty brickearth and clean brickearth containing charcoal and pieces of burnt daub. Fragments of

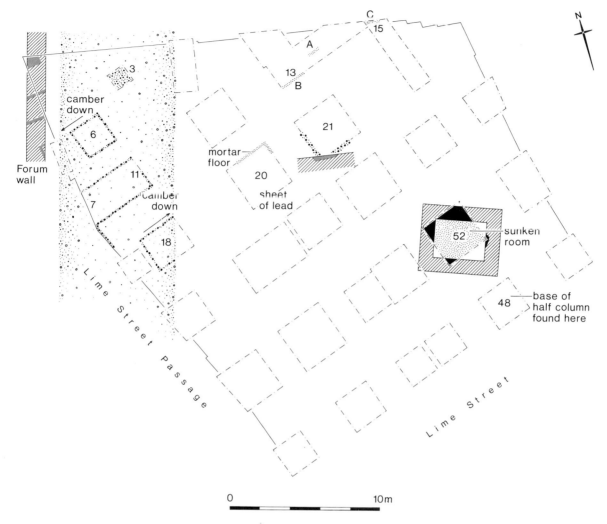

Fig. 97 15–18 Lime Street. Plan of the major Roman features. On the west side is the east wall of the second forum, and beside it a north-south street. The date of the sunken room within the Roman period is not known.

1st-century pottery were found in these deposits, and associated with this phase were some rubbish pits. There was no indication of the nature of the occupation, and no trace of the Boudican burnt layer, suggesting that the site was not then exclusively occupied by buildings. Samian ware stamps apparently of the potters PONTVS and PERRVS, were found in the early deposits, together with coarse pottery of the Flavian period, indicating that this phase of occupation continued until that period.

MAJOR ROMAN FEATURES

Five major groups of structural features were identified which could not be precisely dated, and their relationship remains unknown. However, it seems that they overlay the earliest occupation deposits and

preceded a major fire which swept across the site. The features included a major north-south road which lay adjacent to a wall of the second forum, while on the eastern side were traces of mortar floors, a wall and a sunken room, perhaps of a bath.

1. The Street (Fig. 97). The north-south street flanking the east side of the second forum was traced in the northern part of this site. It was a little over 7m wide, though no side ditches were noted, and was built of hard rammed gravel metalling. No satisfactory cross-section was recorded, but cambered surfaces were sketched in trenches 6 and 18, indicating that the crown of the road lay between them. The bottom of the street lay at a depth of about 1.47m from the modern basement, and survived to a thickness of about 1.07m. The street overlay earlier occupation deposits, including partly filled pits, from which pottery of the Flavian and earlier periods was recovered, including the samian ware already mentioned (bearing stamps of PONTVS, AD 65–95, and PERRVS, AD 55–75) and a coin of Nero of AD 64–68. The street, therefore, was probably constructed after *c* AD 80, at which time the gravel was dumped to fill the pits and hollows to a depth of up to 2.64m thick, though it was seen to overlie the natural surface in places.

2. Forum Wall (Fig. 97). The foundation of the easternmost wall of the second forum was exposed in three trenches at the north-western end of the site. It was 1.2m wide and built of ragstone, some tile fragments and cement. In the central trench the base of the foundation lay at a depth of 2.6m, just above the junction of the natural brickearth and the underlying gravel. The bottom 0.46m of the foundation was constructed of ragstone and tile with layers of cement 0.08m thick. In the southernmost trench the base of the foundation lay at 3.35m–3.5m, but there is no clear reason why this was 0.9m lower than the base in the central trench.

3. The Sunken Room (Fig. 97). On the eastern side of the street a small room, measuring internally 3.5m × 2.54m, was disclosed in trench 52, and was apparently sunken, perhaps for a cold bath or a hypocaust. Its walls, 0.46m wide on the north side, were constructed of tiles, some of which were flanged. A rendering of pinkish cement 38mm thick overlay the internal faces of the walls. The floor itself lay at a depth of 3.66m and was of cement, apparently 0.46m thick, and built on yellow sand. No evidence of *pilae* was noted, suggesting that it was a bath rather than a hypocaust. An 'occupation level' at least 0.6m thick overlay the floor and walls and contained pottery which included a 1st-century sherd of a samian ware form 15/17. This occupation layer continued at a higher level beyond the north wall of the room. The notes suggest that the walls were not standing to any appreciable height, perhaps less than 0.6m.

4. A Wall and a Half Column (Fig. 97). The side of a wall was seen in trench 21 at a depth of 1.52m, and the base of its foundation lay at 2.13m. It is not known how high the wall stood, for at that level it seems to have been simply a foundation. Its construction of tiles, 38mm thick, and irregularly laid in brownish-yellow mortar, suggests that it was part of the building which contained the sunken room. A cement floor was disclosed on its north side at a depth of 1.52m, overlying about 0.6m of gravel layers which in section resembled part of a Roman street. Since the gravel did not appear in other trenches nearby, this is unlikely to have been the case.

The base of a half-column was found in trench 48

at a depth of 1.2m. No further details are known except that there was no sign of any associated walls, and that the top of the natural brickearth lay at 2.13m.

5. Mortar Floors. Traces of mortar floors were also found to the east of the main road, and may have been part of the building with the sunken room. In trenches 13 and 15 floors were found at A, B and C (Fig. 97) as follows: at 'A' was noted a floor of soft mortar 30mm. thick at a depth of 1.52m, overlying a dirty brickearth occupation level which in turn overlay the natural brickearth. At 'B' a floor of mortar and crushed brick 0.076m thick was recorded at a depth of 1.04m above the layer of gravel. It was overlaid by a deposit of brickearth 0.25m thick, which was in turn covered by a burnt layer 2.5m thick. A coin of Nero was found about 0.9m below the floor.

A mortar floor 5–8cm thick was found in trench 20 at a depth of 0.9–1.2m. Its construction included crushed brick, and it overlay about 0.3m of brickearth and gravel, and was itself overlaid by 0.15m of black occupation debris above which was a layer of burnt materials.

THE FIRE LAYER

Traces of red burnt fire debris were noted in some holes at depths between 0.46m and 1.23m below the modern cellar floor (Fig. 98). It is likely that this resulted from a major conflagration which swept across the site during the Roman period, but its date was not established.

In trench 8 the red burnt fire layer was 0.2m thick and lay at a depth of 0.6m. In trenches 9 and 13 burnt debris 0.3m thick contained occasional fragments of wall plaster, and overlay 6mm of charcoal. The bottom of the burnt layer was at a depth of 0.76m. In trench 15, at 'C', a burnt layer occurred between 1.2m and 1.5m and contained a fragment of a ring-necked flagon of 1st–2nd century type. In an unassigned trench, possibly nearby, a burnt layer 0.3m thick and containing tiles was found at a depth of about 0.75m, and this overlay a mortar floor 0.15m thick which included crushed brick. In trench 20 the top of a red burnt layer 0.15m thick lay at a depth of 0.9m. The fire layer occurred at a similar depth in trench 50, but in trench 52 it was found at a depth of about 2.44m, which was about 1.22m above the floor of the sunken room. The greater depth of the burning in this trench may have been due to the sunken room below.

LATER ROMAN BUILDING

Portions of Roman floors were found at levels above the fire debris, showing that a building or buildings of some pretentions had been built on the site after

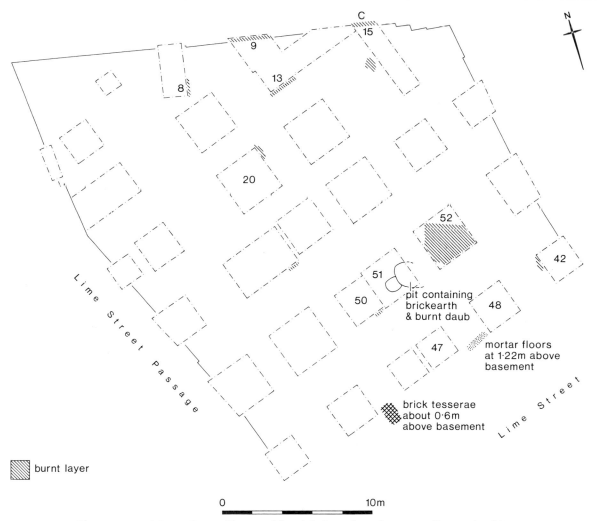

Fig. 98 15–18 Lime Street. Traces of fire debris and a subsequent Roman building.

the fire (Fig. 98). In trench 20 a floor of white cement 0.1m thick and containing crushed brick was found at a depth of about 0.6m (*ie* at 0.3m above the burnt layer). Construction work along the frontage of Lime Street gave an opportunity for some deposits above the basement level to be examined. Workmen reported that between trench 45 and 46 a floor of brick *tesserae* was found at about 0.6m above the basement level; and F. Cottrill recorded a yellow cement floor between trenches 47 and 48 at 1.22m above the basement level. The cement included lumps of brick, and the floor was 0.05m thick. This floor was overlaid by 27mm of pebbles and lumps of brick, and also by a thin layer of mussel shells above which was another cement floor 0.05m thick. Dark clayey soil with charcoal flecks and a layer of bones underlay the lowest floor.

Site 16. Lombard Street, South of All Hallows church, 1933

A 3.7m length of Roman wall was recorded by Frank Cottrill under the north pavement of Lombard Street in October, 1933. To judge from its location it was apparently part of the south or outer wall of the outer portico of the second forum.

The wall lay about 3.35m east of the former entry leading to All Hallows church, while the west end of its north face was situated 2.13m south of the then street frontage, and its east end a few centimetres less.

The top of the wall was overlaid by modern concrete at a depth of 2.13m. The wall itself was built of bricks and extended down another 1.22m, beneath which was a foundation of ragstone rubble more than 0.69m in depth.

The wall was 1.22m thick, and was constructed with red and yellow bricks, each measuring 0.28m × 0.43m × 0.04m, with joints of 0.03m, set in buff cement. The core of the wall was a mixture of courses of tiles and ragstone. An offset of 0.2m occurred on the north face at a depth of 2.95m below the modern pavement. The ragstone foundation was a few inches wider than the brick wall above.

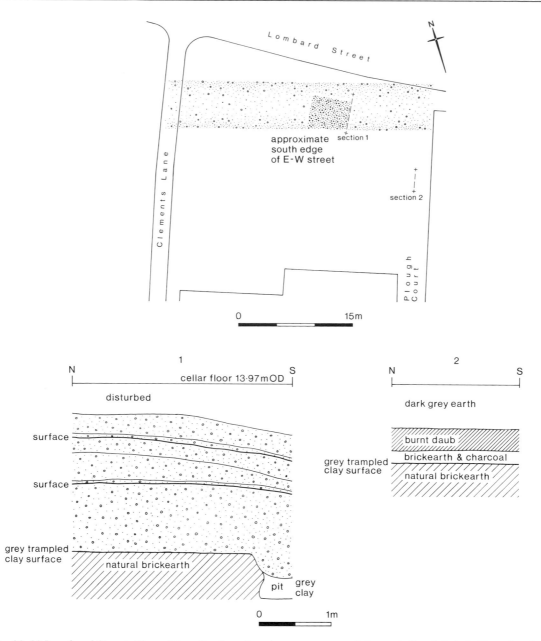

Fig. 99 30–32 Lombard Street. Plan of the site showing the Roman street, the dense stippling showing where the gravel metalling was found. Also sections through the street and through fire debris believed to be of Boudican date, showing that the street is of pre-Boudican origin. The depth of section 2 below the cellar floor is not known.

Site 17.   30–32 Lombard Street, 1962

The rebuilding of this site in 1962–3 was preceded by a rapid and deep mechanical excavation, with the result that the archaeological deposits on the entire site were quickly destroyed and only a very limited record could be made. Nevertheless it was possible to record a major east-west Roman street, south of which were found traces of buildings that had evidently been destroyed by Boudica in AD 60 (Fig. 99).

GEOLOGY

The natural subsoil was brickearth, a spot level on the natural surface under the Roman street at the north end of the site being at about 11.3m above OD. A borehole at the south end of the site close to Clements Lane showed that the brickearth was 0.6–0.9m thick and that it overlay river gravels. The base of the gravel, where it overlay the London Clay, lay at about 6.4m OD at the south end of the site, while at the north end, under the Roman road, it lay at about 3m OD. Clearly the base of the gravel dipped down from south to north.

THE ROMAN STREET

The Roman street was roughly aligned east-west and was clearly the main street beside the south frontage of the forum. The street was built of layers of hard rammed gravel metalling which survived to a height of 1.9m above its base. The north side of the street beside the forum had been destroyed by modern foundations, but the southern edge was indicated by an apparent gradual merging of gravel and earth deposits. As it was not possible to clean the section, many details of the street construction are unknown, including whether or not there was a street-side ditch. But that a ditch might have existed, at least during the early period, is suggested by the gravel-filled hollow recorded in the rapidly drawn section (Fig. 99, Section 1). The width of the street was more than 4.6m, and its many re-metallings show that it was much used and required frequent re-surfacing during the Roman period. Several cambered surfaces each with a thin dark silty layer above them were much in evidence, the silt presumably having been deposited by traffic.

The earliest layer of gravel metalling overlay the trampled grey surface of the natural brickearth which, with a pit filled with grey clay (Fig. 99, Section 1), is witness to some occupation of the area before the street was constructed.

THE FIRE DEPOSIT

During the mechanical excavation a layer of red burnt daub was frequently observed over much of the area south of the Roman street; as this deposit lay close to the natural surface it seems likely that it represented the Boudican destruction of AD 60.

On the east side of the site a section which included the burnt layer was recorded (Fig. 99, Section 2), and confirmed the early dating for the deposit lay only 0.2m above the natural surface. The natural brickearth was initially overlaid by a grey trampled clay surface such as was found beneath the Roman street, but here it was covered by a dump of brickearth containing a scatter of charcoal. This was in turn overlaid by a deposit of red burnt daub 0.3m thick, while above that was a deposit of dark grey earth.

The burnt daub layer was not dated by any artifacts, but its depth indicates its early date. The building that it represents evidently had wattle and daub walls, but as these had been rendered with painted plaster, burnt fragments of which were found in the daub layer, the building was presumably of Roman rather than native type.

The man-made deposit of brickearth and charcoal lying *beneath* the burnt deposit was presumably of Claudian-Neronian date, and represented the make-up for the earliest building. The lowest levels of street metalling in Section 1 must therefore be of equally early date, and it would appear from the evidence on this site that the main east-west street was one of the earliest features of Roman London – evidently pre-dating the Boudican destruction of AD 60.

Site 18.   All Hallows, Lombard Street, 1939
by Adrian Oswald (written about 1946)

INTRODUCTION

The demolition of the Wren Church of All Hallows, Lombard Street, in 1939 for the purpose of an extension to Barclay's Bank, although greatly regretted by lovers of City Churches, provided an excellent opportunity of observing not merely the site of a Saxon foundation but a portion of the baffling forum area of Roman London.

The Guildhall Museum provided the writer as an observer and the Society of Antiquaries made a grant by which it was possible to do some short but vital excavation in the bitter winter of 1939–40. In addition Messrs J.W. Bloe, FSA and the late Francis Taylor, representing the London and Middlesex Archaeological Society, were early in the field and have published their valuable comments on their visits in that Society's *Journal*.[28] An earlier note by the writer may be found in the *Antiquaries Journal*.[29] Full acknowledgements and thanks are due to the late Sir Arthur Clapham and Sir Mortimer Wheeler for their valuable advice, to my late colleague, Quintin Waddington and to the Directors of Barclay's Bank and their architects and contractors.

ROMAN FOUNDATION AND FINDS

The Roman discoveries on the site are the result almost entirely of observation since it was deemed of greater importance to concentrate on the early church in the scanty time available (3 weeks) for planned excavation. Hence chronology is uncertain and the whole of the Roman finds are tantalisingly incomplete. Three different alignments of walls could be seen in the forum area: first, the alignment of the [second] Basilica itself represented by the wall north of Corbet Court; secondly, the building south of Corbet Court and on the opposite side of Gracechurch Street; and, lastly, the walls of the columned building on the All Hallows site and in Lombard Street.[30]

Two of these alignments (Fig. 100), the first and the last, were found in the All Hallows site together

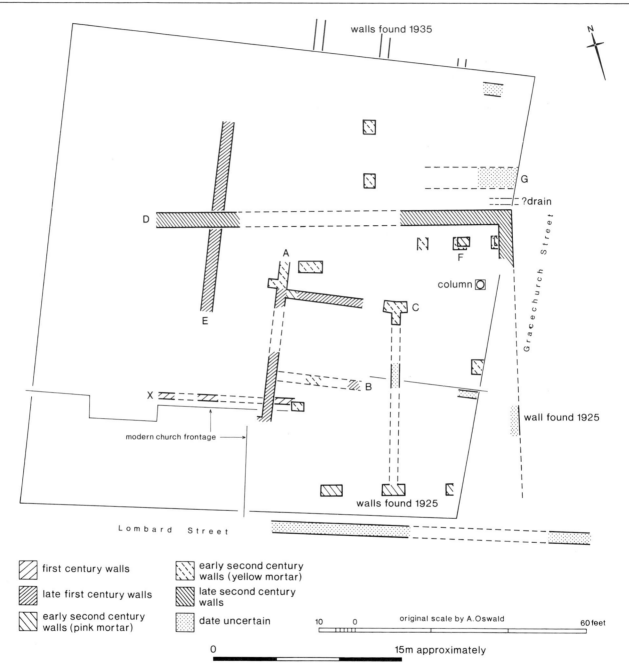

Fig. 100 All Hallows, Lombard Street. Copy of a plan by Adrian Oswald showing all Roman structures found on the site. The metric scale was added in 1986 and is based upon the original irregular imperial scale used on the plan (shown).

with some traces of an earlier wall on yet a different axis.

In seeking to date these walls the main clue was the thin white cement layer found distinctively all over the site and shown on the type section (Fig. 101). This layer was also noted in 1935 by Mr Cottrill on the site immediately to the north (*ie* 17–19 Gracechurch Street, p. 107). It will be seen that it rested on some two feet of sand or builder's rubbish

from which the latest dateable material recovered was a samian sherd of form 18 stamped AVENT (dated Hadrian-Antonine), a form 37 style of FRONTINUS (dated Nero-Trajan) and a small fragment of form 29 style of MEDETVS *c* AD 90–100. On this evidence the white cement floor is unlikely to be earlier than the reign of Hadrian. Quite possibly it represents a deliberate levelling and making up of the area.

The determination of the date of this layer is of the greatest importance in trying to fix the date of the building with square brick piers. The two easternmost of these piers had additions place unsymmetrically on the original bases. These additions were carried out in brick set in pink mortar, as distinct from the original bases in which the mortar was yellow. The white cement layer covered the original yellow mortar bases but stopped flush with the pink mortar additions. It is evident that the pink mortar additions to the piers post-dated or were contemporary with the white cement layers.

With regard to the other walls (Fig. 100) the white cement layer passed over the north-south wall (A) in the basilican alignment – and over wall B (brick and yellow mortar comparable with the bases of the piers). However, it stopped flush with the T-shaped pier (C).

This pier, planned to correspond with the alignments of both buildings, was clearly the connecting link between the two. The western arm aligned with the north-south walls which, in turn, were on the alignment of the basilica; the eastern and southern arms matched with the columned building. This pier was a mixture of brick and rag with yellow mortar and the peculiar angle was certainly due to an addition to an existing wall on the basilican alignment. In the yellow mortar at the angled junction a *quadrans* of Hadrian in excellent condition was found. This is the sole clue to the date of the yellow mortared brickwork of this pier which, on structure and alignment, corresponded closely with buildings found in Lombard Street in 1925 (Plate 7).[31] The piers of this building were of brick and set in pink mortar, the wall to the south of stone with courses of brick in yellow mortar. There is some sound reason for relating these Lombard Street footings to the piers on the All Hallows site. The use of each other's footings makes it also probable that the lapse of time between the buildings in the Basilican alignment, the yellow mortared bases and the pink mortar superstructure was relatively short. The relationship of the 4ft (1.2m) wall (D) with the north-south wall (E) on the basilican alignment must now be considered. Wall E had been heavily robbed over most of its length. The robbing contained exclusively Roman pottery of which the latest might be dated to about the end of the second century – some was recovered in what appeared to be the base of a pit which had been sunk into the robbed wall. The mortar was yellow with ragstone and some yellow tile. Wall D, also heavily robbed, had a foundation trench 2ft (0.6m) higher than that of E and had certainly been cut subsequently.

The white cement floor was noted to the east of wall E, south-east and north-west of the junction between wall E and D a substantial layer of burnt material with quantities of red brick and daub was

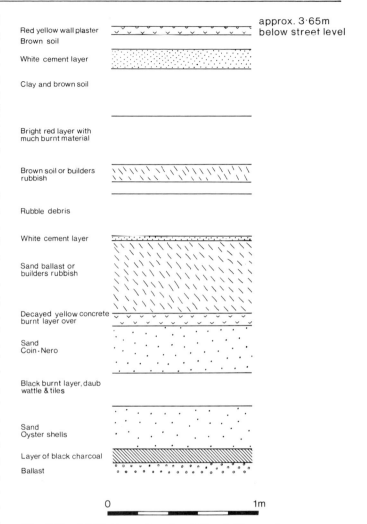

Fig. 101 All Hallows, Lombard Street. Copy of a composite section through Roman strata on the site, by A. Oswald.

observed. This layer, which varied in thickness from 6in–1ft (0.1–0.3m), had been covered in places by 1–2ft (0.3–0.6m) of clean sand or builder's rubbish as make up. Some fragments of mica dusted ware similar to that found in the kilns at Copthall Court, working *c* AD 80–120, were found in this layer, which covered the filling of the large pit in the north-east corner which, in turn, contained pottery of AD 70–90.

It is tempting to relate this red burnt layer to a similar layer noticed by Mr Cottrill to the north of the site, with the Hadrianic burnt layers found elsewhere in the city.

The dating evidence is slight, but suggests that these walls in the basilican alignment were erected at the end of the first or the beginning of the second century. Wall D was standing to a considerable height at the east end of the site where it was constructed of brick with pink mortar and a bonding course of rag (Plate 16). From below it came a

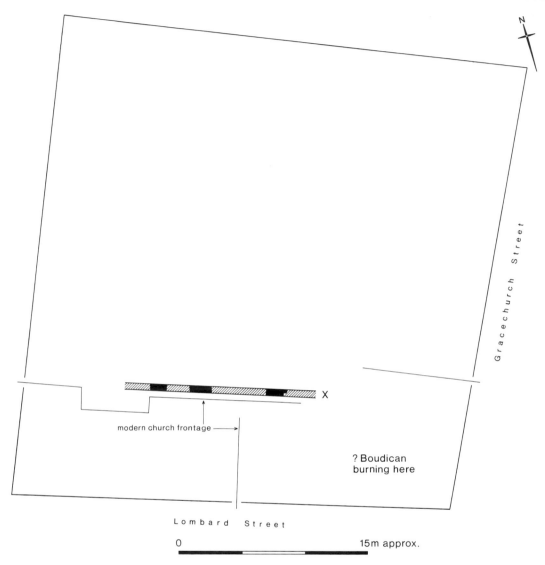

Fig. 102 All Hallows, Lombard Street. Plan showing the earliest wall found on the site.

fragment of samian ware of form 38. On the whole, a late or post second century date for this wall seems probable.

The only other wall for which any sort of date could be postulated was wall G. This had been robbed where encountered and merely comprised ragstone rubble left in the ghost trench. This trench cut through a burnt layer attributable to the Boudican destruction, but was covered by 2ft (0.6m) of yellow sand on which a concrete floor had been placed. From this floor pottery of AD 70–90 was recovered.

Something must be said about the pillar base and core of a column recovered at the eastern end of the site. Both rested on the white cement floor in a mass of building rubble. The column base (since lost) was about 2ft 6in (0.76m) across (Plate 17). The core still

retained a facing of white wall plaster. This column was apparently part of one of the pink mortar bases and was the only Roman architectural feature from the site.

The dates of the other walls on the site could not be ascertained even approximately.

The earliest levels were only reached in a few places, mainly in the underpinning holes in the south and east of the site. The type section shows the general sequence with a marked burnt layer which on pottery evidence and position may represent the Boudican destruction. At some points there was a still lower burnt level containing oyster shell, a little wheel-turned bead-rim pottery and a samian fragment of form 29 style of LICINVS dated AD 45–50. At 25ft (7.6m) below street level this layer apparently represented the earliest occupation on the site. A

Fig. 103 All Hallows, Lombard Street. Plan to show the south-west corner of the first forum. The significance of wall E is not understood.

decayed yellow concrete floor above the possible Boudican burnt layer from which some Flavian potter was recovered may perhaps be linked with the buildings in the basilican alignment.

Such were the unsatisfactory (recoverable) Roman details from the site. The loss on the way by enemy action of much of the excavated pottery accounts for some of the considerable vagueness of these observations.

All Hallows, Lombard Street, 1939
A footnote by Peter Marsden

Although Adrian Oswald's report clearly shows that he was seeking to understand the structures on this site, and in the light of subsequent discoveries on nearby sites the significance of the information now seems clear. Indeed, it is remarkable that Oswald

managed to discover the relationships between the main building phases so that it was clear that wall 'B' (Fig. 102) was the earliest structure found on the site and seems to be part of a post-Boudican building that was also found at 54–58 Lombard Street (see p. 144). This was followed by the first forum, walls 'A' (Fig. 103), but in this phase wall 'E' does not obviously fit any pattern. The rebuilding phase of piers (Fig. 104) in the first forum followed next, but pier 'C' is a little uncertain and seems to belong to two phases – both the piers phase and the second forum phase – since it follows two different alignments. Finally, wall 'D' represents the second forum phase (Fig. 105), with pier 'F' and the pier immediately to its east apparently being part of the row of piers that stood on the north side of the inner portico of the second forum (see p. 63).

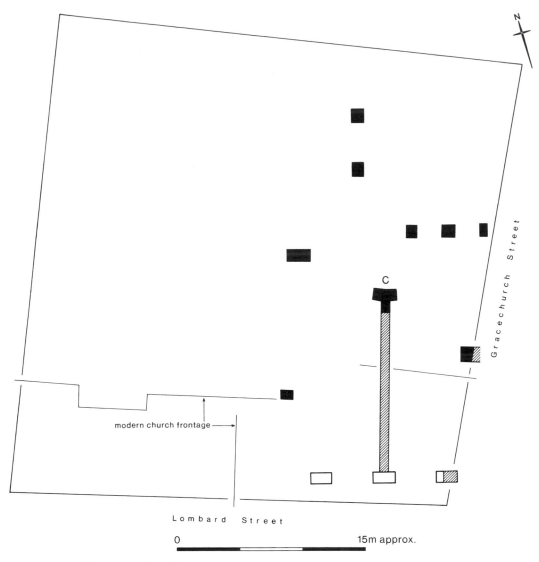

Fig. 104 All Hallows, Lombard Street. Plan to show the phase of piers associated with the first forum.

Site 19.   54–58 Lombard Street, 1960

INTRODUCTION

The Roman deposits were deeply disturbed by the massive concrete foundations of Barclay's Bank, which had previously occupied the site. During its rebuilding in 1960 all the remaining archaeological strata were removed, mostly by two mechanical excavators operating simultaneously and at such a speed that it was impossible to record the ancient features that had survived. At the southern edge of the site, however, a series of large and deep foundation trenches had to be dug by hand, and in these it was possible for Peter Marsden to record some Roman features (Fig. 106).

SUMMARY

Only the southern part of this site is described in this report, the remainder being described under 17–19 Gracechurch Street (p. 113). Evidence of the initial occupation was in the form of a drainage ditch and rubbish pits dating from about the middle of the first century, and it seems that the investigated area was not built-up until after the Boudican revolt. Traces of burnt debris attributable to the destruction of AD 60 were found, but these had clearly been dumped after the fire.

During the Flavian period a stone building with several rooms was constructed beside the main east-west street, and apparently continued in use until the second forum was constructed not earlier

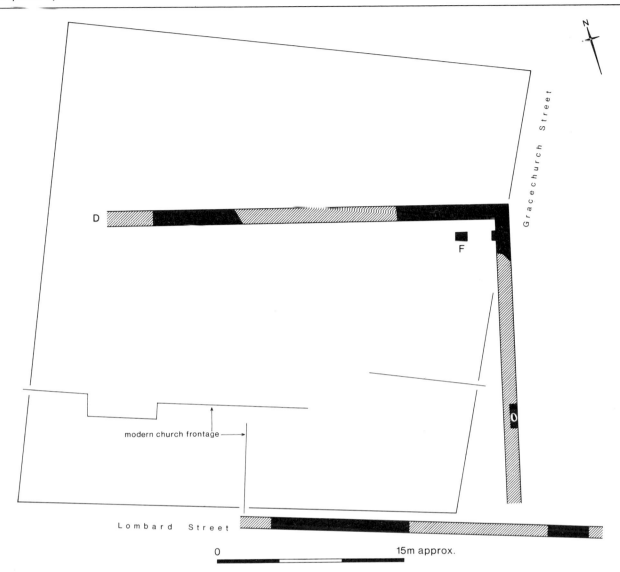

Fig. 105 All Hallows, Lombard Street. Plan to show walls and piers of the second forum. Although pier 'C' in Fig. 100 has been omitted it is thought to have existed in this phase, but its significance is uncertain.

than the late first century. The outer portico of the second forum was located with a stone structure lying within it, and its foundations had evidently been built before a metre thick deposit of brickearth was dumped and the floor was laid on top. Traces of the forum floors were found, but no clear indications of the later history of the building. Parts of the forum walls were robbed during the twelfth century.

GEOLOGY

It was only at the south end of this site that the surface of the natural brickearth subsoil was recorded at 11.20m OD (Fig. 107, Section 2).

THE EARLIEST OCCUPATION LAYERS

In Section 3 (Fig. 107) the natural brickearth was overlaid by deposits of brown and grey clay, which were in turn overlaid by a deposit of gravel. None of these layers indicated the form of occupation. In Section 2 the brickearth was overlaid by black occupation debris 0.18m thick and then by clay. Part of a dish of Pompeian red ware was found in this deposit.[32] The early Roman occupation clearly extended northwards from the excavation to the south end of the site, for a mechanical excavator disclosed a rubbish pit containing pottery of the mid first century.[33]

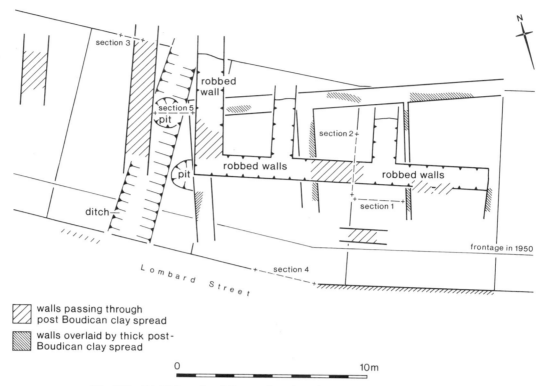

walls passing through
post Boudican clay spread

walls overlaid by thick post-
Boudican clay spread

0   10m

Fig.106   54–58 Lombard Street. South end of the site showing all
Roman features and sections. The frontage of the building is that
which existed during the 1950's, and is shown on Ordnance Survey
maps of that period.

THE DITCH *(Fig. 108)*

Probably the earliest feature in this first occupation
was a large ditch, aligned roughly north-south,
whose filling[34] had been cut by a rubbish pit,[35] Pit 1,
apparently dug from the natural surface. The ditch
was traced for a length of 10m but clearly extended
further. It was U-shaped in cross-section and therefore was not a military defensive ditch, but had
perhaps been dug to drain the land surface before the
site was built upon. Its large size is puzzling for a
drainage ditch, however, since at the north end of the
recorded length it was 1.5m wide, and 1.8m deep,
with a flattish bottom 0.8m wide; whereas at the
south end it was 2.29m wide and only 1.2m deep.
These depths show that it drained northwards, and
that it narrowed distinctly in the direction of flow.

The ditch evidently had a short life as its almost
vertical sides had not been eroded, and it was filled
with large clearly defined dumps of rubbish. At the
north end it was filled with a mass of broken tiles, to
the south of which it contained grey mud, and south
of that were many dumps of gravel and occupation
debris. This occupation debris included pottery of
the Claudian-Neronian period,[36] indicating that the
ditch was filled-in about the middle of the first
century AD. The objects included portions of
amphorae from southern Spain and from Rhodes,

portions of flagons, mortaria, 'Lyon Ware', samian
ware, green glass and a bronze brooch.

The site of the ditch was evidently intended to be
used for some other purpose as its dumped filling
was covered with a spread of gravel, presumably to
make the surface of the ground reasonably stable.

PIT 1 *(Fig. 107, Section 5)*

Although this pit had been cut from the natural
surface, it had also been cut into the gravel filling of
the upper part of the ditch described above. The pit
was 1.52m in diameter and 0.9m deep, its lower
filling being of sand. Above that was a layer of black
occupation debris about 0.05m thick, followed by a
deposit of yellow clay. The upper filling of the pit
was a red burnt clay, which may have been a
continuation of the burnt debris found nearby and
which was likely to have resulted from the destruction of AD 60. If this was so then the pit was in use
and only partly filled when the burning occurred.

Objects recovered from the black occupation
layer[37] in the pit included samian ware, 'Lyon ware',
Pompeian red ware, and coarse wares. A considerable variety of coloured glass was also found including pink, blue, yellow, green, multi-coloured, and

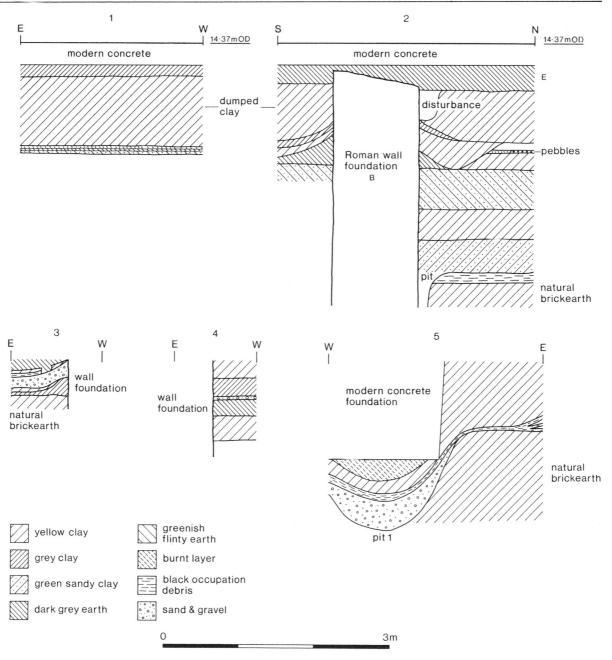

1

E ——————— W   14·37mOD

modern concrete

dumped clay

2

S ——————— N   14·37mOD

modern concrete

E

disturbance

pebbles

Roman wall foundation
B

pit

natural brickearth

3

E   W

wall foundation

natural brickearth

4

E   W

wall foundation

5

W   E

modern concrete foundation

natural brickearth

pit 1

yellow clay

grey clay

green sandy clay

dark grey earth

greenish flinty earth

burnt layer

black occupation debris

sand & gravel

0 ——————— 3m

Fig. 107   54–58 Lombard Street. Sections, whose positions are shown
on Fig. 106. Sections 3, 4 and 5 are not related to Ordnance Datum.

also painted Locano glass. There were also various metal objects including a bronze brooch and two bone knife handles. The whole group dates from about the middle of the first century, and could have been deposited in AD 60.

A black occupation layer examined in Pit 1 (see below) was found to extend up the side of the pit, and to overlie the natural brickearth. Since the pit was dated to the middle of the first century this must be the date of the earliest occupation. This black layer was overlaid by nearly 0.6m of yellow clay containing some oyster shells, suggesting that after the initial activity the site may have been levelled by dumping.

THE FIRE DEPOSIT

Traces of red burnt clay were found in several parts of the excavated area (Fig. 108), and since they occurred at about the same level and in a similar part of the stratigraphical sequence, it is assumed that they formed the debris of the same fire. No evidence of scorching of the underlying deposits was noted,

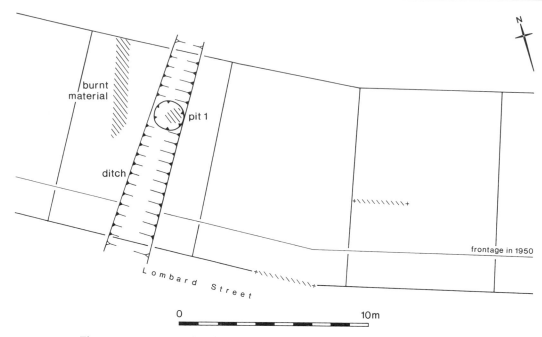

Fig. 108   54–58 Lombard Street. Plan to show the earliest, pre-
Boudican, features discovered on the site. Boudican burnt material was
only found at the west end of the area and in pit 1.

and so it is likely that the fire did not actually occur
in the excavated area but nearby. The patchy occurrence of the burnt debris is consistent with the
spreading and dumping of debris after the fire.

The fire debris itself was recorded as being 0.15m
and 0.23m in thickness and although it occurred
around Pit 1, it was not found in areas to the east (*eg*
Fig. 107, Section 2). This pit provides almost the only
dating evidence, and shows that the fire took place
about the middle of the first century AD. The
presence of the ditch and its filling may explain why
Pit 1 was dug from the natural surface at the side of
the ditch. Elsewhere, where there were no major
earlier excavations, the fire layer lay 0.25m–0.33m
above the natural brickearth surface (Fig. 108). A
mortarium rim from the fire layer[38] in Section 3
cannot be closely dated as it is 'of a type that was
common during the first and second centuries.[39]

THE EARLY OCCUPATION – CONCLUSION

It seems that the initial phase of occupation on this
site dates from the middle of the first century AD,
and that it proved necessary to drain the area for a
short while before a more general form of occupation
and land use could take place. The limited evidence
indicates that the site was not actually occupied by a
building before the fire, which would explain why a
rubbish pit was dug there and why no burning
occurred when the fire took place, probably in AD 60.
Of the objects recovered from this phase on the site,
none was apparently of military type.

SUBSEQUENT DUMPING

Pit 1 was overlaid by a deposit of yellow clay and
oyster shells at least 0.5m thick. It is possible that this
dumping was contemporary with the dumped burnt
debris below, and that it represents a levelling-up
phase after AD 60, in preparation for the construction
of new buildings. Dumping after the initial occupation is also suggested by Section 2 where the
occupation layer overlying the natural surface was
itself overlaid by three dumps of clay and pebbly
earth. These deposits were merely recorded in
section, so it is not clear if they represent either one
or several periods of dumping interspersed with
periods of occupation.

POST-BOUDICAN

A Roman building with stone foundations was
subsequently built at the southern edge of the site,
with an alignment which may not have been quite
parallel to the main east-west Roman street now
beneath Lombard Street (Fig. 109). Very little of the
building was found, but it was characterised by the
use of ragstone and flint set in yellowish-brown
mortar, above which, and presumably at about its
floor level, there lay a course of tiles set in mortar.
Another characteristic was that the walls had been
overlaid by clay dumped as part of the construction
of the second forum.

Fragments of the walls suggested that there had
been at least three rooms. Room 1 was apparently
about 3.8m wide, but the alignment of its presumed

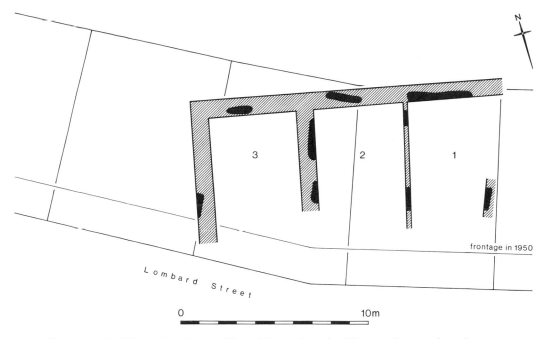

Fig. 109 54–58 Lombard Street. Plan of the earliest building with stone foundations.

east wall, which does not quite match that of the rest of the building, suggests that the wall might have been part of an adjacent structure. On the other hand the stump of the wall was directly overlaid by the thick dump of clay associated with the second forum, so that it presumably continued in use, like the nearby walls, until the construction of that forum.

Within room 1 lay a feature that was overlaid by the dumped clay. Although it may have been a wall foundation, it appeared to be too insubstantial for this purpose. It comprised many small chips of Roman tile and ragstone set in a yellow clayey mortar, and therefore is probably best interpreted as a dump of building debris. The foundation of the wall separating rooms 1 and 2 was only 0.23m thick, and was evidently a minor partition. The foundation was built of ragstone and a little flint and broken brick, all set in white mortar.

Rooms 2 and 3 were 4.57m wide, and were separated by a substantial wall approximately 0.75m thick. Much of the west wall of room 3 had been destroyed by a wall of the second forum, although a short portion remained just south of a pit containing two dateable sherds of the period Nero-Vespasian (Fig. 106).[40] The relationship of this pit to the building remains unclear. The pit is probably earlier than the first stone building on this site, which seems likely to have survived until the second forum was built. If this is correct then the first stone building on the site will be of post-Boudican date, a date indicated both by fragments of a flagon of Brockley Hill pottery recovered from below a gravel surface beneath the level of the top of the foundation

of the walls,[41] and also by a mortarium sherd of the second half of the first century from a deposit of grey occupation debris apparently banked up against the east wall of Room 1.[42] A post-Boudican date would also explain the absence of much fire debris in the building.

The date of the destruction of the building is unclear too, though as it was immediately overlaid by the dumped clay associated with the building of the second forum it is likely that it was demolished at that time. A marked absence of ragstone debris indicates that when the first building was demolished either the debris had been carefully collected for reuse elsewhere, or the upper part of the walls had been built of timber and mud brick.

It is most likely, therefore, that this building was constructed after the destruction by Boudica, and demolished not later than the early 2nd century when, on the evidence from other sites, it seems that the second forum was built.

Other traces of Flavian occupation of the site were found in rubbish pits in the central part of the site. One pit contained pottery dated to the period Nero – early Flavian;[43] and another contained pottery dated to early Flavian period.[44]

THE SECOND FORUM

Substantial Roman foundations were discovered on this site which are now known to be part of the second forum (Fig. 110), but which when found were believed to be part of an earlier Roman building. More recent discoveries on the east side of

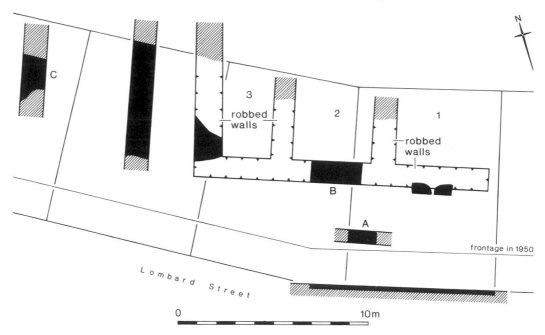

Fig. 110   54–58 Lombard Street. Plan of walls of the second forum phase.

Gracechurch Street enable a much more definite interpretation to be made, and show that they were foundations of the outer portico and central range of shops in the south wing of the second forum. Fortunately, the relationship of the forum foundations to the earlier stone building is clear since the former overlaid the foundation of the wall separating Rooms 2 and 3 in the earlier building, and clearly the first stone building had been demolished before the forum was built and the ground level then artificially raised by dumping.

The outer portico, on the south side of the central range of the south wing, was about 5.18m wide on this site. Its outer wall, lying beside the main east-west street, had not been robbed as far as could be seen, and had been built of ragstone set in white cement. Centrally placed in the portico was an east-west foundation 0.61m thick and of unknown length, built of ragstone and mortar (Fig. 110, A). It seems likely that this was part of the second forum since its construction, which excluded flints and fragments of tiles, was more like that of the second forum than of the earlier stone building on this site.

The stone foundations of the central range of the south wing had been extensively robbed during the early medieval period, the dark earth filling containing sherds of about the 12th century.[45] At one point (Fig. 110, B), however, the forum foundation had not been robbed and stood nearly to the floor level of the forum. It was built of ragstone and a white or buff coloured mortar, and the foundation was not properly faced since it lay below the floor level of the building: The robber trench of the south wall of the central range had an east end in the dumped brickearth showing that the south wing had been built in segments as has been found by B. Philp in Fenchurch Street.[46]

Section 2 was significant in showing that the forum foundation had been constructed *before* the dumping had occurred to raise the floor level of the forum. The dumps were mostly of brickearth and grey clays containing ragstone, wall plaster and tile fragments, together with a little Flavian pottery.[47] At one point the bowl of a Roman bronze spoon was found at the bottom of the dumped clay, resting on top of the west wall of Room 2 of the Flavian stone building, in a position just north of wall B of the second forum. The dumps of clay were up to 1.07m thick above the Flavian surface and were piled up against both north and south faces of wall B. The surviving top of the dumps therefore lay at about 13.87m OD, above which level originally lay the forum floor.

The relationship to the rest of the forum of the apparently isolated foundation of ragstone and white mortar immediately west of Room 2 is unclear; but it seemed that although no foundation linked it with the rest of the central range, it was nevertheless probably part of the second forum to which its thickness, construction, alignment and level was similar. It was built across a mid 1st century rubbish pit.[48]

A foundation (Fig. 110, C) was discovered dug into the dumped clay, and this was clearly a later addition to the forum. It was 1.32m wide and constructed of ragstone and yellow cement. An

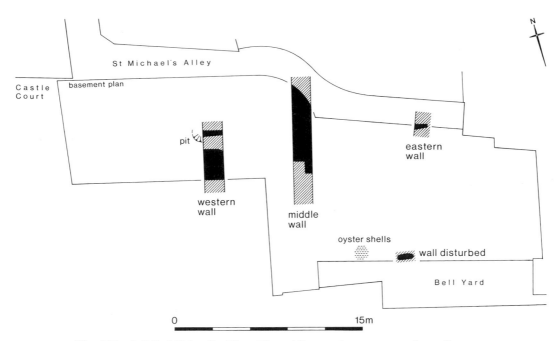

Fig. 111 1–2 St. Michael's Alley. Plan of Roman features, mostly walls of the east wing of the second forum.

interesting aspect of this discovery is that the bottom layer of ragstone fragments in the foundation trench had splashes of pitch on them, suggesting other building activities in the forum while the wall was being constructed.

At the north end of Room 2 traces of a greenish-yellow mortar floor[49] were seen above the level of the top of the dumped clay in sections 1 and 2. Above it was a layer of mixed clayey earth 0.15m thick containing oyster shells and fragments of Roman brick. A white cement floor was seen at a similar level close to the foundation (Fig. 110, C). Here the floor was overlaid by 0.2m of grey earth,[50] which was in turn covered by a layer of loose *opus signinum* suggesting the former existence of a second floor.

The forum floors had been destroyed in sections 1 and 2 either by the construction of a modern cellar floor or by the digging of pits. In section 2, Layer E represents the bottom of an excavation that had been backfilled with dark grey earth containing lumps of ragstone and Roman tiles[51] (Fig. 107).

Site 20.   1–2 St Michael's Alley, 1933
by the late Gerald Dunning

During the greater part of 1932 the premises known as 1 & 2 St Michael's House, St Michael's Alley, on the south side of St Michael's Churchyard, Cornhill, were being demolished, and excavation for the basement of a new building on the site was in progress by February. This excavation involved the greater part of the area shown on the site-plan (Fig. 111), and was carried out to a depth of 29ft (8.8m) below the level of St Michael's Alley and about 19ft (5.8m) below that of the floor of the old basement. During the course of the work early Roman occupation levels and walls were exposed and destroyed, and thanks are due to Barclays Bank Ltd., the owners of the site, for permission to make investigations of these while work was in progress.

The site will be seen to have consisted of two quadrilateral areas, which may be called the eastern and the western half respectively. The eastern half, which was wholly excavated, was about 70ft (21.3m) in length by about 35ft (10.7m) in breadth. The western half, the main axis of which lay to the north of that of the eastern half, was not excavated along most of its northern side or at its western end; it was about 50 feet (15.2m) in length by 27ft (8.2m) in breadth.

1.   THE EARLY OCCUPATION

The excavation was taken everywhere below the level of the lowest made soil into the natural brickearth, the top of which was about 11ft (3.3m) below basement level, and sand and gravel, lying below the brickearth at a further depth of a few feet (about 25ft (7.62m) below pavement level) was also encountered. In the brickearth lay an early Roman occupation layer, the top of which would seem to have been 8ft (2.44m) or somewhat less below basement level. At this point occurred the lowest of the fragmentary cement floors to be described later, which represent a later period when stone buildings were erected on the site. The layer had therefore a minimum thickness of 3ft (0.91m), and it was observed to be at least 4ft (1.22m) thick at a point near the south-east corner of the western half. In character it varied from dirty disturbed brickearth to a mixture of brickearth, charcoal, decayed vegetable matter and oyster shells. It also included patches and layers of pure charcoal a few inches thick, some pieces of burnt daub, considerable quantities of wall-plaster and fragments of tiles and pottery. At the above-mentioned point near the south-east corner of the western half it was found to be divided into an upper and a lower stratum by a band of clean gravel, 4–6ins (0.1–0.15m) thick; the lower stratum, which rested directly on the natural brickearth, was 1ft (0.30m) thick, while the upper, which was 15ins (0.38m) thick, was surmounted by a discontinuous band of gravel 2½ins (0.06m) thick; this stratification was observed over a width of at least 5ft (1.52m) from the eastern face of the westernmost of the three Roman walls which were found crossing the site (see below, p. 149).

Near the north-west corner of the western half was found a well-marked layer of burnt daub and lumps of charcoal, at a depth of 9–11ft (2.74–3.35m) below basement level; it rested immediately on the natural brickearth, and was observed over an area about 8ft (2.44m) square. Another layer of burnt daub, about 5ins (0.13m) thick, was observed near the south-west corner at a depth of 9ft (2.74m).

In the eastern half was a layer consisting purely of oyster shells, occupying the area about 6 by 4ft (1.83–1.27m) roughly indicated on the plan (Fig. 111); it was 1½ft (0.46m) thick, and lay at a depth of about 8ft (2.44m) below basement level. A coin was stated to have been found in this layer.

The wall-plaster varied in thickness from 1⅛ to 2ins (0.028–0.05m), and had a white surface coating which on one sample was measured and found to be ³⁄₆₄in (1mm) thick; the body of the plaster was yellow, and occasionally showed traces of a key on the back. On the white surface had been painted straight bands of brown, red and black, both singly and in groups, and the individual bands, where they occurred on fragments large enough to admit of measurement, were less than ½in (0.01m) wide.

The datable material recovered from the early occupation layer is not considerable in quantity, but it included samian ware and a coin of Vespasian probably minted in AD 71. It affords consistent and reliable evidence of an occupation of the site during the period *c* AD 50–90.[52]

2. RUBBISH PITS

Part of a small rubbish pit was noted in the western half at 18ft (5.49m) below basement level, and against, and partly under, the western face of the Roman wall found in this part of the site (see below). No finds are known from this pit, and its complete excavation must await further work on the site.

A good section of a rubbish pit was obtained in the eastern half. It was made in cutting a face parallel to the south wall of the site, and showed the pit descending 4ft (1.22m) into the brickearth below the bottom of the occupation layer, at which level the mouth of it was 5ft (1.52m) or more in diameter. Its sides sloped inwards to a rounded bottom. Its filling consisted of dirty clay and layers of sand or gravel alternating with layers of carbonised material containing oyster shells. These layers were more obvious in the higher levels of the pit, where they dipped from the sides towards the middle. The pit was sealed by the material of the occupation layer, which here contained a well-marked layer of fragments of wall-plaster. More wall-plaster occurred in the pit itself; one fragment had a pink surface, while another was painted with bands of black, yellow and red on a white ground. The pottery from the pit would indicate a period very much the same as that of the occupation layer.

To the west of this pit was another depression in the brickearth, a section of it being exposed in the same face. It was of uncertain extent, and produced nothing except a lump of fused glass. The filling was of dirty clay and carbonised matter, and was capped by a stony layer. This latter may represent a street of the period of the early occupation; it certainly does not bear any relation to the walls found on the site, as it lies on a level with the footings of one of them.

The Roman structures discovered on the site consisted of parts of three walls running parallel to each other from north to south, besides fragments of cement floors which are probably to be associated with the walls (Fig. 111).

3. THE EASTERN WALL

This wall was satisfactorily observed under the northern or St Michael's Alley frontage of the eastern half; its disturbed remains were also noted, but more vaguely located, under the southern or Bell Yard frontage. The section of it exposed under the northern frontage lay at a depth of 21 to 25ft (6.4m–7.62m) below St Michael's Alley, and showed the lowest 3½ft (1.07m) of the footings, which rested in the brickearth and were 3ft (0.91m) thick. They consisted of undressed lumps of ragstone with yellow mortar containing crushed tile. The mortar did not fill all the interstices, as the stones and the mortar were laid in alternate layers.

At a depth of 9ft (2.74m) below basement level, and about 19ft (5.79m) below modern ground-level, lumps of ragstone and loose tiles set in yellow mortar with crushed tile were noted under the Bell Yard frontage. As indicated above, these are probably the disturbed remains of the same wall, at a higher level.

Building debris, (tiles and undressed blocks of stone) was also encountered under the northern frontage about 8ft (2.43m) east of the wall-section.

4. THE MIDDLE WALL

The middle wall of the three ran across the western end of the eastern half, at a distance of 26½ft (8.08m) from the eastern wall. The bottom of its footings was at 16ft (4.88m) below basement level (26ft (7.92m) below St Michael's Alley), and it stood to a height of 11ft (3.35m), with a thickness of 5ft (1.52m). It was constructed of undressed blocks of ragstone and hard yellow mortar containing crushed chalk. Its footings, laid in the gravel, were composed of alternate layers of mortar and loose lumps of ragstone. At the top of it were observed some pieces of tile laid horizontally, representing a double or possibly triple bonding course.

5. THE WESTERN WALL

This wall ran across the western half of the site, at a distance of 18ft (5.48m) from the middle wall. One of the rectangular pits dug for the new foundations coincided with part of its course exactly, as the pit had a width equal to the thickness of the wall and ran in the same direction. The wall therefore could only be observed for 12ft (3.66m), the length of the pit, from the south wall of the old basement. At the southern end of the pit the bottom of the footings in sand was 16ft (4.88m) below basement level, and a height of 7ft (2.13m) was preserved. It was here constructed of undressed ragstone with hard yellow mortar containing crushed chalk; no tile occurred. At the bottom of the footings was a layer of stones lying under a layer of clay containing flecks of charcoal, and a layer of mortar above the clay; each of the three layers was about 4ins (0.1m) thick. At the northern end of the pit the wall was of different construction and the bottom of it was not reached at 18ft (5.49m) below basement level. At this depth it was constructed of ragstone and yellow mortar with crushed chalk as before, but at a depth of 17ft (5.18m) this was surmounted by a mass of white concrete with a level upper surface and a thickness of 15ins (0.38m). Above this occurred rubbish deposits with layers of charcoal, and it is probable that the masonry stood to its original height at this point. It may be tentatively suggested that these discoveries indicate a sleeper-wall with a pier standing on it at the southern end of the pit. In the two lateral faces of the pit occurred vertical lines of division 3ft (0.91m) from the southern end. South of these lines, the faces showed mixed clay and mortar, indicating contact with masonry; north of them the clay was of a different character,

and contained layers of burnt material, but little or no mortar. These lines may represent the corners of the northern face of a pier.

6. THE FLOORS

Fragments of floors of *opus signinum* were observed in half-a-dozen places, all between the two outermost walls. The floors had suffered a good deal of disturbance, probably in medieval times, but it was certain that floors of different periods were represented. The fragments occurred at various levels, the highest being 4ft (1.22m) below basement level and the lowest 8ft (2.44m). Near the east face of the western wall two adjacent fragments were separated by a vertical distance of 3ft (0.91m); the lower fragment, 4ins (0.1m) thick, was exceptional in being not of *opus signinum* but of white cement without any admixture of broken tile. In the eastern half, to the south of the rubbish pit, but of course at a higher level, a vertical face revealed three floors; the stratification being, from the top downwards:

(1) floor, 7ins (0.18m) thick, 6½ft (1.98m) below basement level:

(2) occupation layer, 2ins (0.05m) thick:

(3) layer of brown clay, 1in (0.03m) thick:

(4) occupation layer, 1½ins (0.04m) thick:

(5) floor, 3½ins (0.09m) thick:

(6) layer of brown clay, 1½ins (0.04m) thick:

(7) floor, 1in (0.03m) thick:

(8) layer of dirty clay, thickness unknown.

Elsewhere the floors varied in thickness from 1½ to 5½ins (0.04–0.14m).

A word may be said here as to the evidence for dating the walls and floors. All the material from the occupation layer described above lay below the general level of the floors. The wall-plaster which was such a constant feature of the early occupation occurred below the lower of the two floors noticed near the western wall (see above, p. 148) but not in the filling between them. Moreover, the middle wall must post-date the pottery, including a jug-neck and a fragment of jug-handle, which was found in the neighbourhood of its footings. The structures on the site would therefore appear to be of the late 1st century, which is also a date assignable on good evidence to the walls and floor, of similar construction and occurring at much the same levels, at 52 Cornhill (Site 3, p. 82).

Of the subsequent history of the site little need be said, as all Roman levels above the floors had been destroyed, and medieval pottery occurred in the first few feet below the basement floor. The medieval deposit also continued above that level, as was shown by a small excavation made under St Michael's Alley, in which a pair of 14th century shoe-soles and a fragment of a medieval cooking-pot were found. In the western half were found some walls the tops of which were immediately under the basement floor, while their foundations were 6ft (1.83m) further down. They were constructed of undressed chalk with occasional pieces of ragstone, flint and brick, and light brown mortar of poor quality. They were associated with a black rubbish deposit in which, about 2ft (0.61m) below basement level, Elizabethan pottery was found, and can hardly be regarded as other than medieval.

FOOTNOTES AND REFERENCES

1   The modern (1986) pavement lies at 18.395m above OD.

2   By relating these depths to the modern (1986) pavement level the natural brickearth is found to lie at 13.51m OD, which is about a metre higher than the natural level on nearby sites (*eg* 68 Cornhill). Similarly the floor of the second basilica apparently lay at 15.56m OD, again about a metre higher than on other sites. Consequently it seems likely that in 1930 the recorded depth of the cellar below Cornhill may have been in error.

3   A. Lowther, 'Excavations at Ashtead, Surrey', *Surrey Archaeological Collections*, 38, 1929, p. 6, pl III.

4   Guildhall Library, *Catalogue of the collection of London antiques in the Guildhall Museum*, London, 1908, p. 74, nos. 108–9.

5   Bricks of both the above types were found built into London Wall, west of Moorgate, in 1882. See E.L. Brock, 'The Roman Wall of London at Moorgate', *Journal of the British Archaeological Association*, 38, 1882, pp. 424–6; Royal Commission on Historical Monuments, *Roman London*, 1928, p. 89; London Museum accession no. A.15293–4.

6   Dr H.H. Thomas, FRS, of H.M. Geological Survey kindly reported on the stones.

7   RCHM. in Note 5, p. 115; *Middlesex and Herts. Notes and Queries*, 1897.

8   The natural surface was brickearth lying at 12.10–12.38m OD.

9   B. Philp, 'The Forum of Roman London: Excavations of 1968–9', *Britannia* VIII, 1977, p. 28.

10   Ibid. in Note 9, pp. 27–8, fig. 11.

11   Ibid. in Note 9, fig. 11.

12   Ibid. in Note 9, plate VI A.

13   Ibid. in Note 9, p. 27, fig. 11.

14   Ibid. in Note 9, pp. 8–10.

15   Ibid. in Note 9, pp. 8–10.

16   Museum of London *Excavation Register*, nos. 905, 906.

17   Ibid. in Note 16, no. 903.

18   Note by F. Cottrill in *Journal of Roman Studies*, 26, 1936, p. 254, fig. 28.

19   R. Merrifield, *The Roman City of London*, London, 1965, pp. 259–260, sites 234–236.

20   Ibid. in Note 18.

21   Ibid. in Note 16, no. 669.

22   Ibid. in Note 16, no. 667.

23   Note by F. Cottrill in *Journal of Roman Studies*, 25, 1935, p. 215.

24   Article in the *Morning Post*, 1934 (date unknown); Ibid. in Note 23.

25   Ibid. in Note 9, p. 25, 40.

26   *The Times*, report of December 1932. Date not known.

27   Note by G. Dunning in *Journal of Roman Studies*, 23, 1933, p. 205.

28   J. Bloe, 'Report of the visits made to the site of All Hallows, Lombard Street', *Transactions of the London and Middlesex Archaeological Society*, 9 (NS), Part II, 1945, pp. 181–189.

29   Note by A. Oswald in *Antiquaries Journal*, 20, 1940, p. 510.

30   It is interesting to note that in this report of 1939 Oswald had identified the first and second forum building phases, but without establishing their purpose. The significance of the 'columned' building on the All Hallows site was unclear.

31   RCHM. in Note 5, p. 129.

32   Ibid. in Note 16, no. 661.

33   Ibid. in Note 16, no. 774.

34   Ibid. in Note 16, no. 648.

35   Ibid. in Note 16, no. 639.

36   Ibid. in Note 16, no. 648.

37   Ibid. in Note 16, no. 639.

38   Ibid. in Note 16, no. 636.

39   See C. Hawkes, *Camulodunum*, Reports of the Research Committee of the Society of Antiquaries of London no. XIV, Oxford, 1947, p. 255, fig. 53, for the type during the Boudican period.

40   Ibid. in Note 16, no. 637.

41   Ibid. in Note 16, no. 623.

42   Ibid. in Note 16, no. 629.

43   Ibid. in Note 16, no. 774.

44   Ibid. in Note 16, no. 775.

45   Ibid. in Note 16, nos. 620, 633, 677.

46   Ibid. in Note 9, p. 25.

47   Ibid. in Note 16, nos. 622, 676, 726.

48   Ibid. in Note 16, no. 635.

49   Ibid. in Note 16, no. 682.

50   Ibid. in Note 16, no. 757.

51   Ibid. in Note 16, no. 631.

52   Although the pottery is now lost, drawings and descriptions of the finds are held in the Museum of London.

Appendix

Carbonised cereal grain from first century London: a summary of the evidence for importation and crop processing.

by Vanessa Straker

A large deposit of carbonised cereal grain was found in a building which is considered to be one of a row of shops at the corner of the main east-west street and market place (see p. 97). There was no definite evidence of the remains of a sack, barrel or other container in which the grain might have been stored, and the pieces of charred wood (oak) which were found in the deposit are as likely to derive from the building itself as from a container. The burning of the building is attributed to the forces of Boudica and the deposit can therefore be very accurately dated to AD 60.

A sub-sample of the deposit was first examined by Boyd[1] and another subsequently by Straker.[2] In the latter investigation the sample was washed gently in water using a series of sieves, the minimum of size being 250 microns. The components were identified and counted as given in Table 1. Details of the criteria used for identification are given by Straker. These concern the morphological characteristics of grain and spikelet fragments. In order to confirm the identification of the einkorn, scanning electron micrographs of the transverse cells of the grains were also taken. Most of the deposit consisted of spelt wheat (76%) with smaller amounts of other wheat species notably emmer (1.4%), bread wheat type (2.7%) and einkorn (0.7%). It is not always possible to identify the grains of spelt and bread wheat on morphological characteristics alone as these can overlap, and it is the spikelet remains that are used to confirm the presence of the different species. Spikelet forks of spelt wheat were identified, but no bread wheat chaff was preserved and the grains noted as bread wheat type exhibit the most extreme features usually suggestive of this species. Hulled barley (1.9%) and oats (0.1%) comprised other minor components in addition to seeds from 'weed' species such as lentil, bitter vetch, corn cockle and others which are listed in Table 1. Spelt wheat is commonly found on Roman sites, with other cereals and weeds seeds constituting 'contaminants' to the crop; but einkorn, lentils and bitter vetch are unex-pected components as Britain is usually regarded as further north than the general distribution of these species. Einkorn (first identified in this deposit by Boyd[3]) has not previously been recorded with certain-ty in a Roman deposit in Britain and neither, to the writers' knowledge, has bitter vetch represented in this sub-sample by a single seed only. Lentils have been found in Roman contexts before.[4] The associa-tion of einkorn, lentils and bitter vetch in the deposit suggests that the crop was not grown in Britain but imported from the Mediterranean or Near East. The significance of this deposit as imported grain will be discussed later.

As Hillman[5] explains, in Britain emmer seems to have been the principal wheat used in agriculture from the Neolithic period to the early Iron Age and was indeed the main cereal in much of Europe and south-west Asia for some 7000 years after domesti-cated cereals first appeared. It is still cultivated today in, for example, parts of Anatolia. During the Iron Age in Britain spelt became more popular than emmer. In most British Roman cereal deposits which contain wheat, spelt is the dominant species. It is a hardy cereal, still grown today in the Alps near Stuttgart. By the Anglo-Saxon period, bread wheat had become the most frequently occurring wheat, this species was a minor component only for at least four millenia after its Neolithic introduction into Britain.[6] The reasons for the changes in the popularity of the different species of wheat are many. Factors including ease of crop processing, suitability of certain soil and climatic conditions for crop growth and agricultural techni-ques, yield, disease tolerance, and taste preference must all have played a part.

The relative proportion of the constituents of the deposit do not suggest that the deliberate or uninten-tional mixing of more than one crop is involved, although this can rarely be completely ruled out. Some of the wheat (23%) had already germinated, as had some of the other components including weed seeds such as corn cockle. This could be attributed to poor storage conditions, as suggested for the Roman granary deposit at Coney Street in York[7] or the grains could even have started to germinate in the ear before harvest. In some cases sprouting in spelt wheat has been induced deliberately, Hillman[8] noted this at Catsgore, and Helbaek[9] also suggested this for the spelt wheat at Isca. In both examples it was suggested that the grain was intended for use in malting. However, there is no particular indication that this was the case for the London deposit.

The deposit was very uncontaminated as far as infestation from weevils is concerned; Boyd[10] noted only two grain weevils (*Sitophilous granarious*) in his sample. This certainly does not suggest an infested crop.

As well as the caryopses of cereals, some chaff was also preserved and it is from an examination of the chaff and weed components in the deposit in relation to the cereals that inferences about crop processing can be drawn. On the basis of detailed observations made in the Near East where primitive forms of wheat are still grown and harvesting and processing techniques appear to have remained unchanged for several millenia, Hillman[11] has constructed a model which provides a useful basis from which to consider the crop processing methods which may have been used in the past. Emmer and spelt are known as 'glume' wheats because the grain is tightly enclosed in the husk and several stages in the crop processing are required to free the grain from the enclosing spikelet. These may involve drying, threshing, raking, winnowing, sieving and pounding. The composition of the deposit under discussion suggests that it corresponds with the 'prime product' of step 12 (third sieving) in Hillman's model. The prime product at this stage of processing should consist of prime grain and many of the spikelet forks and weed seeds of roughly the same size as the prime grain. It has been stressed by Hubbard[12] and Hillman[13] that metrical studies of the prime grain and other components will not allow an estimate for the size of sieve used during crop processing, which Hillman suggests is better calculated from tail grain present in the waste fraction from this same stage of processing. In the Boudican grain sample the ratios of weed seeds, spikelet forks and tail grain to prime grain are consistent with this late stage of processing; these are given below:

spikelet forks: prime grain	1 : 14
tail grain: prime grain	1 : 99
weeds: spikelet forks	1 : 3.8
weeds: prime grain	1 : 52.9

Grain at this stage of processing would usually be consigned to a bulk store, and Hillman[14] suggests that further cleaning of the grain to remove impurities would be done by hand as the grain was required for use. One of the main differences in crop products between wet and dry areas lies at the stage at which crop products are put into long term store. In wet climates, glum wheats are usually stored as semicleaned spikelets[15] as the climate does not allow for the final stages to be undertaken outside. As stated above, the Boudican deposit appears to have been processed further than this, a point in support of the suggestion that the crop was not of local origin. It is not possible to be certain whether the crop was intended for direct consumption or for use as seed, although as seed grain is usually stored in spikelet form perhaps direct consumption is more likely.

The presence of imported grain in first century London is of great importance since it is the only evidence at present to suggest that cereal was in fact being imported into Britain in the first century AD; indeed a comment by Strabo written in the first century BC mentions 'corn' as one of the principal exports at that time.[16] It is thought that as late as the end of the third century AD Britain still possessed abundant crops, pasture and metal ores.[17] In AD 359 the emperor Julian organised a fleet of ships to transport grain from Britain, presumably regarded as reserve of supplies, to the Rhine frontier.[18] Imported exotic foods such as lentil, fig, cucumber, peach and olive are known from Roman London,[19] but with the exception of the Boudican grain there is no evidence for the importation of basic foodstuffs. This deposit need not, however, imply that it was brought in on a large scale. An occasional shipment of grain may have been intended to compensate for a temporary shortage, which may, perhaps, be expected in the early stages in the colonisation of a province. This would seem more likely to have come to Britian from northern Europe and this may have happened on other occasions, but would be difficult to detect as the weed contaminants would be very similar to those of British crops.

Assemblages of Roman date largely consisting of spelt wheat, with smaller amount of other cereals such as other wheat species, barley and oats as well as seeds from wild plants have been found both in Britain and on the continent. The grain deposit from the Roman warehouse excavated at Coney Street in York consisted largely of spelt wheat[20] as did that from, for example, Catsgore,[21] Balkerne Lane, Colchester[22] and Isca.[23] The grain identified from third century Wilderspool, in comparison, consisted of spelt wheat and rye.[24] Jones[25] concludes from an examination of carbonised cereal remains from Iron Age and Roman features on a site in Abingdon that spelt was the predominant wheat throughout the Iron Age and Roman periods, with emmer as a minor constituent at that site.[25] In London, the only other major deposit is early to mid-second century in date and was found on the waterfront of the river Thames. It was sealed within a dump of burnt building debris, thought to represent the clearance of fire damaged structures along the waterfront.[26] This deposit has been described in detail[27] and has some similarities with the Boudican assemblage, consisting largely of spelt wheat, much of it sprouted. The deposit is regarded as being consistent with local production, although the fact that it was also stored as grain and not as spikelets is of interest because storage in spikelet form might be expected in a crop grown in a wet area. It is possible that new farming techniques were among the many innovations brought by the Romans. Grain processing could, perhaps, under the Roman villa system be undertaken on a large scale inside; something possible previously only in areas with dry summers. Until more large deposits of Iron Age and Roman cereals from native farmsteads and Roman villa sites have been examined, the effect of Roman influence on existing crop processing techniques can only be suggested tentatively.

The first century deposit of carbonised grain from London is of great importance because it suggests that cereals were being brought into Britain, albeit probably on a small scale; something that there was previously no direct evidence for, as well as allowing detailed analysis of Roman farming practice.

FOOTNOTES AND REFERENCES

1 P. Boyd, 'Carbonised cereals and associated weed seeds from Roman London, AD 60'. *Ancient Monuments Laboratory Report 3135*, 1980.

2 V. Straker, 'First and second century carbonised cereal grain from Roman London', in W. van Zeist and W.A. Casparie (eds), *Plants and Ancient Man*, Rotterdam, 1984, pp. 323–329.

3 Ibid. in Note 1.

4 G. Willcox, 'Exotic plants from Roman waterlogged sites in London', *Journal of Archaeological Science*, 4, 1977, pp. 269–282; H. Helbaek, 'The Isca grain, A Roman plant introduction into Britain', *New Phytologist*, 63, 1964, pp. 158–164.

5 G. Hillman, 'Charred remains of crops from a hut entrance behind the ramparts', in C. Musson and A. Smith (editors), *Excavations at the Breiddin Hillfort*, Cambrian Archaelogical Society, Cardiff (forthcoming).

6 M. Jones, 'The plant remains', in M. Parrington, *The excavation of an Iron Age settlement, Bronze Age ring-ditches and Roman features at Ashville Trading Estate, Abingdon (Oxfordshire) 1974–1976*, Council for British Archaeology Research Report 28, 1978.

7 D. Williams, 'The plant remains', in H. Kenward and D. Williams (editors), *Biological evidence from the Roman warehouses in Coney Street*. The Archaeology of York, vol. 14, fascicule 2, London, Council for British Archaeology, 1979.

8 G. Hillman, 'Evidence for spelt malting at Catsgore', in R. Leech (ed), *Excavations at Catsgore, 1970–1973*, 1982, pp. 137–141, Bristol.

9 H. Helbaek, 1964, in Note 4.

10 Ibid. in Note 1.

11 G. Hillman, 'Reconstructing crop practices from charred remains of crops', in R. Mercer (ed), *Farming practice in British prehistory*, Edinburgh, 1981, pp. 123–162.

12 R. Hubbard, 'On the strength of the evidence for prehistoric crop processing activities'. *Journal of Archaeological Science*, 3, 1976, pp. 257–65.

13 G. Hillman forthcoming, 'Interpretation of archaeological plant remains: the application of ethnographic models from Turkey'. *Plants and Ancient Man*.

14 Ibid. in Note 11.

15 Ibid. in Note 11, stage 7.

16 Strabo, *Geography*, IV, 199.

17 P. Salway, *Roman Britain*, Oxford, 1981, p. 359.

18 Ibid. in Note 17.

19 G. Willcox, 'Exotic plants from Roman waterlogged sites in London', *Journal of Archaeological Science*, 4, 1977, pp. 269–282.

20 Ibid. in Note 7.

21 Ibid. in Note 8.

22 P. Murphy forthcoming, 'Balkerne Lane, Colchester: Carbonised cereals and crop weeds'.

23 H. Helbaek, 1964, in Note 4.

24 G. Hillman, 'Crop processing at 3rd century AD. Wilderspool', in J. Hinchcliffe and J. Williams (eds), *Excavations at Wilderspool 1966–1968*. Cheshire County Council Monograph, 1983.

25 Ibid. in Note 6.

26 N. Bateman and G. Milne, 'A Roman harbour in London'. *Britannia*, 14, 1983, pp. 207–226.

27 Ibid. in Note 2.

Table 1.   Carbonised cereals and weed seeds

Taxon		Components	Number	% of total
Triticum (Wheat)	T. monococcum (einkorn)	spikelet forks grains	13 46	0.7
	T. dicoccum (emmer)	spikelet forks (lateral) grain grain (terminal)	14 74 31	1.4
	T. monococcum/dicoccum (einkorn/emmer)	spikelet forks grain	4 65	0.8
	T. spelta (spelt)	spikelet forks (lateral) rachis internodes grain	89 1 6318	76.5
	T. dicoccum/spelta (emmer/spelt)	spikelet forks (lateral) spikelet forks (terminal)	62 5	0.8
	T. aestivum (bread wheat)	grain	224	2.7
	Triticum sp (indeterminate wheat– poorly preserved)	spikelet forks rachis internode frag grain grain (tail)	339 9 592 74	12.1
	Triticum/Secale (wheat/rye)	grain	96	1.1
Hordeum (Barley)	H. sativum (hulled barley)	straight grain twisted grain indeterminate grain	35 76 27	1.9
	Hordeum sp. (poorly preserved)	grain lemma base (indet.)	41 1	
Avena (Oats)	A. fatua/ludiviciana (wild type oats)	lemma bases	2	0.1
	Avena sp.	floret fragments awn fragment grain	11 1 7	
Cereals	Indeterminate	grain	9	
		cereal culm node	1	
		cereal fragments	many (157.3g)	

Table 1 continued

WEED SEEDS	Agrostemma githago	corn cockle	66	
	Lens culinaris	lentil	20	
	cf. Lens culinaris		1	
	Vicia/Lathyrus	vetches	24	
	Vicia ervilia	bitter vetch	1	
	Galium sp.	bedstraw	1	
	Malva sp.	mallow	1	1.7
	Rumex sp.	dock etc.	2	
	Umbelliferae	gen. et sp. indet.	3	
	Gramineae	grasses Lolium/Festuca	15	
		cf. Bromus sp.	1	
	unidentified	weed seeds	5	

Total number of identifiable components: 8377

CHARCOAL	Quercus sp.	Oak	5.3g

Plates

Plate 1   160–162 Fenchurch Street. The east face of mud-brick wall 3 of the Phase 2 building burnt in the Boudican destruction. The unplastered face of the wall had a herringbone pattern impressed in its clay rendering. The black deposit behind the scale is carbonised grain (see p. 97). The scale is in 10cm divisions. (*See p. 151 and Fig. 73*).

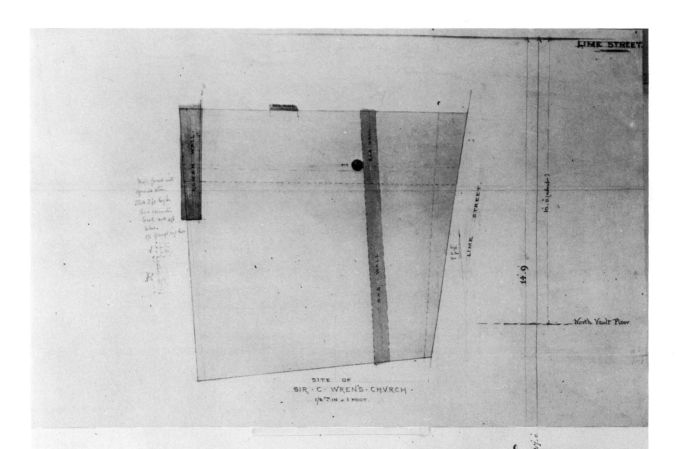

LIME STREET.

ROMAN WALL

RAG WALL

PIT

LIME STREET

LIME STREET

10. 0 (about)

14. 9

North Vault Floor

SITE OF
SIR · C · WREN'S · CHVRCH.
1/8 TH IN = 1 FOOT.

EXCAVATION LEVEL
DEBRIS AND MADE
GROVND

RED SEAM

BLACK SEAM

YELLOW AND BROWN
LOAMY EARTH

GRAVEL STRATVM

27. 0

7. 6

4. 9

S·DIONIS·BACKCHVRCH·
FENCHVRCH STREET.

THE PIT & BIN

THE RAG WALL

ANCIENT PIT AND WALLS

Feb. 1892

Plate 2 St. Dionis Backchurch site, Lime Street, 1882. Plan and section by Henry Hodge of walls of the second Roman forum and an early Roman pit or well. On the plan (north is to the top) the western (left hand) Roman wall is annotated showing that the upper 3 feet was faced with squared stone, and below an offset at the base of this facing was a rough ragstone foundation 5 feet deep. The section shows a pit 3 feet in diameter dug into the natural brickearth and gravel. This was overlaid by black and red deposits that presumably represent the Boudican destruction. The pit is described as being "Filled with gravel, chalk, red and buff brick, rag, oyster shells, brown and red mortar fragments. Black colour filling in 5 oak round wood stakes shaped to points". (*See p. 90 and Figs. 25, 76*). Copyright: Guildhall Library.

Plate 3 3–6 Gracechurch Street. The north face of the wall separating the nave from the north aisle of the first basilica. The upper half of the wall, between the two triple courses of tiles, was built of ragstone, and the lower half was of flints. The base of the foundation has been slightly undercut to the right of the scale. The scale is in foot divisions. (*See p. 104 and Figs. 77 and 80*).

Plate 4 (*top left*)   79 Gracechurch Street. The north-south foundation of the east wing of the first forum (A), with the impression of a robbed pier (B) which originally extended beyond the width of the foundation. At top left is a section through the thick dump of gravel associated with the second forum, which buried the first forum. A spread of mortar contemporary with the first forum is visible to the east (top right) and west (bottom left) of the forum foundation. Scale in 10cm divisions. (*See Figs. 87, 88*).

Plate 6 (*above*)   17–19 Gracechurch Street. Internal corner of the Roman temple at point 13. (See Fig. 81). The walls, made from the flanges of roof tiles, are standing about 0.68m high.

Plate 5   79 Gracechurch Street. View of a north-south foundation of the first forum (A), with the impression, partly outlined, of the robbed pier (B) upon both the foundation and the mortar spread to the west (left). Above is the dump of gravel associated with the second forum, which is in turn cut by the base of a medieval chalk foundation. Scale in 10cm divisions. (*See Figs. 87, 88*).

Plate 7 Lombard Street, east end. Pier 22, found in 1925, which is believed to be associated with the rebuilding of the first forum. View looking west. (*See p.36 and Fig. 24*).

Plate 8 The Post Office tunnel excavated below Gracechurch Street in 1977. This view shows John Maloney of the Museum of London recording a section in the nave of the second basilica. Such recording could only be carried out during the short periods when the workmen were not extending the tunnel.

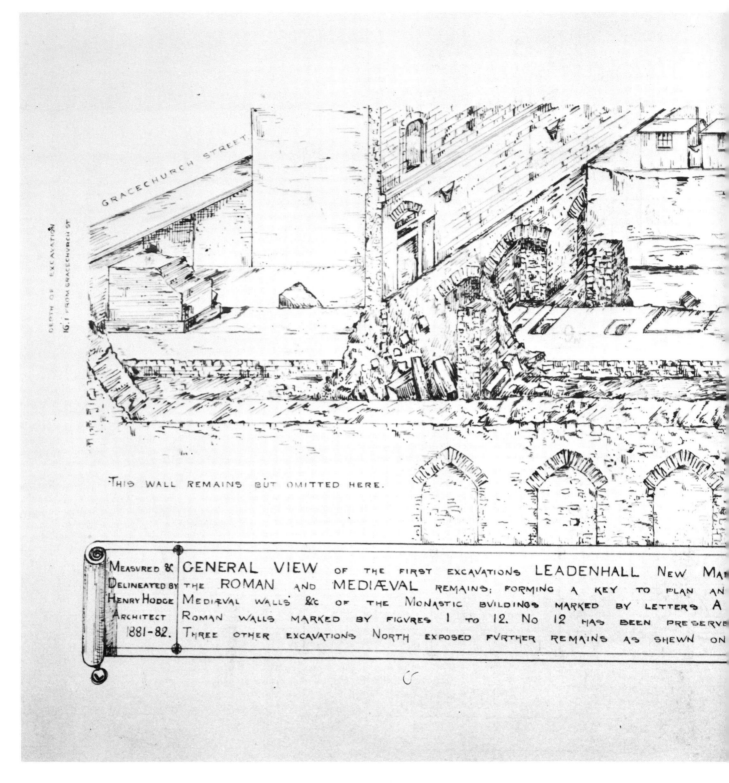

Within the illustration:

GRACECHURCH STREET

DEPTH OF EXCAVATION 16.1 FROM GRACECHURCH ST

THIS WALL REMAINS BUT OMITTED HERE.

MEASURED & DELINEATED BY HENRY HODGE ARCHITECT 1881-82.

GENERAL VIEW OF THE FIRST EXCAVATIONS LEADENHALL NEW MAR... THE ROMAN AND MEDIÆVAL REMAINS; FORMING A KEY TO PLAN AN... MEDIÆVAL WALLS &c OF THE MONASTIC BUILDINGS MARKED BY LETTERS A... ROMAN WALLS MARKED BY FIGURES 1 TO 12. NO 12 HAS BEEN PRESERVE... THREE OTHER EXCAVATIONS NORTH EXPOSED FURTHER REMAINS AS SHEWN ON...

Plate 9 The Leadenhall Market site in 1881–2 viewed from the south and drawn by Henry Hodge. The walls of the second Roman basilica and various medieval walls are shown, but the wall numbers mentioned in the drawn caption are rather faint, but are given in Fig. 30.

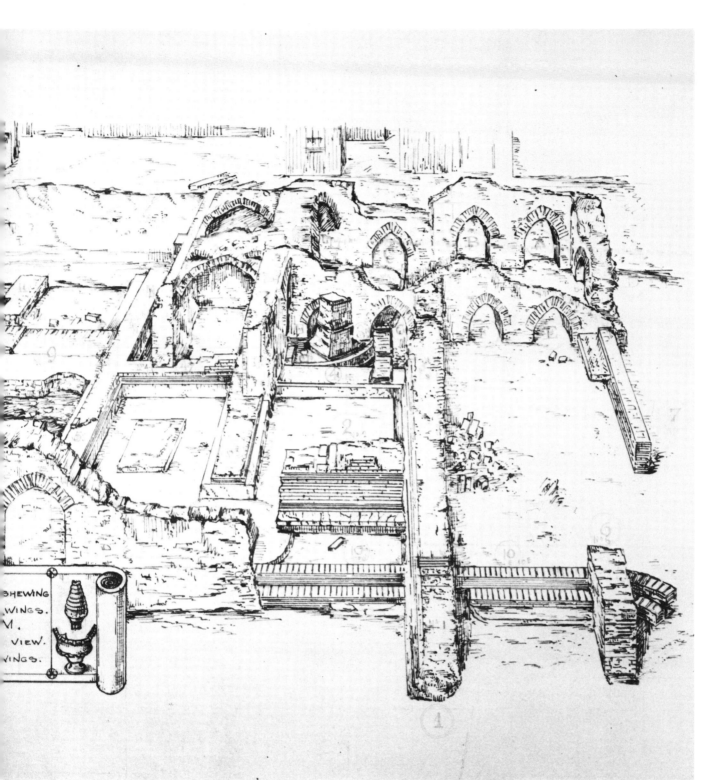

Plates 10 and 11   The Post Office tunnel below Gracechurch Street, 1977. Two sections through the nave of the second basilica showing the thick primary white mortar floor, and a little above it a second thinner mortar floor. Between the two floors are various trampled surfaces, some silt-like, suggesting a slow accumulation of soil resulting from the use of the building. The dark

soil above the latest mortar floor in Plate 10 contained building debris and may represent the abandonment and gradual decay of the basilica. No layer of concentrated rubble debris was found that might have represented a deliberate demolition of the building. Scale in 10cm divisions. (*See p. 49 and Fig. 49*).

Plate 12 52 Cornhill. Section across one of the two north-south walls (probably that in the north-east corner of the site) that extended beneath Cornhill. These walls lay immediately north of the north aisle of the second basilica. (*See p. 85 and Fig. 63*). Scale of 2 feet.

Plate 13 52 Cornhill. Pier 4N, constructed of bricks upon a base of stone blocks, lay on the north sleeper wall of the second basilica. (*See p. 84 and Figs. 28, 63 and 64*).

Plate 14 (*top*) 90 Gracechurch Street, 1986. Photograph of Pier 10S by J. Scrivener. Scale in 10cm divisions. Although Hodge notes that there were 'inscribed bricks in this wall' (See Fig. 30) none was found when the pier was cleaned in 1986. (See p. 43 and Fig. 29). Scale in 10cms divisions.

Plate 15 Lombard Street, east end. The north face of the southern outer portico wall of the second forum, found beneath the pavement on the north side of Lombard Street in 1925. (*See Fig. 24*).

Plate 16 (*top left*)   All Hallows church, Lombard Street, 1939. The northernmost inner east-west portico wall of the second forum. Built of tiles and pink mortar with 'a bonding course of rag'. (*See p. 137 and Figs. 100 (wall D) and 105*).

Plate 18 (*above*)   160–162 Fenchurch Street, 1976. The west face of the easternmost wall of the east wing of the second forum. The chalk foundation beside the scale is of medieval date, and the scale is in 10cm divisions. (*See p. 97 and Fig. 76*).

Plate 17   All Hallows church, Lombard Street, 1939. A stone column base, about 0.76m across, found in debris associated with the second forum. (*See p. 138 and Fig. 100*).

Plate 19 The Post Office tunnel below Gracechurch Street, 1977. A view of a section through the floors of the central 'pool' in the second forum courtyard. This section is shown in Fig. 55, centre. Scale in 10cm divisions. (*See p. 65*).

Plate 20 83–87 Gracechurch Street, 1867. A lifesize bronze hand found on *The Spread Eagle* Inn site, now 83–87 Gracechurch Street, may be derived from a monument in the forum (*See p. 66*). The hand is a poor quality work of art, and is 241mm long. (Museum of London accession number: 2079).